REFLECTIONS
ON LANGUAGE

NOAM CHOMSKY

Reflections on Language

Temple Smith · London

in association with
Fontana Books

First published in Great Britain 1976
by Maurice Temple Smith Ltd
37 Great Russell Street, London WC1

Published by arrangement with Pantheon Books, a
division of Random House Inc.

ISBN 0 85117 1052

Printed in Great Britain by offset lithography by
Billing & Sons Limited, Guildford, London and Worcester

Contents

Preface

Part I of this book is an elaboration of the Whidden Lectures, delivered in January 1975 at McMaster University. Part II is a revised version of my contribution to a volume of essays in honor of Yehoshua Bar-Hillel (Kasher, ed., forthcoming), submitted for publication in June 1974. The latter essay considers some critical discussion of the general point of view developed here, as it had been presented in earlier work. To preserve the internal coherence of the discussion in part II, I have retained some material that recapitulates themes that are developed in a somewhat different form in the Whidden Lectures.

I have presented much of this material in lectures at MIT and elsewhere and am indebted to many students, colleagues, and friends for valuable comments and criticism. The work reviewed in chapter 3 of part I, in particular, incorporates suggestions and research to which many people have contributed, as the citations only partially serve to indicate. Among others, Harry Bracken, Donald Hockney, Ray Jackendoff, Justin Leiber, Julius Moravcsik, and Henry Rosemont have made helpful comments on an earlier version of this manuscript. I have also profited greatly from lively and extensive discussions with members of the faculty of McMaster University.

Noam Chomsky

Cambridge, Massachusetts
April 1975

PART I

CHAPTER 1

On
Cognitive Capacity

These reflections on the study of language will be non-technical for the most part, and will have a somewhat speculative and personal character. I am not going to try to summarize the current state of knowledge in the areas of language study that I know something about, or to discuss ongoing research in any depth. I want to consider, rather, the point and purpose of the enterprise, to ask—and I hope explain—why results obtained in technical linguistics might interest someone who is not initially enchanted by the relation between question formation and anaphora, the principles of rule ordering in phonology, the relation of intonation to the scope of negation, and the like. I will sketch what seems to me an appropriate framework within which the study of language may prove to have more general intellectual interest, and will consider the possibilities for constructing a kind of theory of human nature on a model of this sort.

Why study language? There are many possible answers, and by focusing on some I do not, of course, mean to disparage others or question their legitimacy. One may, for example, simply be fascinated by the elements of language in themselves and want to discover their order and arrangement, their origin in history or in the individual, or the ways in which they are used in thought, in science or in art, or in normal social interchange. One reason for studying language—and for me personally the most compelling reason—is that it is tempting to regard language, in the traditional phrase, as "a mirror of mind." I do not mean by this simply that the concepts expressed and distinctions developed in normal language use give us insight into the patterns of thought and the world of "common sense" constructed by the human mind. More intriguing, to me at least, is the possibility that by studying language we may discover abstract principles that govern its structure and use, principles that are universal by biological necessity and not mere historical accident, that derive from mental characteristics of the species. A human language is a system of remarkable complexity. To come to know a human language would be an extraordinary intellectual achievement for a creature not specifically designed to accomplish this task. A normal child acquires this knowledge on relatively slight exposure and without specific training. He can then quite effortlessly make use of an intricate structure of specific rules and guiding principles to convey his thoughts and feelings to others, arousing in them novel ideas and subtle perceptions and judgments. For the conscious mind, not specially designed for the purpose, it remains a distant goal to reconstruct and comprehend what the child has done intuitively and with minimal effort. Thus language is a mirror of mind in a deep and significant sense. It is a product of human intelligence, created anew in each individual by operations that lie far beyond the reach of will or consciousness.

By studying the properties of natural languages, their structure, organization, and use, we may hope to gain some understanding of the specific characteristics of human intelligence. We may hope to learn something about human nature; something significant, if it is true that human cognitive capacity is the truly distinctive and most remarkable characteristic of the species. Furthermore, it is not unreasonable to suppose that the study of this particular human achievement, the ability to speak and understand a human language, may serve as a suggestive model for inquiry into other domains of human competence and action that are not quite so amenable to direct investigation.

The questions that I want to consider are classical ones. In major respects we have not progressed beyond classical antiquity in formulating clear problems in this domain, or in answering questions that immediately arise. From Plato to the present time, serious philosophers have been baffled and intrigued by the question that Bertrand Russell, in one of his later works, formulated in this way: "How comes it that human beings, whose contacts with the world are brief and personal and limited, are nevertheless able to know as much as they do know?" (Russell, 1948, p. 5). How can we gain such rich systems of knowledge, given our fragmentary and impoverished experience? A dogmatic skeptic might respond that we do not have such knowledge. His qualms are irrelevant to the present point. The same question arises, as a question of science, if we ask how comes it that human beings with such limited and personal experience achieve such convergence in rich and highly structured systems of belief, systems which then guide their actions and interchange and their interpretation of experience.

In the classical tradition, several answers were suggested. One might argue, along Aristotelian lines, that the world is structured in a certain way and that the human mind is able to perceive this structure, ascending from particulars to species to genus to further generalization and thus attaining knowledge of universals from perception of particulars. A "basis of pre-existent knowledge" is a prerequisite to learning. We must possess an innate capacity to attain developed states of knowledge, but these are "neither innate in a determinate form, nor developed from other higher states of knowledge, but from sense-perception." Given rich metaphysical assumptions, it is possible to imagine that a mind "so constituted as to be capable of this process" of "induction" might attain a rich system of knowledge.[1]

A more fruitful approach shifts the main burden of explanation from the structure of the world to the structure of the mind. What we can know is determined by "the modes of conception in the understanding";[2] what we do know, then, or what we come to believe, depends on the specific experiences that evoke in us some part of the cognitive system that is latent in the mind. In the modern period, primarily under the influence of Cartesian thought, the question of what we can know became again a central topic of inquiry. To Leibniz and Cudworth, Plato's doctrine that we do not attain new knowledge but recover what was already known seemed plausible, when this doctrine was "purged of the error of preexistence."[3] Cudworth argued at length that the mind has an "innate cognoscitive power" that provides the principles and conceptions that constitute our knowledge, when provoked by sense to do so. "*But sensible things themselves* (as, for example, light and colors) *are not known and understood either by the passion or the fancy of sense, nor by anything merely foreign and adventitious, but by intelligible ideas exerted from the mind itself, that is, by something native and domestic to it....*"[4] Thus knowledge "consisteth in the awakening and exciting of the inward active powers of the mind," which "exercise[s] its own inward activity upon" the objects presented by sense, thus coming "to know or understand, ... actively to comprehend a thing by some abstract, free and universal ratio's, reasonings...." The eye perceives, but the mind can compare, analyze, see cause-

and-effect relations, symmetries, and so on, giving a comprehensive idea of the whole, with its parts, relations, and proportions. The "book of nature," then, is "legible only to an intellectual eye," he suggests, just as a man who reads a book in a language that he knows can learn something from the "inky scrawls." "The primary objects of science and intellection," namely, "the intelligible essences of things," "exist no where but in the mind itself, being its own ideas. . . . And by and through these inward ideas of the mind itself, which are its primary objects, does it know and understand all external individual things, which are the secondary objects of knowledge only."

Among the "innate ideas" or "common notions" discussed in the rich and varied work of seventeenth-century rationalists are, for example, geometrical concepts and the like, but also "*relational* ideas or categories which enter into every presentation of objects and make possible the unity and interconnectedness of rational experience," [5] including such "relative notions" as "Cause, Effect, Whole and Part, Like and Unlike, Proportion and Analogy, Equality and Inequality, Symmetry and Asymmetry," all "*relative* ideas . . . [that are] . . . no material impresses from without upon the soul, but *her own active conception proceeding from herself whilst she takes notice of external objects.*" [6] Tracing the development of such ideas, we arrive at Kant's rather similar concept of the "conformity of objects to our mode of cognition." The mind provides the means for an analysis of data as experience, and provides as well a general schematism that delimits the cognitive structures developed on the basis of experience.

Returning to Russell's query, we can know so much because in a sense we already knew it, though the data of sense were necessary to evoke and elicit this knowledge. Or to put it less paradoxically, our systems of belief are those that the mind, as a biological structure, is designed to construct. We interpret experience as we do because of our special mental design. We attain knowledge when the "inward ideas of the mind itself" and the structures it creates conform to the nature of things.

Certain elements of the rationalist theories must be discarded, but the general outlines seem plausible enough. Work of the past years has shown that much of the detailed structure of the visual system is "wired in," though triggering experience is required to set the system in operation. There is evidence that the same may be true of the auditory structures that analyze at least some phonetic distinctive features. (Cf. Eimas et al., 1971.) As techniques of investigation have improved, Bower argues, "so has the apparent sophistication of the infant perceptual system." He reviews evidence suggesting that "the infant perceptual system seems capable of handling all of the traditional problems of the perception of three-dimensional space"—perception of solidity, distance, size-distance invariants, and size constancy. Thus "contrary to the Berkeleian tradition the world of the infant would seem to be inherently tridimensional" (Bower, 1972). There is evidence that before infants are capable of grasping, they can distinguish graspable from ungraspable objects, using purely visual information (Bruner and Koslowski, 1972).

Gregory observes that "the speed with which babies come to associate the properties of objects and go on to learn how to predict hidden properties and future events would be impossible unless some of the structure of the world were inherited—somehow innately built into the nervous system." [7] He suggests further that there may be a "grammar of vision," rather like the grammar of human language, and possibly related to the latter in the evolution of the species. Employing this "grammar of vision"—largely innate—higher animals are able to "read from retinal images even hidden features of objects, and predict their immediate future states," thus "to classify objects according to an internal grammar, to read reality from their eyes." The neural basis for this system is gradually coming to be understood since the pioneering work of Hubel and Wiesel (1962). More generally, there is every reason to suppose that "learning behavior occurs via modification of an already functional structural organization"; "survival would be improbable if learning in nature required the lengthy repetition characteristic of most conditioning procedures," and it is well known that animals acquire complex systems of behavior in other ways (John, 1972).

Despite the plausibility of many of the leading ideas of the rationalist tradition, and its affinity in crucial respects with the point of view of the natural sciences, it has often been dismissed or disregarded in the study of behavior and cognition. It is a curious fact about the intellectual history of the past few centuries that physical and mental development have been approached in quite different ways. No one would take seriously a proposal that the human organism learns through experience to have arms rather than wings, or that the basic structure of particular organs results from accidental experience. Rather, it is taken for granted that the physical structure of the organism is genetically determined, though of course variation along such dimensions as size, rate of development, and so forth will depend in part on external factors. From embryo to mature organism, a certain pattern of development is predetermined, with certain stages, such as the onset of puberty or the termination of growth, delayed by many years. Variety within these fixed patterns may be of great importance for human life, but the basic questions of scientific interest have to do with the fundamental, genetically determined scheme of growth and development that is a characteristic of the species and that gives rise to structures of marvelous intricacy.

The species characteristics themselves have evolved over long stretches of time, and evidently the environment provides conditions for differential reproduction, hence evolution of the species. But this is an entirely different question, and here too, questions can be raised about the physical laws that govern this evolution. Surely too little is known to justify any far-reaching claims.

The development of personality, behavior patterns, and cognitive structures in higher organisms has often been approached in a very different way. It is generally assumed that in these domains, social environment is the dominant factor. The structures of mind that develop over time are taken to be arbitrary and accidental; there is no "human nature" apart from what develops as a specific historical product. According to this view, typical of empiricist speculation, certain general principles of learning that are common in their essentials to all (or some large class of) organisms suffice to account for the cognitive structures attained by humans, structures which incorporate the principles by which human behavior is planned, organized, and controlled. I dismiss without further comment the exotic though influential view that "internal states" should not be considered in the study of behavior.[8]

But human cognitive systems, when seriously investigated, prove to be no less marvelous and intricate than the physical structures that develop in the life of the organism. Why, then, should we not study the acquisition of a cognitive structure such as language more or less as we study some complex bodily organ?

At first glance, the proposal may seem absurd, if only because of the great variety of human languages. But a closer consideration dispels these doubts. Even knowing very little of substance about linguistic universals, we can be quite sure that the possible variety of languages is sharply limited. Gross observations suffice to establish some qualitative conclusions. Thus, it is clear that the language each person acquires is a rich and complex construction hopelessly underdetermined by the fragmentary evidence available. This is why scientific inquiry into the nature of language is so difficult and so limited in its results. The conscious mind is endowed with no advance knowledge (or, recalling Aristotle, with only insufficiently developed advance knowledge). Thus, it is frustrated by the limitations of available evidence and faced by far too many possible explanatory theories, mutually inconsistent but adequate to the data. Or—as unhappy a state—it can devise no reasonable theory. Nevertheless, individuals in a speech community have developed essentially the same language. This fact can be explained only on the assumption that these individuals employ highly restrictive principles that guide the construction of grammar. Furthermore, humans are, obviously, not designed to learn one human language rather than another; the system of principles must be a species property. Powerful constraints must be operative restricting the variety of languages. It is natural that in our daily life we should concern ourselves only with differences among people, ignoring uniformities of structure. But different intellectual demands arise when we seek to understand what kind of organism a human really is.

The idea of regarding the growth of language as analogous to the development of a bodily organ is thus quite natural and plausible. It is fair to ask why the empiricist belief to the contrary has had such appeal to the modern temper. Why has it been so casually assumed that there exists a "learning theory" that can account for the acquisition of cognitive structures through experience? Is there some body of evidence, established through scientific inquiry, or observation, or introspection, that leads us to regard mental and physical development in such different ways? Surely the answer is that there is not. Science offers no reason to "accept the common maxim that there is nothing in the intellect which was not first in the senses," or to question the denial of this maxim in rationalist philosophy.[9] Investigation of human intellectual achievements, even of the most commonplace sort, gives no support for this thesis.

Empiricist speculation and the "science of behavior" that
has developed within its terms have proved rather barren,
perhaps because of the peculiar assumptions that have
guided and limited such inquiry. The grip of empiricist
doctrine in the modern period, outside of the natural sciences, is to be explained on sociological or historical
grounds.[10] The position itself has little to recommend it on
grounds of empirical evidence or inherent plausibility or
explanatory power. I do not think that this doctrine would
attract a scientist who is able to discard traditional myth
and to approach the problems afresh. Rather, it serves as an
impediment, an insurmountable barrier to fruitful inquiry,
much as the religious dogmas of an earlier period stood in
the way of the natural sciences.

It is sometimes argued that modern empiricism overcomes the limitations of the earlier tradition, but I think
that this belief is seriously in error. Hume, for example,
presented a substantive theory of "the secret springs and
principles, by which the human mind is actuated in its
operations." In his investigation of the foundations of
knowledge, he suggested specific principles that constitute
"a species of natural instincts." Modern empiricists who disparage Hume have simply replaced his theory by vacuous
systems that preserve empiricist (or more narrowly, behaviorist) terminology while depriving traditional ideas of their
substance. I have discussed this matter elsewhere (cf. chapter 4), and will not pursue it here.

In recent years, many of these issues, long dormant, have
been revived, in part in connection with the study of language. There has been much discussion of the so-called
"innateness hypothesis," which holds that one of the faculties of the mind, common to the species, is a faculty of
language that serves the two basic functions of rationalist
theory: it provides a sensory system for the preliminary
analysis of linguistic data, and a schematism that determines, quite narrowly, a certain class of grammars. Each

grammar is a theory of a particular language, specifying formal and semantic properties of an infinite array of sentences. These sentences, each with its particular structure, constitute the language generated by the grammar. The languages so generated are those that can be "learned" in the normal way. The language faculty, given appropriate stimulation, will construct a grammar; the person knows the language generated by the constructed grammar. This knowledge can then be used to understand what is heard and to produce discourse as an expression of thought within the constraints of the internalized principles, in a manner appropriate to situations as these are conceived by other mental faculties, free of stimulus control.[11] Questions related to the language faculty and its exercise are the ones that, for me at least, give a more general intellectual interest to the technical study of language.

I would now like to consider the so-called "innateness hypothesis," to identify some elements in it that are or should be controversial, and to sketch some of the problems that arise as we try to resolve the controversy. Then, we may try to see what can be said about the nature and exercise of the linguistic competence that has been acquired, along with some related matters.

A preliminary observation is that the term "innateness hypothesis" is generally used by critics rather than advocates of the position to which it refers. I have never used the term, because it can only mislead. Every "theory of learning" that is even worth considering incorporates an innateness hypothesis. Thus, Hume's theory proposes specific innate structures of mind and seeks to account for all of human knowledge on the basis of these structures, even postulating unconscious and innate knowledge. (Cf. chapter 4.) The question is not whether learning presupposes innate structure—of course it does; that has never been in doubt—but rather what these innate structures are in particular domains.

What is a theory of learning? Is there such a theory as *the* theory of learning, waiting to be discovered? Let us try to sharpen and perhaps take some steps towards answering these questions.

Consider first how a neutral scientist—that imaginary ideal—might proceed to investigate the question. The natural first step would be to select an organism, O, and a reasonably well delimited cognitive domain, D, and to attempt to construct a theory that we might call "the learning theory for the organism O in the domain D." This theory— call it LT(O,D)—can be regarded as a system of principles, a mechanism, a function, which has a certain "input" and a certain "output" (its domain and range, respectively). The "input" to the system LT(O,D) will be an analysis of data in D by O; the output" (which is, of course, internally represented, not overt and exhibited) will be a cognitive structure of some sort. This cognitive structure is one element of the cognitive state attained by O.

For example, take O to be humans and D language. Then LT(H,L)—the learning theory for humans in the domain language—will be the system of principles by which humans arrive at knowledge of language, given linguistic experience, that is, given a preliminary analysis that they develop for the data of language. Or, take O to be rats and D to be maze running. Then LT(R,M) is the system of principles used by rats in learning how to run mazes. The input to LT (R,M) is whatever preliminary analysis of data is used by rats to accomplish this feat, and the output is the relevant cognitive structure, however it should properly be characterized as a component of the state achieved by the rat who knows how to run a maze. There is no reason to doubt that the cognitive structure attained and the cognitive state of which it is a constituent will be rather complex.

To facilitate the discussion, let us make two simplifying assumptions. Assume first that individuals of the species O under investigation are essentially identical with respect to their ability to learn over the domain D—for example, that humans do not differ in language-learning capacity. Second, assume that learning can be conceptualized as an instantaneous process in the following sense: assume that LT(O,D) is presented with a cumulative record of all the data available to O up to a particular moment, and that LT(O,D), operating on that data, produces the cognitive structure attained at that moment. Neither of these assumptions is true: there are individual differences, and learning takes place over time, sometimes extended time. I will return later to the question of just "how false" these assumptions are. I think that they give a useful first approximation, helpful for the formulation of certain issues and possibly much more.

To pursue the study of a given LT(O,D) in a rational way, we will proceed through the following stages of inquiry:

1. Set the cognitive domain D.

2. Determine how O characterizes data in D "pretheoretically," thus constructing what we may call "the experience of O in D" (recall the idealization to "instantaneous learning").

3. Determine the nature of the cognitive structure attained; that is, determine, as well as possible, what is learned by O in the domain D.

4. Determine LT(O,D), the system that relates experience to what is learned.

Step 4 relies on the results attained in steps 2 and 3.

To avoid misunderstanding, perhaps I should stress that the ordering of steps is a kind of rational reconstruction of rational inquiry. In practice, there is no strict sequence. Work at level 4, for example, may convince us that our original delimitation of D was faulty, that we have failed to abstract a coherent cognitive domain. Or, it may lead us to conclude that we have misconstrued the character of what is learned, at step 3. It remains true, nevertheless, that we can hope to gain some insight at the level of step 4 only to the extent that we have achieved some understanding at levels 2 and 3 and have selected, wisely or luckily, at level 1. It is senseless to try to relate two systems—in this case, experience and what is learned—without some fairly good idea of what they are.

Parenthetically, we might observe that step 3 is missing in many formulations of psychological theory, much to their detriment. In fact, even the concept "what is learned" is missing in familiar "learning theories." Where it is missing, the basic questions of "learning theory" cannot even be formulated.

How does the study of behavior fit into this framework? Surely a prerequisite to the study of behavior is a grasp of the nature of the organism that is behaving—in the sense of "prerequisite" just explained. An organism has attained a certain state through maturation and experience. It is faced with certain objective conditions. It then does something. In principle, we might want to inquire into the mechanism M that determines what the organism does (perhaps probabilistically) given its past experience and its present stimulus conditions. I say "in principle," because I doubt that there is very much that we will be able to say about this question.

No doubt what the organism does depends in part on its experience, but it seems to me entirely hopeless to investigate directly the relation between experience and action. Rather, if we are interested in the problem of "causation of behavior" as a problem of science, we should at least analyze the relation of experience to behavior into two parts: first, LT, which relates experience to cognitive state,[12] and second, a mechanism, M_{cs}, which relates stimulus conditions to behavior, given the cognitive state CS.

To put it schematically, in place of the hopeless task of

investigating M as in (I), we may more reasonably under-take research into the nature of LT as in (II) and M_{CS} as in (III).

(I)   M: (experience, stimulus conditions) ———→ be-havior

(II) LT: experience ———→ cognitive state CS

(III) M_{CS}: stimulus conditions ———→ behavior (given CS)

I think that we can make considerable progress towards understanding LT as in (II); that is, towards understanding particular LT(O,D)'s, for various choices of D given O, and the interaction among them. It is this problem that I want to consider here. I doubt that we can learn very much, as scientists at least, about the second of these two parts, M_{CS}.[13] But it seems to me most unlikely that there will be any scientific progress at all if we do not at least analyze the problem of "causation of behavior" into the two com-ponents LT and M_{CS} and their elements. An attempt along the lines of (I) to study directly the relation of behavior to past and current experience is doomed to triviality and sci-entific insignificance.

Returning to the problem of learning, suppose that we have determined a number of LT(O,D)'s, for various choices of organism O and cognitive domain D. We can now turn to the question: What is "learning theory"? Or better: Is there such a theory as learning theory? The question might be put in various ways, for example, the following two:

(1)   Is it the case that however we select O and D, we find the same LT(O,D)?

(2)   Are there significant features common to all LT(O,D)'s?

Before considering these questions, let us return to the first of our simplifying assumptions, namely, with regard to variability within the species O. I would like to suggest that the interesting questions of "learning theory, those that might lead to a theory that is illuminating and that will ultimately relate to the body of natural science more generally, will be those for which our first assumption is essentially correct. That is, the interesting questions, those that offer some hope of leading to insight into the nature of organisms, will be those that arise in the investigation of learning in domains where there is a nontrivial structure uniform for members of O (with certain parameters relating to rapidity of learning, scope of learning, rate of forgetting, and other such marginal phenomena for which variability is to be expected). These are the questions that deal with significant characteristics of the species, or perhaps, of organisms generally. Again, I see no reason why cognitive structures should not be investigated rather in the way that physical organs are studied. The natural scientist will be primarily concerned with the basic, genetically determined structure of these organs and their interaction, a structure common to the species in the most interesting case, abstracting away from size, variation in rate of development, and so on.

If we can accept this judgment, then LT(O,D) can be characterized for O taken not as an individual but as a species—hence for individuals apart from gross abnormalities. And we may proceed to qualify question (1), asking whether LT(O,D) is identical with LT(O′,D′) apart from such matters as rapidity, facility, scope, and retention, which may vary across species and, to a lesser extent, among individuals of a given species.

Consider now question (1), so qualified. Surely the answer must still be a firm No. Even the crudest considerations suffice to show that there is no hope of reaching a positive answer to this question. Take O to be humans (H) and O′ rats (R); D to be language (L) and D′ maze running (M). If even some vague approximation to question (1) had a positive answer, we would expect humans to be as much superior to rats in maze-learning ability as they are in language-learning ability. But this is so grossly false that the question cannot be seriously entertained. Humans are roughly comparable to rats in the domain M but incomparable in the domain L. In fact, it seems that "white rats can even best college students in this sort of learning"—namely, maze-learning (Munn, 1971, p. 118). The distinction between the pair $(LT(H,L), LT(R,L))$ on the one hand and the pair $(LT(H,M), LT(R,M))$ on the other cannot be attributed to sensory processing systems and the like, as we can see by "transposing" language into some modality accessible to rats. (Cf. chapter 4, note 14.) As far as is now known—and I say this despite suggestions to the contrary—the same is true if we consider other organisms (say, chimpanzees) in place of rats. Putting this interesting but peripheral question to the side, it is surely obvious at once that no version of question (1) is worth pursuing.

Let us turn to the more plausible speculation formulated in question (2). No answer is possible, for the present. The question is hopelessly premature. We lack an interesting conception of $LT(O,D)$ for various choices of O and D. There are, I believe, some substantive steps possible towards $LT(H,L)$, but nothing comparable in other domains of human learning. What is known about other animals, to my knowledge, suggests no interesting answer to (2). Animals learn to care for their young, build nests, orient themselves in space, find their place in a dominance structure, identify the species, and so on, but we should not expect to find significant properties which are common to the various $LT(O,D)$'s that enter into these achievements. Skepticism about question (2) is very much in order, on the basis of the very little that is known. I should think that for the biologist, the comparative physiologist, or the physiological psychologist, such skepticism would appear quite unremarkable.

Thus, for the present, there seems to be no reason to

suppose that learning theory exists. At least, I see no interesting formulation of the thesis that there is such a theory that has initial plausibility or significant empirical support.

Within the odd variant of empiricism known as "behaviorism," the term "learning theory" has commonly been used, not as the designation of a theory (if it exists) that accounts for the attainment of cognitive structures on the basis of experience (namely, (II) above), but rather as a theory that deals with the relation of experience to behavior (namely, (I) above). Since there is no reason to suppose that learning theory exists, there is certainly no reason to expect that such a "theory of behavior" exists.

We might consider contentions more plausible than those implicit in questions (1) and (2). Suppose that we fix the organism O, and let D range over various cognitive domains. Then we might ask whether there is some interesting set of domains $D_1, \ldots, D_n$ such that:

(3) $LT(O,D_i) = LT(O,D_j)$; or $LT(O,D_i)$ is similar in interesting ways to $LT(O,D_j)$.

There might be some way of delimiting domains that would yield a positive answer to (3). If so, we could say that within this delimitation, the organism learns in similar or identical ways across cognitive domains. It would be interesting, for example, to discover whether there is some cognitive domain D other than language for which $LT(H,L)$ is identical to or similar to $LT(H,D)$. To date, no persuasive suggestion has been made, but conceivably there is such a domain. There is no particular reason to expect that there is such a domain, and one can only be surprised at the dogmatic view, commonly expressed, that language learning proceeds by application of general learning capacities. The most that we can say is that the possibility is not excluded, though there is no evidence for it and little plausibility to the contention. Even at the level of sensory processing there appear to be adaptations directly related to language, as already noted.[14] The proposal that language learning is simply an instance of "generalized learning capacities" makes about as much sense, in the present state of our knowledge, as a claim that the specific neural structures that provide our organization of visual space must be a special case of the class of systems involved also in language use. This is true, so far as we know, only at a level so general as to give no insight into the character or functioning of the various systems.

For any organism O, we can try to discover those cognitive domains D for which the organism O has an interesting LT(O,D)—that is, an LT(O,D) that does not merely have the structure of trial-and-error learning, generalization along physically given dimensions, induction (in any well-defined sense of this notion), and so on. We might define the "cognitive capacity" of O as the system of domains D for which there is an interesting learning theory LT(O,D) in this sense.[15] For D within the cognitive capacity of O, it is reasonable to suppose that a schematism exists delimiting the class of cognitive structures that can be attained. Hence it will be possible, for such D, for a rich, complex, highly articulated cognitive structure to be attained with considerable uniformity among individuals (apart from matters of rate, scope, persistence, etc.) on the basis of scattered and restricted evidence.

Investigating the cognitive capacity of humans, we might consider, say, the ability to recognize and identify faces on exposure to a few presentations, to determine the personality structure of another person on brief contact (thus, to be able to guess, pretty well, how that person will react under a variety of conditions), to recognize a melody under transposition and other modifications, to handle those branches of mathematics that build on numerical or spatial intuition, to create art forms resting on certain principles of structure and organization, and so on. Humans appear to have characteristic and remarkable abilities in these domains, in that they construct a complex and intricate intellectual system, rapidly and uniformly, on the basis of degenerate evidence. And structures created by particularly talented individuals within these constraints are intelligible and appealing, exciting and thought-provoking even to those not endowed with unusual creative abilities. Inquiry, then, might lead to nontrivial LT(H,D)'s, for D so chosen. Such inquiry might involve experimentation or even historical investigation—for example, investigation of developments in forms of artistic composition or in mathematics that seemed "natural" and proved fruitful at particular historical moments, contributing to a "mainstream" of intellectual evolution rather than diverting energy to an unproductive side channel.[16]

Suppose that for a particular organism O, we manage to learn something about its cognitive capacity, developing a system of LT(O,D)'s for various choices of D with the rough properties sketched above. We would then have arrived at a theory of the mind of O, in one sense of this term. We may think of "the mind of O," to adapt a formulation of Anthony Kenny's,[17] as the innate capacity of O to construct cognitive structures, that is, to learn.

I depart here from Kenny's formulation in two respects, which perhaps deserve mention. He defines "mind" as a second-order capacity to acquire "intellectual abilities," such as knowledge of English—the latter "itself a capacity or ability: an ability whose exercise is the speaking, understanding, reading of English." Moreover, "to have a mind is to have the capacity to acquire the ability to operate with symbols in such a way that it is one's own activity that makes them symbols and confers meaning on them," so that automata operating with formal elements that are symbols for us but not for them do not have minds. For the sake of this discussion, I have generalized here beyond first-order capacities involving operations with symbols, and am thus considering second-order capacities broader than "mind" in Kenny's quite natural sense. So far there is no issue beyond terminology. Secondly, I want to consider mind (in the narrower or broader sense) as an innate capacity to form cognitive structures, not first-order capacities to act. The cognitive structures attained enter into our first-order capacities to act, but should not be identified with them. Thus it does not seem to me quite accurate to take "knowledge of English" to be a capacity or ability, though it enters into the capacity or ability exercised in language use. In principle, one might have the cognitive structure that we call "knowledge of English," fully developed, with no capacity to use this structure; [18] and certain capacities to carry out "intellectual activities" may involve no cognitive structures but merely a network of dispositions and habits, something quite different. [19] Knowledge, understanding, or belief is at a level more abstract than capacity.

There has been a tendency in modern analytic philosophy to employ the notion "disposition" or "capacity" where the more abstract concept of "cognitive structure" is, I believe, more appropriate. (Cf. chapter 4; also Chomsky, 1975a.) I think we see here an unfortunate residue of empiricism. The notions "capacity" and "family of dispositions" are more closely related to behavior and "language use"; they do not lead us to inquire into the nature of the "ghost in the machine" through the study of cognitive structures and their organization, as normal scientific practice and intellectual curiosity would demand. The proper way to exorcise the ghost in the machine is to determine the structure of the mind and its products. [20] There is nothing essentially mysterious about the concept of an abstract cognitive structure, created by an innate faculty of mind, represented in some still-unknown way in the brain, and entering into the system of capacities and dispositions to act and interpret. On the contrary, a formulation along these lines, embodying the conceptual competence-performance distinction (cf. Chomsky, 1965, chap. 1) seems a prerequisite for a serious investigation of behavior. Human action can be understood only on the assumption that first-order capacities and families of dispositions to behave involve the use of cognitive structures that express systems of (unconscious) knowledge, belief, expectation, evaluation, judgment, and the like. At least, so it seems to me.

Returning to the main theme, suppose that we now select a problem in a domain D that falls outside of O's cognitive capacity. O will then be at a loss as to how to proceed. O will have no cognitive structure available for dealing with this problem and no LT(O,D) available to enable it to develop such a structure. O will therefore have to proceed by trial and error, association, simple induction, and generalization along certain available dimensions (some questions arise here, which I put aside). Taking O to be humans, we will not expect the person to be able to find or construct a rich and insightful way to deal with the problem, to develop a relevant cognitive structure in the intuitive, unconscious manner characteristic of language learning and other domains in which humans excel.

Humans might be able to construct a conscious scientific theory dealing with problems in the domain in question, but that is a different matter—or better, a partially different matter, since even here there are crucial constraints. An intellectually significant science, an intelligible explanatory theory, can be developed by humans in case something close to the true theory in a certain domain happens to fall within human "science-forming" capacities. The LT(H,D)'s involved in scientific inquiry, whatever they may be, must be special and restrictive, or it would be impossible for scientists to converge in their judgment on particular explanatory theories that go far beyond the evidence at hand, as they customarily do in those few fields where there really is significant progress, while at the same time rejecting much evidence as irrelevant or beside the point, for the moment at least. The same LT(H,D)'s that provide for the vast and impressive scope of scientific understanding must also sharply constrain the class of humanly accessible sciences. There is, surely, no evolutionary pressure that leads humans to have minds capable of discovering significant explanatory theories in specific fields of inquiry. Thinking of humans as biological organisms in the natural world, it is only a lucky accident if their cognitive capacity happens to be well matched to scientific truth in some area. It should come as no surprise, then, that there are so few sciences, and that so much of human inquiry fails to attain any intellectual depth. Investigation of human cognitive capacity might give us some insight into the class of humanly accessible sciences, possibly a small subset of those potential sciences that deal with matters concerning which we hope (vainly) to attain some insight and understanding.

As a case in point, consider our near-total failure to discover a scientific theory that provides an analysis of Mcs of (III) on page 17—that is, our very limited progress in developing a scientific theory of any depth to account for the normal use of language (or other aspects of behavior). Even the relevant concepts seem lacking; certainly, no intellectually satisfying principles have been proposed that have explanatory force, though the questions are very old. It is not excluded that human science-forming capacities simply do not extend to this domain, or any domain involving the exercise of will, so that for humans, these questions will always be shrouded in mystery.

Note, incidentally, how misleading it would be to speak simply of "limitations" in human science-forming capacity. Limits no doubt exist, but they derive from the same source as our ability to construct rich cognitive systems on the basis of limited evidence in the first place. Were it not for the factors that limit scientific knowledge, we could have no such knowledge in any domain.[21]

Suppose that in investigating organisms, we decide, perversely, to restrict ourselves to tasks and problems that lie outside their cognitive capacity. We might then expect to discover simple "laws of learning" of some generality. Suppose further that we define a "good experiment" as one that provides smooth learning curves, regular increments and extinction, and so on. Then there will be "good experiments" only in domains that lie outside of O's cognitive capacity. For example, there will be no "good experiments" in the study of human language learning, though there may be if we concentrate attention on memorization of nonsense syllables, verbal association, and other tasks for which humans have no special abilities.

Suppose now that some branch of inquiry develops, limited in principle to "good experiments" in something like this sense. This discipline may, indeed, develop laws of learning that do not vary too greatly across cognitive domains for a particular organism and that have some cross-species validity. It will, of necessity, avoid those domains in which an organism is specially designed to acquire rich cognitive structures that enter into its life in an intimate fashion. The discipline will be of virtually no intellectual interest, it seems to me, since it is restricting itself in principle to those questions that are guaranteed to tell us little about the nature of organisms. For we can learn something significant about this nature only by inquiry into the organism's cognitive capacity, inquiry that will permit no "good experiments" in the strange sense just specified, though it may lead to the discovery (through experiment and observation) of intricate and no doubt highly specific LT(O,D)'s. The results and achievements of this perversely limited, rather suicidal discipline are largely an artifact. It will be condemned in principle to investigation of peripheral matters such as rate and scope of acquisition of information, the relation between arrangement of reinforcers and response strength, control of behavior, and the like. The discipline in question may continue indefinitely to amass information about these matters, but one may question the point or purpose of these efforts.

A more elaborate study of cognitive capacity raises still further questions. Thus, some intellectual achievements, such as language learning, fall strictly within biologically determined cognitive capacity. For these tasks, we have "special design," so that cognitive structures of great complexity and interest develop fairly rapidly and with little if any conscious effort. There are other tasks, no more "complex" along any absolute scale (assuming that it is possible even to make sense of this notion), which will be utterly baffling because they fall beyond cognitive capacity. Consider problems that lie at the borderline of cognitive capacity. These will provide opportunity for intriguing intellectual play. Chess, for example, is not so remote from cognitive capacity as to be merely a source of insoluble puzzles, but is at the same time sufficiently beyond our natural abilities so that it is challenging and intriguing. Here, we would expect to find that the slight differences between individuals are magnified to striking divergence of aptitude.

The study of challenging intellectual tasks might give some insight into human intelligence, at the borders of cognitive capacity, just as the study of the ability to run a four-minute mile may give useful information about human physiology. But it would be pointless to study the latter feat at a very early stage of our understanding of human locomotion—say, if we knew only that humans walk rather than fly. Correspondingly, in the present state of our understanding of mental abilities, it seems to me that, for example, the study of chess-playing programs may teach something about the theory of chess, but is unlikely to contribute much to the study of human intelligence. It is good procedure to study major factors before turning to tenth-order effects, to study the basic character of an intricate system before exploring its borders, though of course one can never know in advance just what line of inquiry will provide sudden illumination.[22]

In the case of human cognition, it is the study of the basic cognitive structures within cognitive capacity, their development and use, that should receive priority, I believe, if we are to attain a real understanding of the mind and its workings.

The preceding discussion is not very precise. I hope that it is at least suggestive as to how a rational study of learning might proceed. Let me now turn to the particular questions in the "theory of learning" that concern language.

Let us take O to be humans (H) and D to be language (L). What is LT(H,L)? Of the two simplifying assumptions mentioned earlier, the first—invariability across the species—is, so far as we know, fair enough. It seems to provide a close approximation to the facts. Let us therefore accept it with no further discussion, while keeping a cautious and skeptical eye on the second assumption, that learning is "instantaneous." I will return to the latter in chapter 3.

LT(H,L) is the system of mechanisms and principles put to work in acquisition of knowledge of language—acquisition of the specific cognitive structure that we are calling "grammar"—given data which are a fair and adequate sample of this language.[23] The grammar is a system of rules and principles that determine the formal and semantic properties of sentences. The grammar is put to use, interacting with other mechanisms of mind, in speaking and understanding language. There are empirical assumptions and conceptual distinctions embedded in this account, and they might be wrong or misguided, but I think it is not unreasonable, given present understanding, to proceed with them.

To relate these remarks to earlier discussion, note that I am insisting that the relation of experience to action be subdivided into two systems: LT(H,L), which relates experience to cognitive state attained, and M_{CS}, which relates current conditions to action, given cognitive state attained (cf. (II)–(III), p. 17). One of the cognitive structures entering into the cognitive state CS attained and put to use by M_{CS} is grammar. Again, I see few present prospects for the scientific study of M_{CS}, though the study of LT(H,L), it seems to me, can be profitably pursued.

Let us define "universal grammar" (UG) as the system of principles, conditions, and rules that are elements or properties of all human languages not merely by accident but by necessity—of course, I mean biological, not logical, necessity. Thus UG can be taken as expressing "the essence of human language." UG will be invariant among humans. UG will specify what language learning must achieve, if it takes place successfully. Thus UG will be a significant component of LT(H,L). What is learned, the cognitive structure attained, must have the properties of UG, though it will have other properties as well, accidental properties. Each human language will conform to UG; languages will differ in other, accidental properties. If we were to construct a language violating UG, we would find that it could not be learned by LT(H,L). That is, it would not be learnable under normal conditions of access and exposure to data. Possibly it could be learned by application of other faculties of mind; LT(H,L) does not exhaust the capacities of the human mind. This invented language might be learned as a puzzle, or its grammar might be discovered by scientific inquiry over the course of generations, with the intervention of individual genius, with explicit articulation of principles and careful experimentation. This would be possible if the language happened to fall within the bounds of the "science-forming" component of human cognitive capacity. But discovery of the grammar of this language would not be comparable to language learning, just as inquiry in physics is qualitatively different from language learning.

UG will specify properties of sound, meaning, and structural organization. We may expect that in all of these domains, UG will impose conditions that narrowly restrict the variety of languages. For familiar reasons, we cannot conclude from the highly restrictive character of UG that there is a translation procedure of any generality or significance, even in principle (cf. Chomsky, 1965). And quite obviously, nothing is implied about the possibility of translating actual texts, since a speaker or writer naturally presupposes a vast background of unspecified assumptions, beliefs, attitudes, and conventions. The point is perhaps worth noting, since there has been much confusion about the matter. For some discussion, see Keyser (1975).

We can gain some insight into UG, hence LT(H,L), whenever we find properties of language that can reasonably be supposed not to have been learned. To make the discussion more concrete, consider a familiar example, perhaps the simplest one that is not entirely trivial. Think of the process of forming questions in English. Imagine again our neutral scientist, observing a child learning English. Suppose that he discovers that the child has learned to form such questions as those of (A), corresponding to the associated declaratives:

(A)   the man is tall—is the man tall?
      the book is on the table—is the book on the table?
      etc.

Observing these facts, the scientist might arrive at the following tentative hypothesis as to what the child is doing, assuming now that sentences are analyzed into words:

Hypothesis 1: The child processes the declarative sentence from its first word (i.e., from "left to right"), continuing until he reaches the first occurrence of the word "is" (or others like it: "may," "will," etc.); he then preposes this occurrence of "is," producing the corresponding question (with some concomitant modifications of form that need not concern us).

This hypothesis works quite well. It is also extremely simple. The scientist has every right to be satisfied, and will be able to find a great deal of evidence to support his tentative hypothesis. Of course, the hypothesis is false, as we learn from such examples as (B) and (C):

(B) the man who is tall is in the room—is the man who is tall in the room?

(C) the man who is tall is in the room—is the man who tall is in the room?

Our scientist would discover, surely, that on first presentation with an example such as "the man who is tall is in the room," the child unerringly forms the question (B), not (C) (if he can handle the example at all). Children make many mistakes in language learning, but never mistakes such as exemplified in (C). If the scientist is reasonable, this discovery will surprise him greatly, for it shows that his simple hypothesis 1 is false, and that he must construct a far more complex hypothesis to deal with the facts. The correct hypothesis is the following, ignoring complications that are irrelevant here:

Hypothesis 2: The child analyzes the declarative sentence into abstract phrases; he then locates the first occurrence of "is" (etc.) that follows the first noun phrase; he then preposes this occurrence of "is," forming the corresponding question.

Hypothesis 1 holds that the child is employing a "structure-independent rule"—that is, a rule that involves only analysis into words and the property "earliest" ("leftmost") defined on word sequences. Hypothesis 2 holds that the child is employing a "structure-dependent rule," a rule that involves analysis into words and phrases, and the property "earliest" defined on sequences of words analyzed into abstract phrases. The phrases are "abstract" in the sense that neither their boundaries nor their categories (noun phrase, verb phrase, etc.) need be physically marked. Sentences do not appear with brackets, intonation boundaries regularly marking phrases, subscripts identifying the type of phrase, or anything of the sort.

By any reasonable standards, hypothesis 2 is far more complex and "unlikely" than hypothesis 1. The scientist would have to be driven by evidence, such as (B), (C), to postulate hypothesis 2 in place of the simpler and more elementary hypothesis 1. Correspondingly, the scientist must ask why it is that the child unerringly makes use of the structure-dependent rule postulated in hypothesis 2, rather than the simpler structure-independent rule of hypothesis 1. There seems to be no explanation in terms of "communicative efficiency" or similar considerations. It is certainly absurd to argue that children are trained to use the structure-dependent rule, in this case. In fact, the problem never arises in language learning. A person may go through a considerable part of his life without ever facing relevant evidence, but he will have no hesitation in using the structure-dependent rule, even if all of his experience is consistent with hypothesis 1. The only reasonable conclusion is that UG contains the principle that all such rules must be structure-dependent. That is, the child's mind (specifically, its component LT(H,L)) contains the instruction: Construct a structure-dependent rule, ignoring all structure-independent rules. The principle of structure-dependence is not learned, but forms part of the conditions for language learning.

To corroborate this conclusion about UG (hence LT(H,L)), the scientist will ask whether other rules of English are invariably structure-dependent. So far as we know, the answer is positive. If a rule is found that is not structure-dependent, the scientist will be faced with a problem. He will have to inquire further into UG, to discover what additional principles differentiate the two categories of rules, so that the child can know without instruction that one is structure-dependent and the other not. Having gotten this far, the scientist will conclude that other languages must have the same property, on the assumption that humans are not specifically designed to learn one rather than another language, say English rather than Japanese. On this reasonable assumption, the principle of structure-dependence (perhaps, if necessary, qualified as indicated above) must hold universally, if it holds for English. Investigating the consequences of his reasoning, the scientist would discover (so far as we know) that the conclusion is correct.

More complex examples can be produced, but this simple one illustrates the general point. Proceeding in this way, the scientist can develop some rich and interesting hypotheses about UG, hence LT(H,L). Thus, learning theory for humans in the domain of language incorporates the principle of structure-dependence along with other more intricate (and, I should add, more controversial) principles like it. I will return to some of these in the third chapter.

Keeping this single example of a principle of UG in mind, let us return now to the "innateness hypothesis." Recall that there is no issue as to the necessity for such a hypothesis, only as to its character.

Assuming still the legitimacy of the simplifying assumption about instantaneous learning, the "innateness hypothesis" will consist of several elements: principles for the preliminary, pretheoretic analysis of data as experience, which serves as input to LT(H,L); properties of UG, which determine the character of what is learned; other principles of a sort not discussed in the foregoing sketch.

We might, quite reasonably, formulate the *theory of language* so as to reflect this way of looking at LT(H,L). A theory is a system of principles expressed in terms of certain concepts. The principles are alleged to be true of the subject matter of the theory. A particular presentation of a theory takes some of the concepts as primitive and some of the principles as axioms. The choice of primitives and axioms must meet the condition that all concepts are defined in terms of the primitives and that all principles derive from the axioms. We might choose to formulate linguistic theory by taking its primitive concepts to be those that enter into the preliminary analysis of data as experience, with the axioms including those principles expressing relations between the primitive concepts that enter into this preliminary analysis (thus, the primitive notions are "epistemologically primitive"; they meet an external empirical condition apart from sufficiency for definition). The defined terms belong to UG, and the principles of UG will be theorems of this theory. Linguistic theory, so construed, is a theory of UG incorporated into LT(H,L) in the manner described.

The "innateness hypothesis," then, can be formulated as follows: Linguistic theory, the theory of UG, construed in the manner just outlined, is an innate property of the human mind. In principle, we should be able to account for it in terms of human biology.

To the extent that our simplifying assumption about instantaneous learning must be revised, along lines to which

I will return, we must accordingly complicate the "innateness hypothesis."

A fuller version of the "innateness hypothesis" for humans will specify the various domains belonging to cognitive capacity, the faculty of mind LT(H,D) for each such domain D, the relations between these faculties, their modes of maturation, and the interactions among them through time. Alongside of the language faculty and interacting with it in the most intimate way is the faculty of mind that constructs what we might call "common-sense understanding," a system of beliefs, expectations, and knowledge concerning the nature and behavior of objects, their place in a system of "natural kinds," the organization of these categories, and the properties that determine the categorization of objects and the analysis of events. A general "innateness hypothesis" will also include principles that bear on the place and role of people in a social world, the nature and conditions of work, the structure of human action, will and choice, and so on. These systems may be unconscious for the most part and even beyond the reach of conscious introspection. One might also want to isolate for special study the faculties involved in problem solving, construction of scientific knowledge, artistic creation and expression, play, or whatever prove to be the appropriate categories for the study of cognitive capacity, and derivatively, human action.

In the next two chapters I want to say something more about a few of these mental faculties and their interaction.

CHAPTER 2

The
Object of Inquiry

I hope it will not be too repetitive if I begin by summarizing briefly what I have said so far, elaborating here and there along the way.

The theory of language is simply that part of human psychology that is concerned with one particular "mental organ," human language. Stimulated by appropriate and continuing experience, the language faculty creates a grammar that generates sentences with formal and semantic properties. We say that a person knows the language generated by this grammar. Employing other related faculties of mind and the structures they produce, he can then proceed to use the language that he now knows.[1]

With the progress of science, we may come to know something of the physical representation of the grammar and the language faculty—correspondingly, the cognitive state attained in language learning and the initial state in which there is a representation of UG (universal grammar) but of no specific grammar conforming to UG. For the present, we can only characterize the properties of grammars and of the language faculty in abstract terms.

It is sometimes argued that this contingency, inescapable for the present, deprives the theory of language of empirical content. The conclusion is incorrect. Thus, the single example I have so far given, the principle of structure-dependence, can easily be falsified if false, and the same is true of other proposals within UG or particular grammars. Similarly, it is possible to imagine discoveries in neurophysiology or in the study of behavior and learning that might lead us to revise or abandon a given theory of language or particular grammar, with its hypotheses about the components of the system and their interaction. The abstract nature of these theories permits some latitude in interpretation of particular results, especially insofar as we do not have a clear picture of how cognitive structures are embedded within the theory of performance. Latitude is not total license, however. The theoretical psychologist (in this case, the linguist), the experimental psychologist, and the neurophysiologist are engaged in a common enterprise, and each should exploit as fully as possible the insights derived from all approaches that seek to determine the initial state of the organism, the cognitive structures attained, and the manner in which these cognitive structures are employed. Care is necessary, however. Not infrequently in the psycholinguistic literature we read that particular conclusions about the nature of grammar, or about UG, or about the role of grammar in language use, must be rejected because they are inconsistent with what is known about the organization of memory, behavior, and so on. But what is actually known or even plausibly surmised about these matters is limited and generally still quite remote from the questions that arise in the theoretical study of language. There are some suggestive relations between sentence complexity and processing difficulty, and some other matters. Such evidence should be seriously considered for its possible bearing on the nature of the cognitive state attained and the mechanisms for attaining it.[2] But the evidence available does not support conclusions that are blandly presented in the literature, without argument, as if they were somehow established fact.[3]

A physical organ, say the heart, may vary from one person to the next in size or strength, but its basic structure and its function within human physiology are common to the species. Analogously, two individuals in the same speech community may acquire grammars that differ somewhat in scale and subtlety.[4] What is more, the products of the language faculty vary depending on triggering experience, ranging over the class of possible human languages (in principle). These variations in structure are limited, no doubt sharply, by UG; and the functions of language in human life are no doubt narrowly constrained as well, though no one has as yet found a way to go much beyond a descriptive taxonomy in dealing with this question.[5]

Restricting ourselves now to humans, suppose that we understand psychology to be the theory of mind, in the sense outlined earlier. Thus psychology is that part of human biology that is concerned at its deepest level with the second-order capacity to construct cognitive structures that enter into first-order capacities to act and to interpret experience. Psychology has as its primary concern the faculties of mind involved in cognitive capacity. Each such faculty of mind is represented as one of the LT(H,D)'s of earlier discussion. These faculties enable a person to attain intricate and uniform cognitive structures that are vastly underdetermined by triggering experience, and that need not relate to such experience in any simple way (say, as generalizations, higher-order generalizations, etc.). Rather, the relation of a cognitive structure to experience may be as remote and intricate as the relation of a nontrivial scientific theory to data; depending on the character of the "innateness hypothesis," the relation might be even more partial and indirect.

Such cognitive structures form part of the cognitive state achieved by the person at a given stage of maturation. This state also incorporates habit structures, dispositions, and capacities to employ cognitive structures. The primary concern of the study of learning is to identify the domains within cognitive capacity and to discover LT(H,D) for each such domain D. Furthermore, this inquiry will seek to map out the full system of cognitive capacity, exploring the relations between various domains, the interaction between LT(H,D)'s in learning, common properties or similarities (if any) between them, the ordering of accessibility of cognitive structures or accessibility relative to attained structures, and so on.

Psychology will also explore the organization of behavior under given situations, as these are analyzed by available cognitive structures (this is the study of M_{CS}; cf. (III), p. 17). We might try to approach the classic problem of accounting for action that is appropriate to situations but uncontrolled by stimuli in these terms. Given a partially structured system that provides an evaluation of outcomes, choices that are random except for maximizing "value" may have the appearance of free, purposeful, and intelligent behavior—but one must remain skeptical about this approach, though it is the only one that seems to fall within any conceptual framework intelligible to us.

Within cognitive capacity, the theory of mind has a distinctly rationalist cast. Learning is primarily a matter of filling in detail within a structure that is innate. We depart from the tradition in several respects, specifically, in taking the "*a priori* system" to be biologically determined.[6] Outside the bounds of cognitive capacity, an empiricist theory of learning applies, by unfortunate necessity. Hence little learning is possible, the scope of discovery is minimal, and uniformities will be found across domains and across species.

The language faculty is a particularly interesting element of cognitive capacity. We might inquire into its nature (specifically, the study of UG), its relation to other domains, and its uniqueness. We may ask whether Cartesian doctrine is correct in contending that this faculty is specific to the human species, the unique thinking creature. Does the inability of other species to develop languages of the human type derive from their lack of a specific quality of intelligence rather than from a mere limitation in a common intelligence, as Descartes thought? The dispute is a traditional one. There were, for example, those dismissed contemptuously by Antoine Le Grand, a leading expositor of Cartesian ideas in seventeenth-century England, who speaks of the opinion of "some certain *People* of the *East Indies*, who think that *Apes* and *Baboons*, which are with them in great numbers, are imbued with *understanding*, and that they can *speak* but will not for fear they should be imployed, and set to work." [7] In some ill-considered popularizations of interesting current research, it is virtually argued that higher apes have the capacity for language but have never put it to use—a remarkable biological miracle, given the enormous selectional advantage of even minimal linguistic skills, rather like discovering that some animal has wings but has never thought to fly.

It is a reasonable surmise, I think, that there is no structure similar to UG in nonhuman organisms and that the capacity for free, appropriate, and creative use of language as an expression of thought, with the means provided by the language faculty, is also a distinctive feature of the human species, having no significant analogue elsewhere. The neural basis for language is pretty much of a mystery, but there can be little doubt that specific neural structures and even gross organization not found in other primates (e.g., lateralization) play a fundamental role.[8]

We might expect that the procedures used to train apes in forms of symbolic behavior will succeed as well for humans with severe damage to the neural structures involved directly in language. There is some evidence that this is true.[9] Efforts to induce symbolic behavior in other species might illuminate the specific properties of human language, just as the study of how birds fly might be advanced, in principle, by an investigation of how people jump or fish swim. Some might argue that more is to be expected in the latter case: after all, flying and jumping are both forms of locomotion; both involve going up and coming down; with diligent effort and special training people can jump higher and farther. Perhaps some hopelessly confused observer might argue, on these grounds, that the distinction between jumping and flying is arbitrary, a matter of degree; people can really fly, just like birds, only less well. Analogous proposals in the case of language seem to me to have no greater force or significance.

Returning to human psychology, consider the question how the language faculty fits into the system of cognitive capacity. I have been assuming that UG suffices to determine particular grammars (where, again, a grammar is a system of rules and principles that generates an infinite class of sentences with their formal and semantic properties). But this might not be the case. It is a coherent and perhaps correct proposal that the language faculty constructs a grammar only in conjunction with other faculties of mind. If so, the language faculty itself provides only an abstract framework, an idealization that does not suffice to determine a grammar.

Suppose that there is no sharp delimitation between those semantic properties that are "linguistic" and those that form part of common-sense understanding, that is, the cognitive system dealing with the nature of things named, described, or discussed. Thus, lexical items might be related by principles that form a kind of central core for a system of common-sense beliefs,[10] with no sharp distinction between analytic and synthetic propositions. Or, imagine that terms for "natural kinds" are in part characterized by "stereotypes" in Hilary Putnam's sense.[11] A tiger, then, is something not too unlike given exemplars, and with the same internal structure (perhaps unknown) as the stereotype. Under this assumption, lexical items are located in a "semantic space" generated by the interaction of the language faculty and other faculties of mind. Few if any of these words will have "senses" in the sense of Frege, strictly speaking. The "criterion in mind" that determines the applicability of the term "tiger" will involve actual exemplars. The essential rolè of possibly unknown inner structure permits change of presumed reference without a change in the concept itself ("a change of sense"); and the reference of the term will be a function of the place of the associated concept in the nonlinguistic system of common-sense understanding. Only through its association with the latter system will the term "tiger" acquire something on the order of a Fregean "sense," though the linguistic system may provide some more abstract semantic properties (say, some "semantic markers" of the sort that Katz discusses[12]).

Suppose further that the operation of rules of grammar is in part determined by semantic properties of lexical items; to form passive sentences, for example, we must take into account semantic properties of verbs and their "thematic relations" to surrounding noun phrases.

These are by no means implausible ideas. If they are correct, the language faculty does not fix a grammar in isolation, even in principle. The theory of UG remains as a component of the theory of mind, but as an abstraction. Note that this conclusion, if correct, does not imply that the language faculty does not exist as an autonomous component of mental structure. Rather, the position we are now considering postulates that this faculty does exist, with a physical realization yet to be discovered, and places it within the system of mental faculties in a fixed way. Some might regard this picture as overly complex, but the idea that the system of cognitive structures must be far more simple than the little finger does not have very much to recommend it.

The place of the language faculty within cognitive capacity is a matter for discovery, not stipulation. The same is true of the place of grammar within the system of acquired cognitive structures. My own, quite tentative, belief is that there is an autonomous system of formal grammar, determined in principle [13] by the language faculty and its component UG. This formal grammar generates abstract structures that are associated with "logical forms" (in a sense of this term to which I will return) by further principles of grammar. But beyond this, it may well be impossible to distinguish sharply between linguistic and nonlinguistic components of knowledge and belief. Thus an actual language may result only from the interaction of several mental faculties, one being the faculty of language. There may be no concrete specimens of which we can say, These are solely the product of the language faculty; and no specific acts that result solely from the exercise of linguistic functions.[14]

Questions of this nature face us no matter what corner of language we try to investigate. There is no "sublanguage" so primitive as to escape these complexities, a fact that comes as no surprise to someone who is persuaded of the essential correctness of the rationalist framework outlined earlier. For in accordance with this view, a grammar is not a structure of higher-order concepts and principles constructed from simpler elements by "abstraction" or "generalization" or "induction." Rather, it is a rich structure of predetermined form, compatible with triggering experience and more highly valued, by a measure that is itself part of UG, than other cognitive structures meeting the dual conditions of compatibility with the structural principles of UG and with relevant experience.[15] There need be no isolable "simple" or "elementary" components within such a system.

Consider, for example, the category of names and the act of naming, which might be regarded as somehow primitive and isolable. A name, let us suppose, is associated with a thing by an original stipulation, and the association is then conveyed in some manner to others. Consider the original stipulation. The name is drawn from the system of language, and the thing is chosen in terms of the categories of "common-sense understanding." Thus two major faculties of mind, at least, place conditions on the stipulation. There are complex conditions—poorly understood, though illustrative examples are not hard to find—that an entity must satisfy to qualify as a "naturally nameable" thing: these conditions involve spatiotemporal contiguity, *Gestalt* qualities, functions within the space of human actions. (Cf. chapter 4, p. 203.) A collection of leaves on a tree, for example, is not a nameable thing, but it would fall within this category if a new art form of "leaf arrangement" were devised and some artist had composed the collection of leaves as a work of art. He could then stipulate that his creation was to be named "serenity." Thus it seems that there is an essential reference even to willful acts, in determining what is a nameable thing.

Furthermore, in determining that an entity is a nameable thing, we assign it to a "natural kind" that might be designated by a common noun, a "sortal predicate." Otherwise (excluding mass terms), it is not nameable. This assignment involves assumptions about the nature of the thing named, some conceptual and some factual. In our system of common-sense understanding, natural kinds are defined by internal structure, constitution, origin, function (for artifacts), and other properties. This is not to say that we necessarily know the defining structure, and so on, but that we assume that it exists and that new entities are assigned correctly to the "sort" and designated by the sortal predicate just in case they share the "essential properties," whatever they are. We may not know just what internal structure determines that such-and-such is a tiger, but something looking and acting just like a tiger is not properly assigned to this category if it in fact differs from "stereotypic" tigers in internal structure. This is a conceptual requirement, drawn from the structure of common-sense understanding. But factual beliefs and common-sense expectations also play a role in determining that a thing is categorizable and hence nameable. Consider Wittgenstein's disappearing chair. In his terms, we have no "rules saying whether one may use the word 'chair' to include this kind of thing" (Wittgenstein, 1953, p. 38). Or to put it differently, we keep certain factual assumptions about the behavior of objects fixed when we categorize them and thus take them as eligible for naming or description.[16]

At least this much of the system of common-sense understanding seems to be involved in the stipulation that a thing is named so-and-so. Furthermore, the cognitive structure of language imposes its own conditions. Languages do not seem to have a category of pure names, in the logician's sense. Rather there are personal names, place names, color names, and so on. Discussing the Aristotelian theory of language, Julius Moravcsik (1975a) has argued that in it "there are no expressions that perform solely the task of referring. Individuals are given by certain privileged terms that specify domains of discourse." I think this is true of natural language. The domains of discourse must be related to the categories of common-sense understanding, though how closely is a fair question. Needless to say, the structure of the two interacting systems that enter into the act of naming need not be open (or even accessible) to the conscious mind. It is, again, an empirical problem to determine the character of the cognitive structures that are involved in the apparently simple act of naming.

Names are not associated with objects in some arbitrary manner. Nor does it seem very illuminating to regard them as "cluster terms" in the Wittgensteinian sense.[17] Each name belongs to a linguistic category that enters in a determinate way into the system of grammar, and the objects named are placed in a cognitive structure of some complexity. These structures remain operative as names are "transferred" to new users.[18] Noting that an entity is named such-and-such, the hearer brings to bear a system of linguistic structure to place the name, and a system of conceptual relations and conditions, along with factual beliefs, to place the thing named. To understand "naming," we would have to understand these systems and the faculties of mind through which they arise.

I mentioned the notion "essential properties," referring it, however, to the systems of language and common-sense understanding. But it has sometimes been argued that things have "essential properties" apart from such designation and categorization. Consider the sentences:

(1) Nixon won the 1968 election
(2) Nixon is an animate object [19]

Surely statement (1) is in no sense a necessary truth. There is a possible state of the world, or a "possible world," in which it is untrue, namely, if Humphrey had won. What about (2)? It is not true *a priori;* that is, we might discover that the entity named "Nixon" is in fact an automaton. But suppose that in fact Nixon is a human being. Then, it might be argued, there is no possible world in which (2) is false; the truth of (2) is a matter of "metaphysical necessity." It is a necessary property of Nixon that he has the property, animacy. Entities can have necessary properties, apart from their designation.

These conclusions seem unnecessarily paradoxical. The sentence (2) is, let us say, a necessary truth (given that in fact Nixon is human). But the term "Nixon" in our language system is not simply a name; rather, it is a personal name. Thus (2) has (approximately) the same meaning as (3):

(3)   the person Nixon is an animate object

The necessity of this statement follows without any attribution of necessary properties to individuals apart from their designation. It is a case of modality *de dicto* rather than *de re*, somewhat like the statement that the man who lives upstairs lives upstairs. The necessary truth of (3) (hence (2), given the linguistic category of the name "Nixon") is a consequence of the necessary truth of the statement that people are animate. This necessary truth may be grounded in a necessary connection between categories of common-sense understanding, or an analytic connection between the linguistic terms "person" and "animate." Under any of these assumptions, we need not suppose that an essential property is assigned to an individual, Nixon, apart from the way he is named or the category of common-sense understanding to which he is assigned.

Suppose, on the other hand, we were to add to natural language a new category of "pure names," including the name "N," for Nixon. Then there would no longer be any intuitive support for a distinction between (1) and (2), with "Nixon" replaced by "N." If we can wrench ourselves from the framework of language and common-sense understanding, within which "Nixon" is a personal name and the thing named is assigned to the natural kind Person (hence Animate), then (1) and (2) are true statements with the same logical status. The argument gives no support to the view that objects as such have essential properties, apart from their designation or the conceptual category in which they are placed. Within this new invented system, divorced from language and common-sense understanding, we have no relevant intuitions to guide us, I believe. Thus we might want to say that there is no way for the thing N to have been anything other than what it is, for then it would have been a different thing; thus, in an uninteresting sense, all its properties are "essential." Or, we might want to say that any of its properties might have been other than what they are. The expository recourse to distinctions between (1) and (2) (for example), between what might have been and what could not have been otherwise, is no longer available to us within the new system we are imagining. For this recourse presupposes the systems of thought and language constructed by the faculties of language and common-sense understanding.[20]

Returning to our familiar cognitive structures of thought and language, suppose that we were to discover that the entity named "Nixon" was in fact an automaton, so that (2) was false. We might then conclude that the personal name "Nixon" had been misused (so we now discover), or we might choose to interpret sentences involving this name within the framework of personification metaphor, one of the natural, if derivative, uses of language. Still, nothing leads us to the notion of essential properties, in this case, to the idea that "some properties of an object may be essential to it, in that it could not have failed to have them" (Kripke, 1972, p. 273).

Similar considerations apply in the case of other examples that have been discussed in connection with the problem of *de re* modality. Kripke (1972) suggests that there could be no situation in which Queen Elizabeth II of England, this very woman, might have had different parents; it is a necessary truth that she had the particular parents she had (though again, we do not know it *a priori*).

His conclusion is that "anything coming from a different origin would not be this object" (p. 314). Having a particular origin, in this case two given parents, is another "essential property" of the object.

My own intuitions differ about the example. Thus, it does not seem to me that a logical problem would arise if Queen Elizabeth II were to write a fictionalized autobiography in which she, this very person, had different parents; we might, I think, take this as a description of the history of this person in a different "possible world," a description of a possible state of this world with the very objects that appear in it.

But suppose that this is not so, and that having a particular origin is an "essential property." Is it, then, an essential property of the thing itself, apart from its designation or categorization in common-sense understanding? I think not. We name the entity with a personal name, "Queen Elizabeth II." We assign it to a category of common-sense understanding, Person. It might be (though as noted, I doubt it) that an object taken to be a person could not be the same person if it had parents other than its own. If so, this is a property of the conceptual system of common-sense understanding, and perhaps also of the related system of language; it is a property of the concept Person. Given the cognitive structures, we can distinguish necessary and contingent properties. We can distinguish between what might have been true of an object categorized and designated within these systems, and what could not have been otherwise. The intuitive force of the argument for essential properties seems to me to derive from the system of language in which the name is placed and the system of common-sense understanding, with its structure, in which the object is located. Dropping this framework, with its *de dicto* modalities and conceptual connections, there seems to remain no intuitive force to the proposal that the object as such has essential properties.

To take another case, Kripke suggests that "(roughly) *being a table* seems to be an essential property of the table" (1972, p. 351), that is, of a particular thing that is a table. Exactly what weight is being carried by the qualification "(roughly)" is unclear. If we drop the qualification, the proposal can hardly stand. Suppose we discover that the designer of this particular object had intended it to be a hard bed and that it is so used. Surely we would then say that the thing is not a table but a hard bed that looks like a table. But the thing is what it is. Neither a gleam in the eye of the inventor nor general custom can determine its essential properties, though intention and function are relevant to determining what we take an artifact to be. Suppose further that the thing in question is a table nailed to the floor. We would be inclined to say that it would have been the same thing had it not been nailed to the floor, but it could not have been other than a table. Thus it is necessarily a table but only accidentally immovable. Consider now another creature with a different language and a different system of common-sense understanding, in which such categories as movable-immovable are fundamental but not function and use. These creatures would say that this immovable object would have been a different thing had it not been nailed to the floor, though it could have been other than a table. To them, immovability would appear to be an essential property of the thing, not "being a table." If this is so, a property may be essential or not, depending on which creature's judgments prevail.

We might discover that humans, operating within cognitive capacity, will not develop "natural" systems of the sort postulated for this hypothetical creature. If true, this would be a discovery about human biology, but I do not see how such biological properties of humans affect the "essence" of things.

Intuitive arguments concerning essential properties must account for the whole range of our intuitions, including the ones just offered if they are indeed .correct. An account of the full range of intuitions seems simple enough, if we explain the intuitive force of the argument that such-and-such is an essential property of a thing on the basis of the systems of language and common-sense understanding that we bring to bear in making such judgments. The intuitive differences that Kripke cites are often quite clear, but it seems to me that they have to do with the structure of the systems of common-sense understanding and of language, not with essential properties of things considered in abstraction from our characterization of them in terms of these systems of categorization and representation. A study of human judgments concerning essential and accidental properties may give considerable insight into the cognitive structures that are being employed, and perhaps beyond, into the nature of human cognitive capacity and the range of structures that are naturally constructed by the mind. But such a study can carry us no further than this.

It may well be true that in the case of a natural kind, say tigers, the dictionary definition with its defining properties does not provide criterial conditions for something to be a tiger.[21] Thus, were we to "discover an animal which, though having all external appearances of a tiger as described here, has an internal structure completely different from that of the tiger," we would not conclude that it is a tiger; not because the concept of tiger has changed or because the term "tiger" marks a "cluster concept," but because if "tigers form a certain species or natural kind," then we suppose that some fixed internal structure—even if this is unknown—is required for an object to be a tiger (Kripke, 1972, pp. 317–18). Accepting all of this, it does not follow that if an object is in fact a tiger and tigers are in fact a natural kind, then having this internal structure is an essential property of the object apart from its designation or categorization as a tiger, though it is a necessary truth that a tiger has this internal structure, by virtue of properties of the system of common-sense understanding and the system of language.

In the Aristotelian framework,[22] there are certain "generative factors" that enter into the essential constitution of objects; we gain understanding of the nature of an object insofar as we grasp the generative factors which enable it to be what it is—a person, a tiger, a house, or whatever. Constitution and structure, agent responsible for generation within a system of natural law, distinguishing factors for particular species, are among the generative factors. These generative factors are close, it seems, to Kripke's "essential properties."[23] Under this formulation, there are essential properties of things because of the way the world is in fact constituted, but we may easily drop the metaphysical assumptions and say that x is a generative factor of y under the description D [24] (or, perhaps, when y is categorized as a C within the system of common-sense understanding). It seems to me that this formulation keeps fairly close to what little we can determine, on the basis of introspection and intuition, about our judgments and the logical categories of our statements.

I am raising no objection to the construction of formal theories involving languages with pure names designating entities with individuating essential properties apart from the way they are designated or categorized. One may ask, however, whether the study of such systems, whatever its interest, will provide much insight into the workings of human language and human thought.

What is true of names holds as well of other linguistic categories. There is no simple "point of entry" into the system of language. Color terms have often been taken in empiricist speculation to be particularly simple, learnable in isolation by conditioning, ostension, or association. But in fact, these terms seem to be learned as part of a system of color expressions at a rather advanced stage of language learning.[25] There is no general reason to suppose that a human language has "primitive subsystems" in any interesting sense, and no convincing evidence for such a belief.

Observation of early stages of language acquisition may be quite misleading in this regard. It is possible that at an early stage there is use of languagelike expressions, but outside the framework imposed, at a later stage of intellectual maturation, by the faculty of language—much as a dog can be trained to respond to certain commands, though we would not conclude, from this, that it is using language. The most that we can say with any plausibility is that a relation of "compatibility" holds between the grammar constructed at a given stage of mental growth and linguistic experience, as analyzed at that stage by mechanisms of mind. Given the idealization to instantaneous acquisition, discussed earlier, we may say that the primitives of linguistic theory, selected by the criterion of epistemological priority, provide an analysis of linguistic experience that serves as one term in the relation of compatibility. But beyond this, there is little to say at the moment, and even this much may involve seriously falsifying assumptions, a matter to which I must yet return. But even if legitimate as a first approximation, these assumptions will not carry the burden required by much philosophical speculation about how language is or must be learned. As for the further claim that language is not only learned but taught, and that this "teaching" is essential to establishing the meaning of linguistic expressions, this view receives no support on either empirical or conceptual grounds.[26]

John Searle has urged a distinction between "brute facts" and "institutional facts" (Searle, 1969, pp. 50 f.). Among the former are those described by the so-called observation sentences of the reconstruction of scientific knowledge: "the litmus paper is red," "the pointer reads 23.6," and the like. The existence of "institutional facts," no less objective, "presupposes the existence of certain human institutions." It is an objective fact, say, that Mr. Smith married Miss Jones, but "it is only given the institution of marriage that certain forms of behavior constitute Mr. Smith's marrying Miss Jones." Human institutions are "systems of constitutive rules" of the form "X counts as Y in context C." Searle proposes that "speaking a language is performing acts according to constitutive rules" which determine institutional facts. He argues further that institutional facts cannot be explained in terms of brute facts, but only "in terms of the constitutive rules which underlie them."

In the view we have been considering, the statement of "brute facts" takes place within (at least) a dual framework, involving the interaction of the system of language and the system of common-sense understanding. Likewise, the statement of institutional facts presupposes a theory of human institutions and a related linguistic system. I doubt that the principles entering into the theory of human institutions that persons have developed (largely without awareness) can be reduced simply to the form "X counts as Y in context C," as Searle suggests. An analysis of institutional structure appears to require principles of much more abstract nature. Abandoning empiricist bias, there is little reason to shy away from this conclusion. Again, it is a matter for discovery, not stipulation; discovery, in this case, in the course of investigation of still another faculty of mind and its operation.

In general, cognitive structures of varied sorts are constructed as a person matures, interacting with grammar and providing conditions for language use. An integrated study of cognition should try to make these connections precise, thus leading—we may speculate—to further innate properties of mind.

Note again that there is no inconsistency between this view and the thesis of autonomy of formal grammar, that is, the thesis that the language faculty constructs an abstract formal skeleton invested with meaning by interpretive rules, an integrated structure that fits in a definite manner into a system of language use.

Searle has suggested elsewhere that the latter thesis, while not internally inconsistent, nevertheless derives from an approach to language which "runs counter to quite ordinary, plausible, and common-sense assumptions about language." He takes the "common-sense picture of human language" to be something like this:

> The purpose of language is communication in much the same sense that the purpose of the heart is to pump blood. In both cases it is possible to study the structure independently of function but pointless and perverse to do so, since structure and function so obviously interact. We communicate primarily with other people, but also with ourselves, as when we talk or think in words to ourselves.

Language is the communicative system *par excellence*, and it is "peculiar and eccentric" to insist on studying the structure of language apart from its communicative function.

Searle presents my competing picture in the following terms:

> . . . except for having such general purposes as the expression of human thoughts, language doesn't have any essential purpose, or if it does there is no interesting connection between its purpose and its structure. The syntactical structures of human languages are the products of innate features of the human mind, and they have no significant connection with communication, though, of course, people do use them for, among other purposes, communication. The essential thing about languages, their defining trait, is their structure.

Searle suggests that I have "arbitrarily assumed" that "use and structure . . . [do not] . . . influence each other," and that this rather perverse approach has prevented the construction of a theory of meaning, indeed, that I am fighting "a rearguard action" against "the study of speech acts," which offers the way out of traditional problems in semantics. It is this "failure to see the essential connection between language and communication, between meaning and speech acts," that is the greatest "defect of the Chomskyan theory," he suggests.[27]

Let us examine these objections, and ask whether the picture that Searle rejects is in fact as pointless and perverse as he suggests.

First, I should clarify that I have always rejected some of the positions that Searle attributes to me. Thus, I have never suggested that "there is no interesting connection" between the structure of language and "its purpose," including communicative function, nor have I "arbitrarily assumed" that use and structure do not influence one another, though I have argued—correctly, I think—that particular proposals about this relation are wrong.[28] Surely there are significant connections between structure and function; this is not and has never been in doubt.[29] Furthermore, I do not hold that "the essential thing about languages . . . is their structure." I have frequently described what I have called "the creative use of language" as an essential feature, no less than the distinctive structural properties of language. Study of structure, use, and acquisition may be expected to provide insight into essential features of language.

Consider now Searle's other points. He claims that language has an "essential purpose," communication, and regards my denial of this claim as counter to common sense and implausible. It is difficult to argue about common sense. There is, in fact, a very respectable tradition, which I have reviewed elsewhere,[30] that regards as a vulgar distortion the "instrumental view" of language as "essentially" a means of communication, or a means to achieve given ends. Language, it is argued, is "essentially" a system for expression of thought. I basically agree with this view. But I suspect that little is at stake here, given Searle's concept of "communication" as including communication with oneself, that is, thinking in words. We do, I am sure, think without words too—at least so introspection seems to show. But insofar as we are using language for "self-communication," we are simply expressing our thoughts, and the distinction between Searle's two pictures collapses. Thus I agree with Searle that there is an essential connection between language and communication once we take "communication" in his broader sense—an unfortunate move, I believe, since the notion "communication" is now deprived of its essential and interesting character. But I remain unconvinced by his contention that there is an essential connection of the sort he claims between meaning and speech acts.

Before turning to this point of disagreement—the only one, I think, when the issues are properly stated—consider Searle's contention that it is "pointless and perverse" to study the structure of language "independently of function," bearing in mind the qualifications just noted. Pursuing his analogy, there is no doubt that the physiologist, studying the heart, will pay attention to the fact that it pumps blood. But he will also study the structure of the heart and the origin of this structure in the individual and the species, making no dogmatic assumptions about the possibility of "explaining" this structure in functional terms.

Similarly in the case of language. Consider, again, the principle of structure-dependence discussed earlier. This seems to be a general property of an interesting class of linguistic rules, innate to the mind. Following what I take to be Searle's suggestion, let us try to account for it in terms of communication. I see no way of doing so. Surely this principle enters into the function of language; we might well study the ways in which it does. But a language could function for communication (or otherwise) just as well with structure-independent rules, so it would seem. For a mind differently constituted, structure-independent rules would be far superior, in that they require no abstract analysis of a sentence beyond words. I think that the example is typical. Where it can be shown that structures serve a particular function, that is a valuable discovery. To account for or somehow explain the structure of UG, or of particular grammars, on the basis of functional considerations is a pretty hopeless prospect, I would think; it is, perhaps, even "perverse" to assume otherwise. Perhaps Searle has something else in mind, but I frankly see no issue here, no counterproposal that has any plausibility to the picture Searle rejects.

Searle argues that "it is quite reasonable to suppose that the needs of communication influenced the structure" of language, as it evolved in human prehistory. I agree. The question is: What can we conclude from this fact? The answer is: Very little. The needs of locomotion influenced the fact that humans developed legs and birds wings. This observation is not very helpful to the physiologist concerned with the nature of the human body. Like physical structures, cognitive systems have undoubtedly evolved in certain ways, though in neither case can we seriously claim to understand the factors that entered into a particular course of evolution and determined or even significantly influenced its outcome. True, if genetically based systems had been seriously dysfunctional the evolutionary development might have been aborted, and insofar as they facilitated differential reproduction they contributed to evolution. But observations at this level of generality are not of much interest. Among the systems that humans have developed in the course of evolution are the science-forming capacity and the capacity to deal intuitively with rather deep properties of the number system. As far as we know, these capacities have no selectional value, though it is quite possible that they developed as part of other systems that did have such value.[31] We know very little about what happens when 10^{10} neurons are crammed into something the size of a basketball, with further conditions imposed by the specific manner in which this system developed over time. It would be a serious error to suppose that all properties, or the interesting properties of the structures that have evolved, can be "explained" in terms of natural selection. Surely there is no warrant for such an assumption in the case of physical structures.

When Searle says that "in general an understanding of syntactical facts requires an understanding of their function in communication since communication is what language is all about," I agree only in part. If we take communication to include expression of thought, as he does, then the statement becomes at least a half-truth; thus we will have only a partial understanding of syntax if we do not consider its role in the expression of thought, and other uses of language. This much should arouse no controversy. But from this unexceptionable remark, it does not at all follow that the thesis of the autonomy of syntax is "peculiar and eccentric." If language is to be thought of on the analogy of a physical organ such as the heart, then functional explanations are unlikely to carry us very far, and we should concern ourselves with the structure of the organ that serves these functions.[32] It is, again, a question of fact, not a matter for stipulation, whether the organization of language involves an autonomous syntax in the sense that has been proposed. One can have no *a priori* intuitions about this question, any more than one can sensibly argue, on grounds of intuition, that a certain theory of the structure of the heart is "perverse."

Let us turn now to the sole serious point of disagreement, the "essential connection" that Searle claims to exist between language and communication, between meaning and speech acts. Taking these issues to be related, Searle

(1972) argues against the theory that "sentences are abstract objects that are produced and understood independently of their role in communication," on the grounds that
"any attempt to account for the meaning of sentences
within such assumptions is either circular or inadequate."
He claims further that the account offered by philosophers that he cites (Wittgenstein, Austin, Grice, Searle,
Strawson) has "provided us with a way out of this dilemma," by explaining "meaning" in terms of *what the
speaker intends the audience to believe or to do*. Others
too have made this claim, and have argued that there is a
gain in an approach that explains the meaning of linguistic
expressions in terms of speaker's intentions, in that this approach permits us to escape "the orbit of conceptual space"
that includes the concepts "idea," "semantic marker," Fregean sense, and so on.[33] This approach avoids the "circularity" to which Searle objects in his critique of classical
semantics, and in particular, my version of it.

The account to which Searle alludes would, if it were
correct, avoid the "circularity" that he claims to exist.[34]
But this account fails in many respects. In particular, it
offers no way to deal with the many cases in which language is not used for communication (in the narrower
sense), normal cases, for which the speaker's intention
with regard to an audience offers no particular insight into
the literal meaning of what he says. Furthermore, an analysis of the proposals that have been put forth shows that
"literal meaning" is reintroduced as an unexplained notion.
The approach thus remains within the "orbit of conceptual space" from which one had sought an escape.

Consider first the alleged "essential" connection between
language and communication. Searle objects to my statement that meaningful use of language "need not involve
communication or even the attempt to communicate," as
when "I use language to express or clarify my thoughts,

with the intent to deceive, to avoid an embarrassing silence, or in a dozen other ways." In these cases, I suggested, "my words have a strict meaning and I can very well mean what I say, but the fullest understanding of what I intend my audience (if any) to believe or to do might give little or no indication of the meaning of my discourse" (Chomsky, 1971, p. 19).

Despite Searle's qualms, all of this seems to me commonplace and obvious. I can be using language in the strictest sense with no intention of communicating. Though my utterances have a definite meaning, their normal meaning, nevertheless my intentions with regard to an audience may shed no light on this meaning. Take some concrete examples. As a graduate student, I spent two years writing a lengthy manuscript, assuming throughout that it would never be published [35] or read by anyone. I meant everything I wrote, intending nothing as to what anyone would believe about my beliefs, in fact taking it for granted that there would be no audience. Once a year, along with many others, I write a letter to the Bureau of Internal Revenue explaining, with as much eloquence as I can muster, why I am not paying part of my income tax. I mean what I say in explaining this. I do not, however, have the intention of communicating to the reader, or getting him to believe or do something, for the simple reason that I know perfectly well that the "reader" (probably some computer) couldn't care less. What my statements in the letter mean, what I mean—in one sense—in making these statements, is not explicable in terms of what I mean, what I intend, in writing the letter, namely to express support for people undertaking resistance to the criminal violence of the state in more meaningful ways. Once, I had the curious experience of making a speech against the Vietnam war to a group of soldiers who were advancing in full combat gear, rifles in hand, to clear the area where I was speaking. I meant what I said—my statements had their strict and literal meaning—but this had little to do with my intentions at that moment.[36]

These examples are misleading because they are, perhaps, out of the ordinary. In fact, the situation they illustrate is commonplace. Under innumerable quite normal circumstances—research, casual conversation, and so on—language is used properly, sentences have their strict meaning, people mean what they say or write, but there is no intent to bring the audience (not assumed to exist, or assumed not to exist, in some cases) to have certain beliefs or to undertake certain actions. Such commonplace examples pose a difficulty for an analysis of meaning in terms of speaker's intention with regard to an audience, even if it were possible, for the case where there is intent to communicate, to account for what a sentence means in these terms—and this too I doubt, for reasons to which I will return.

Searle (forthcoming) asserts that:

> (A) The simplest cases of meaning are those where the speaker utters a sentence and means exactly and literally what he says. In such cases the speaker intends to produce a certain illocutionary effect in the hearer, and he intends to produce this effect by means of getting the hearer to recognize his intention to produce it, and he intends to get the hearer to recognize this intention in virtue of the hearer's knowledge of the rules that govern the utterance of the sentence.

He then proceeds to an interesting discussion of other, less simple "cases of meaning," such as "in hints, insinuations, irony, and metaphor." But the problem remains that (A) is often false even for the simplest cases. The speaker may mean exactly and literally what he says, but with no intention of the sort that Searle claims must exist. The speaker's actual intentions may vary widely even in these "simplest cases," and may shed no light at all on the meaning of what he says.

Searle has not entirely overlooked these problems. Thus, he considers Grice's theory that "To say that a speaker S meant something by X is to say that S intended the utterance of X to produce some effect in a hearer H by means of the recognition of this intention." As Searle notes, the account fails because it "does not show the connection between one's meaning something by what one says, and what that which one says actually means in the language." To overcome this difficulty, Searle revises Grice's definition in several respects. He introduces the notion of rules for using expressions and develops a broader notion of "effects produced in the hearer." For Searle, these effects include "understanding what I said." Thus, in his revised account (1969, p. 48), the meaning of a sentence is determined by rules, and uttering a sentence and meaning it is a matter of intending to get the hearer to know that certain states of affairs specified by the rules obtain, with the corollary intention of getting the hearer to know these things by recognizing the first intention, and intending him to recognize the first intention by virtue of his knowledge of the rules for the sentence uttered—essentially, (A) above.

Later, I will turn to the question whether crucial questions are not begged by this reference to rules and so on; I think they are. But let us ask how these revisions deal with one general problem that Searle raises against Grice's theory, namely: "I may make a statement without caring whether my audience believes it or not but simply because I feel it my duty to make it." Or, the examples that I just mentioned, which are in a sense even worse, since it is assumed that there is no audience (cf. note 36). Unfortunately, the difficulty Searle cites against Grice survives the revisions. In the cases cited, I, the speaker, have no intention of getting the hearer to know anything or to recognize anything, but what I say has its strict meaning, and

I mean what I say. Thus Searle's revision, for this reason alone, fails to capture the intended notion of meaning; as a factual claim, it is false. The same is true of all other attempts that I know of to explain "meaning" in terms of "speaker's intention in communicating."

In elaborating the issue that he raises against Grice, Searle switches without comment from a discussion of meaning to a discussion of communication. The shift is important. The theory of speaker's intention may well be a contribution to a theory of successful communication. Searle has, however, offered no way to escape the problems he raises against alternative approaches. Still other problems arise, as we shall see, when we consider the nature of the rules involved in the Grice-Searle theories.

Other philosophers have argued in a similar vein. Thus P. F. Strawson (1970) speaks of a "Homeric struggle" over a central issue of philosophy between "theorists of communication-intention" and "theorists of formal semantics." Like Grice and Searle, Strawson opts for the theory of communication-intention. Before examining his reasons, let us try to clarify just what is at issue.

It turns out on investigation that there is actually a fair amount of agreement among the parties to this "struggle on what seems to be such a central issue in philosophy." In particular, all agree, Strawson says, that "the meanings of the sentences of a language are largely determined by the semantic and syntactic rules or conventions of that language." Thus there is a common project—and it is this that interests me particularly—namely, to discover these semantic and syntactic rules and conventions, and more specifically, to extract the universal element in them.

When the theorist of communication-intention wants to distinguish a promise to go to the store from a promise to dry the dishes, he will refer to the results of this common enterprise, which finds its place, in his theory, in the principle that "the meaning of a sentence is determined by rules, and those rules specify both conditions of utterance of the sentence and also what the sentence counts as" (Searle, 1969, p. 48); in one case, the utterance counts as a promise to go to the store, in the other, as a promise to dry the dishes. About this part of the theory, theorists of communication-intention have little to say. It is just this part that concerns me—and, I suspect, others whom Strawson calls "theorists of formal semantics" (I am cited as one).

Similarly, suppose that Searle and Strawson can distinguish a promise from a warning or a prediction or a threat. Then their results will be of immediate interest to the most unregenerate exponent of abstract "meanings," who wishes to express somehow the fact that a given linguistic form— say, "drinks will be served at five"—can be used as a promise, a prediction, a warning, a threat, a statement, or an invitation.

This is not to deny that there is an issue between Strawson and his opponents, but it is less clear where the issue lies. According to Strawson, "where [the two views] differ is as to the relations between the meaning-determining rules of the language, on the one hand, and the function of communication on the other: one party insists, and the other (apparently) refuses to allow, that the general nature of those rules can be understood only by reference to this function."

Strawson then proceeds to inquire into the import of this refusal. But from the initial formulation, his discussion is misleading. It would have been more appropriate to shift the implicit burden of proof, and to say that one party claims that the general nature of the meaning-determining rules can be understood by reference to (and only by reference to) the function of communication, while the other party asks for an argument, and is not too impressed by what is forthcoming. Strawson's misleading formulation persists throughout. Thus, he poses the "central issue" in these terms: "It consists in nothing other than the simple-seeming question whether the notion of truth-conditions can itself be explained or understood without reference to the function of communication." To reformulate the issue more properly, it consists in the question whether reference to the function of communication is essential to analysis of meaning or to explaining "the notion of truth-conditions," as Strawson alleges, or indeed whether it gives us any help in dealing with the central problems of meaning. The "theorist of formal semantics" is unconvinced.

Placing the burden of proof where it belongs, consider Strawson's defense of his claims. He suggests that we take as a primitive the notion "audience-directed belief-expression" (ADBE). To illustrate, "an utterer might have, as one of his intentions in executing his utterance, that of bringing his audience to think that he, the utterer, believes some proposition, say the proposition that p; and he might intend this intention to be wholly overt, to be clearly recognized by the audience." So he might—and he might also have the intention of expressing the proposition honestly, perhaps to clarify his thoughts, perhaps out of a sense of personal integrity, caring little whether his audience believes that he believes it, or even whether there is an audience. Surely such cases are commonplace. Or perhaps his intention is to amuse the audience, to keep the conversation going, or innumerable other possibilities.

What the communication theorist must show, somehow, is that ADBE is central and that communication is, as claimed, the "essential function" of language. He must show that reference to ADBE, reference to the speaker's intentions with regard to what the audience will believe or do, explains something—for example, explains why the statement that p is meaningful when produced with no intention other than honest self-expression. This the communication theorist cannot do. But he must do still more, to establish his claims. He must show how reference to ADBE helps in developing an account of what sentences mean. The prospects seem still more dubious. If we can give an account of the notion "the utterer believes the proposition that p," which appears without explanation in Strawson's example cited above, and explain how this differs from "believing the proposition that q," then it would seem that the central problems have been solved and that further reference to ADBE is not very interesting. But the crucial notion, "the utterer believes the proposition that p (not q)," is common to the contestants in Strawson's struggle, and is in no way clarified by reference to ADBE, contrary to what Strawson suggests. Given this notion, we can (uninterestingly) expound "linguistic meaning" along lines that Strawson reviews; without it, it appears that we cannot.

Strawson suggests that an analysis by Paul Grice gives reason to think that "it is possible to expound such a concept of communication-intention or, as he calls it, utterer's meaning, which is proof against objection and which does not presuppose the notion of linguistic meaning," thus avoiding Searle's "circularity." But Grice's analysis fails in the crucial cases. Observing more closely how it fails, we discover that the differences between opponents in this perhaps less-than-Homeric struggle seem to narrow still further.

Grice considers the crucial notion "occasion meaning in the absence of an audience"—for example, the use of an utterance for self-expression, clarification of thought, and so on (Grice, 1969). He argues that to say that the speaker means such-and-such by uttering x is to say that there is a property P such that x is uttered with the intention that anyone who has P would think what an appropriate audience is supposed to think in the "normal" case of communication to an audience (with various refinements that we may ignore here).

But I see no reason to believe that the speaker must have such intentions as are specified in Grice's definiendum. In cases of the sort mentioned, the speaker has no relevant intentions with regard to what a hearer with P, however chosen, would think. In the case of honest self-expression, the speaker doesn't care. In the case of casual conversation, the speaker's intentions with regard to a hypothetical audience need not go beyond his intentions with regard to the actual audience, and plainly there need be no intention that the actual audience believe that the speaker's beliefs are such-and-such. Furthermore, consider the property P that appears in Grice's definition. This property, Grice suggests, might be, for example, the property of being an English speaker. But this won't do. Suppose the speaker believes that there are native English speakers who habitually misunderstand what they read or hear—the reviewers of his books, for example. Then even if this speaker happens to have the intention that Grice assumes to be necessary, it will be necessary to take P to be something like "is a speaker of English who will think that the utterer believes that Q upon hearing x," where Q is the literal meaning of x. It is only for such "hearers" that the speaker intends that the cognitive response correspond to his meaning in the required way. But now all questions are begged. The notion "literal meaning," or some equivalent, again intrudes, and no way has been offered to escape the "orbit of conceptual space" that includes the suspect abstract notions "linguistic meaning" and the like, even if the utterer happens to have the postulated intentions with regard to a hypothetical audience, as is by no means necessary in the normal use of language.[37]

One can imagine modifications of the proposed definition that would not involve incorrect claims about intentions, but not, so far as I can see, without introducing some notion like "linguistic meaning." As we will see directly, Grice's more explicit and comprehensive theory fails on this count as well. The point is, I think, that the "communication theorists" are not analyzing "meaning" but rather something else: perhaps "successful communication." This concept may indeed involve essential reference to Grice's notion of

"M-intending," namely, the intention of a speaker to produce in the listener an effect by means of the listener's
recognition of his intentions, with the elaborations suggested by Searle, Grice, and others. But communication is
only one function of language, and by no means an essential
one. The "instrumental" analysis of language as a device for
achieving some end is seriously inadequate, and the "language games" that have been produced to illuminate this
function are correspondingly misleading.[38] In contemplation,
inquiry, normal social interchange, planning and guiding
one's own actions, creative writing, honest self-expression,
and numerous other activities with language, expressions
are used with their strict linguistic meaning irrespective of
the intentions of the "utterer" with regard to an audience;
and even in the cases that the communication theorist regards as central, the implicit reference to "rules" and "conventions" in his account seems to beg the major questions, a
matter to which I will return directly.

In any event, it seems that there are a host of interesting
problems in the common ground shared by the two theories
that Strawson counterposes: namely, the problems of analyzing how the meanings of the sentences of a language are
determined by the rules of the language, that is, the grammar—possibly in interaction with other cognitive structures,
along lines outlined earlier.

Strawson has failed to establish the claims of the "communication theorist," and the sources to which he refers do
no better. Consider now his argument against the theorist
of formal semantics. Note that this argument might well be
correct without advancing his primary claim. Is it correct?

Strawson finds the opposing theory inadequate because
it relies on the unanalyzed and unexplicated notion of "expressing a belief." The "meaning-determining rules for a
sentence of the language," in this view, "are the rules which
determine *what* belief is conventionally articulated by one
who, in given contextual conditions, utters the sentence";

"determining what this belief is, is the same thing as determining what assertion is made." But the notion of "an essentially independent concept of belief-expression," with no
reference to communicative intention, requires further explanation, Strawson argues. It is wanting, because "we are
debarred from making reference to the end or goal of communication an essential part of our story." The description
does not tell us what need of the speaker is satisfied by
expressing his belief. Furthermore, it appears on this account that it is "a quite contingent truth about language
that the rules or conventions which determine the meanings
of the sentences of a language are public or social rules or
conventions. This will be, as it were, a natural fact, a fact
of nature, in no way essential to the concept of a language. . . ." Thus, on this theory, people learn a language
in which they can express beliefs,[39] and also "acquire the
secondary skill of communicating their beliefs," but the
latter is "simply something added on, an extra and conceptually uncovenanted benefit, quite incidental to the description of what it is to have mastered the meaning-rules
of the language." Listeners may assume that belief-expres-
sions do in fact express beliefs and are intended for this
purpose, but that is a mere contingent fact: "As far as the
central core is concerned, the function of communication
remains secondary, derivative, conceptually inessential."

With no further argument,[40] Strawson dismisses this account as "too perverse and arbitrary to satisfy the requirements of an acceptable theory." Thus the communication
theorist "must be allowed to have won [the game]."

Note that the question whether communication *is* "primary" and "conceptually essential" is begged throughout
in Strawson's counterargument. Furthermore, the picture
that Strawson rejects as perverse and arbitrary seems quite
reasonable and probably correct, though not very illuminating. The organism is so constituted that it acquires a system
of language that includes "meaning-determining rules"

(again, perhaps, in interaction with other faculties of mind). These rules are then used by the speaker to express his beliefs (*inter alia*). The learner has no "reason" for acquiring the language; he does not choose to learn, and cannot fail to learn under normal conditions, any more than he chooses (or can fail) to organize visual space in a certain way—or, for that matter, any more than certain cells in the embryo choose (or can fail) to become an arm or the visual centers of the brain under appropriate environmental conditions. Having acquired the system of language, the person can (in principle) choose to use it or not, as he can choose to keep to or disregard his judgments concerning the position of objects in space. He cannot choose to have sentences mean other than what they do, any more than he can choose to have objects distributed in perceptual space otherwise than the way they are. Communication is one function that the system may serve; as noted several times, it is by no means the only function, and Strawson nowhere offers a plausible argument that it is the "essential function" (unless we trivialize the issue by introducing "self-communication" as an instance of "communication"), nor does he even enlighten us as to what it means for one use of language to be its "essential function." As for "what need of his it satisfies" to express his beliefs, the answers may range widely: perhaps the need to be honest and forthright, or to impress others and advance his career, or to do himself in, or to maintain certain social relations in a group, among many other possibilities.

As for the fact that the rules of language are "public rules," this is, indeed, a contingent fact. It is a fact of nature that the cognitive structures developed by people in similar circumstances, within cognitive capacity, are similar, by virtue of their similar innate constitution. Thus we share rules of language with others as we share an organization of visual space with them. Both shared systems play a role in successful communication. Hearers sometimes assume that the speaker is expressing beliefs that he holds, at other times not, depending on the circumstances. There is nothing surprising about any of this, though we still understand very little about the cognitive structures developed and their basis in faculties of mind; and questions can be raised about problems that are common to both approaches, specifically, the problem of clarifying the notions "use a linguistic rule," "express the belief that p," and so on.

Strawson's belief that this picture is perverse and arbitrary derives, perhaps, from his unargued assumption that language is consciously taught by conditioning and training and is thus quite different from cognitive or physical structures that develop in the organism by virtue of its nature, under appropriate environmental conditions. Surely there are important differences between the growth of language, the construction of perceptual space, the development of organs in the embryo, and other processes of physical and cognitive development. But these differences are not, I think, of anything like the sort that Strawson seems to suppose. With regard to the questions he raises, the processes are similar in important respects. In none of these cases do issues of "choice" or "reason" or "ends and purposes" arise in accounting for the development of the structures in question in the particular person. We are dealing here with systems that develop in a natural way as a species of animal instinct, in Hume's phrase, entirely without conscious choice, without reasons (for the organism), and certainly without any necessity for training and conditioning. The nature of the structures that develop is in large measure predetermined by the biologically given organization of the mind. If what I am suggesting here is generally true, as I believe it is, then it is the questions that Strawson raises that are "perverse," not the answers that the "theorist of formal semantics" might give to them, along the lines just indicated.

I stress again, however, that even if the proposals of the

"theorist of formal semantics" were as "perverse and arbitrary" as Strawson believes, this would in no way vindicate the "communication theorist." Rather, a positive demonstration is required for the claims of the "communication theorist," and this is lacking.

Searle speculates that my reason for (allegedly) fighting a "rearguard action against [the study of speech acts]" is that I see in this theory a reversion to behaviorism (Searle, 1972). The conclusion is incorrect. My objections to the theory of speech acts, as it has so far been developed, are basically those just stated: it may help to analyze successful communication, and it has led to interesting discoveries about the semantic properties of utterances, but it gives us no way to escape the orbit of conceptual space that includes such notions as "linguistic meaning." Without such intrusion, the theory simply expresses false statements about meaning.

As for the reversion to behaviorism, it seems true of the most careful work within the theory. In what is, to my knowledge, the most careful and comprehensive effort to explain the meaning of linguistic expressions within this framework,[41] Grice presents a system of definitions that rest not only on intentions but also on the speaker's "policy," "practice," and "habit," on the idea of a "repertoire of procedures." To have a procedure in one's repertoire is to have "a standing readiness (willingness, preparedness), in some degree to . . . ," where "a readiness (etc.) to do something [is] a member of the same family . . . as an intention to do that thing." Grice recognizes the inadequacy of this analysis, but gives only some "informal remarks" as to how a proper definition might be constructed. He cites "three main cases in which one may legitimately speak of an established procedure in respect of utterance-type X." One, which we may disregard, has to do with a system of communication that has been devised artificially but never put into operation. Analysis of the other two cases reveals very clearly just how the whole approach leads in an entirely wrong though quite familiar direction.

The two relevant cases reduce to "practice," that is, custom and habit. One is the case in which a speaker has the "practice to utter X in such-and-such circumstances," and thus "*will* have a readiness to utter X in such-and-such circumstances." But this is inadequate, since a speaker may not have "*any* degree of readiness to utter the expression in any circumstances whatsoever." The problem, as Grice notes, is that we seem to need "the idea of [the speaker's] being *equipped* to use the expression"; that is, we need the notion of "competence," in the familiar sense of linguistic theory, outlined earlier. This notion Grice takes to be "problematic," though he does not explain why. It would indeed be problematic to a behaviorist, but not, it seems, within an approach that takes humans to be organisms within the natural world. True, there is much that is not well understood, but there seems no problem in principle in investigating the nature, use, and acquisition of cognitive structures, if we dispense with the *a priori* and completely unwarranted strictures on legitimate theory construction that are part of the behaviorist program.

Grice's final case is intended to deal with the problem that a speaker may be "equipped" to use expressions properly but have no readiness to do so. He suggests that a person may have a "procedure for X" in the required sense if "to utter X in such-and-such circumstances is part of the practice of many members of" the group to which the person belongs. That is, other members of the group "*do* have a readiness to utter X in such-and-such circumstances." But for familiar reasons, this analysis is useless. There are no practices, customs, or habits, no readiness, willingness, or preparedness, that carry us very far in accounting for the normal creative use of language, whether we consider the practices of a person or of a group. Thus, any speaker of English is "equipped," in the sense that Grice requires, to speak or understand an arbitrary sentence on this page, but neither a given speaker nor any group has a practice or readiness to utter these sentences under any circumstances. The same is true even of single words, if we take the notions "practice" and "readiness" seriously.

All of these efforts lead in the wrong track, a furrow already plowed by proponents of empiricist myth, and more recently, of the curious deviation from normal scientific practice called "behaviorism."

A related difficulty has to do with the move from unstructured signals to structured utterances. The move is made in terms of a notion of "resultant procedure," which, as Grice remarks, "has been left pretty unilluminated." His attempt to clarify it involves a shift from "procedure" in the sense of "customary practice" to "procedure" in the sense of "rule," a very different notion, belonging to a totally different "conceptual space." The heart of the matter is, as Grice points out, that we in some sense implicitly accept and appear to follow certain linguistic rules—"an as yet unsolved problem," as he puts it, but the central problem, not a marginal one. Grice remarks that "the proper interpretation of the idea that we *do* accept these rules becomes something of a mystery, if the 'acceptance' of the rules is to be distinguished from the existence of the related practices; but it seems like a mystery which, for the time being at least, we have to swallow."

Since the central problems remain unsolved, and since there is, furthermore, not a hint of an idea as to how to proceed to solve them, it seems that Searle, Strawson, and others have gone well beyond what is appropriate in their claims for the theory of communication-intention and speech acts. Following this approach, we are back with the old mysteries: in what sense do we "accept" the rules of language and how do we follow them to express our thoughts, our beliefs, our wishes, and so on? Reference to customs and practices is simply beside the point, completely unhelpful. Furthermore, we now face new problems, such as the problem of accounting for the normal uses of language cited earlier. The theory of communication-intention seems a blind alley.[42]

We must distinguish between the literal meaning of the linguistic expression produced by S and what S meant by producing this expression (or by saying that so-and-so, whatever expressions he used). The first notion is the one to be explained in the theory of language. The second has nothing particular to do with language; I can just as well ask, in the same sense of "meaning," what S meant by slamming the door. Within the theory of successful communication, we can, perhaps, draw a connection between these notions. The theory of meaning, however, seems quite unilluminated by this effort.

The mystery that Grice cites can be slightly reduced by distinguishing two notions of "acceptance" of rules: in the acquisition of language, and in the use of language. In either case, "acceptance" of rules must be "distinguished from the existence of the related practices." In general, there are no related practices. But in the first case, we should abandon the notion of "acceptance" of rules altogether, with the associated idea that rules are "chosen" and that we have reasons for these choices, as in Strawson's discussion. The rules of language are not accepted for certain reasons, but rather are developed by the mind when it is placed under certain objective conditions, much as the organs of the body develop in their predetermined way under appropriate conditions. So far, there is no mystery. A mystery would arise if we were to attempt to account for the development of rules in terms of practices and customs. Similarly, there would be a mystery if we were to attempt to account for the "acceptance" of the principles by which we organize visual space in terms of our practices and customs. Thus far, at least, the mystery can be resolved by abandoning the residue of empiricism and undertaking the analysis of cognitive capacity along lines sketched earlier.

Mysteries do remain, however, when we turn to the "acceptance" of the rules in language use. Once the system of language and other cognitive structures are developed by the mind, the person has a certain range of choices available as to how to use these systems. What does it mean to say that a person "accepts" the rules, in this context? Perhaps, that he chooses to follow the rules that are part of his current cognitive state, that belong to the cognitive structures his mind has produced. I cannot see what else it might mean. Now, however, we face some real mysteries, namely, those relating to the theory of human action (the theory of M_{cs}; cf. p. 17). The rules that a person "accepts" do not tell him what to say. We may ask how or why we put to use the system of rules that the mind has developed. Under what circumstances do we choose to violate these rules? What kinds of sophistication are involved in this choice, and what are its conceptual limitations? And so on. Appeal to customs and practices is notoriously unhelpful, but appeal to other modes of explanation does not carry us very far either.

The study of the development of cognitive structures ("acceptance of rules," in the first sense) poses problems to be solved, but not, it seems, impenetrable mysteries. The study of the capacity to use these structures and the exercise of this capacity, however, still seems to elude our understanding.

CHAPTER 3

Some General Features
of Language

The discussion so far has been rather abstract. I have mentioned only one general property that I think can plausibly be attributed to the language faculty, namely, the principle of structure-dependence of grammatical rules; though if the speculations on semantics and on the interaction of the language faculty and common-sense understanding can be given real substance and pressed beyond a few illustrative examples, then this too would count as a proposal concerning the innate organization of the human mind.

Pursuing these reflections further, I would like to take up three topics. First, I want to add some structure to the account of the language faculty. Then, I would like to return to the simplifying assumption that language learning is instantaneous, tentatively adopted earlier. And finally, I will return to some of the questions raised at the outset concerning the possibilities for a broader theory of human nature and its implications.

In discussing various approaches to the semantics of natural language, I noted that there is a project common to all, namely, to discover "the semantic and syntactic rules or conventions [that determine] the meanings of the sentences of a language" (Strawson, 1970), and more important, to discover the principles of universal grammar (UG) that lie beyond particular rules or conventions. Some believe that "the general nature of such rules and conventions can be ultimately understood only by reference to the concept of communication-intention" (Strawson, 1970). For reasons already discussed, I do not believe that the claim has been substantiated and doubt that it can be. It seems to me to misconceive the general character of language use and to ignore an intellectual element that cannot be eliminated from any adequate account of it. But whatever the future holds on that score, we can still turn with profit to the common project. What, then, can plausibly be said about the rules that determine the formal and semantic properties of the sentences of a language, that is, its grammar?

In the past few years, a number of approaches to the question have been developed and fruitfully applied. I will not be able to survey them here, or to give any compelling reasons in support of those that seem to me most promising, or even to deal with objections that have been raised to the point of view I will present.[1] In the present context, these deficiencies are perhaps less serious than they might seem. My primary purpose is to give some idea of the kinds of principles and the degree of complexity of structure that it seems plausible to assign to the language faculty as a species-specific, genetically determined property. Alternative approaches, while differing in a number of respects,[2] are comparable, I believe, in their implications concerning the more general questions that I have in mind.

Let us begin by considering some implications of the principle of structure-dependence. If it is correct, then the rules of grammar apply to strings of words analyzed into abstract phrases, that is, to structures that are called "phrase markers" in the technical literature. For example, the sentence (1) might be assigned a phrase marker giving the structure indicated in the obvious way by the bracketing, along with other structures omitted here:

(1) $[_S[_{NP}[_{DET}$ the$]$ $[_N$ man$]$ $[_S$ who $[_{VP}$ is tall$]]]]$ $[_{VP}$ *is* here$]]$

(S = sentence; NP = noun phrase; DET = determiner; N = noun; VP = verb phrase)

The italicized occurrence of "is" is the one following the first noun phrase; it is this occurrence that is preposed to give the corresponding yes-or-no question, with its phrase marker.

The rule that carries out this operation is called a "(grammatical) transformation." Thus, transformations map phrase markers into phrase markers. One component of the syntax of a language consists of such transformations, with whatever structure (say, ordering) is imposed on this set. Call this the "transformational component."

For the transformational component to function in the generation of structured sentences, it is necessary for some class of initial phrase markers to be provided. Suppose, then, that the syntax contains also a "base component" that generates a class of "initial phrase markers." We take this class to be infinite, thus assigning to the base component the recursive property that any grammar must possess.

The base, in turn, consists of two subcomponents: a "categorial component" and a lexicon. The categorial component presents the basic abstract structures by means of "rewriting rules" that state how a syntactic category can be analyzed into a sequence of such categories. One such rule, for example, would state that Sentence consists of Noun Phrase followed by Verb Phrase (in symbols: S ⟶ NP VP). Among the categories that figure in the categorial component are the "lexical categories," Noun (N), Verb (V), Adjective (A), and others. It is a simple matter to devise a procedure by which rules of the categorial component can generate phrase markers of the appropriate type, with lexical categories in place of the lexical items that must ultimately appear in these positions.

The lexicon consists of the lexical items that belong to the lexical categories, each with its phonological, semantic, and syntactic properties. It also contains rules of "word formation" that delimit the class of lexical items and express their general properties.[3] "Lexical transformations" insert items from the lexicon into the abstract phrase markers generated by the categorial component, giving the initial phrase markers.[4] The latter are also abstract, in that only through the application of grammatical transformations and other rules do they become sequences of words that count as sentences of the language, phonologically represented.[5]

Thus, the various components of the base interact to generate initial phrase markers, and the transformational component converts an initial phrase marker, step by step, into a phonologically represented sentence with its phrase marker. The latter complex we call a "surface structure." The sequence of phrase markers generated in this way we call a "transformational derivation."

There is a good deal more to say about the structure of the categorial component of the base and the lexicon, but I will not pursue this topic here.[6]

In the so-called "standard theory,"[7] the initial phrase markers were called "deep structures," but I will avoid the term here, for several reasons. In the standard theory, deep structures were characterized in terms of two properties: their role in syntax, initiating transformational derivations; and their role in semantic interpretation. As for the latter, it was postulated that deep structures give all the information required for determining the meaning of sentences.[8] Clearly, these characterizations are independent; it might turn out that the structures that initiate transformational derivations are not those that determine semantic interpretation. I believe that this is the case.[9] The "extended standard theory" postulates that surface structures contribute in a definite way to semantic interpretation. In the version that I will outline here, I will suggest that perhaps all semantic information is determined by a somewhat enriched notion of surface structure. In this theory, then, the syntactic and semantic properties of the former "deep structures" are dissociated. Either class of properties might, then, be taken as defining the technical notion "deep structure." To avoid the issue, with the possible attendant confusion, I will simply drop the term, speaking only of "initial phrase markers" and "surface structures."

There is another reason for this terminological change. The term "deep structure" has, unfortunately, proved to be very misleading. It has led a number of people to suppose that it is the deep structures and their properties that are truly "deep," in the nontechnical sense of the word, while the rest is superficial, unimportant, variable across languages, and so on. This was never intended. Phonological theory includes principles of language that are deep, universal, unexpected, revealing, and so on; and the same, I believe, is true of the theory of surface structures and other elements of grammar. On occasion, the term "deep structure" has even been used to mean "grammar" or "universal grammar" or "abstract properties of rules," or in other confusing ways. No one, I hope, will be misled into believing that the properties of abstract initial phrase markers necessarily exhaust what may be "deep," or that assumptions about such structures constitute the fundamental thesis of transformational grammar, without which it collapses.

In part, the belief that "deep structures" are uniquely important derives from the role assigned to them in semantic interpretation. There is a widespread feeling that semantics is the part of language that is really deep and important, and that the study of language is interesting primarily insofar as it contributes to some understanding of these questions of real profundity. There is some merit to this view. Thus, the questions having to do with what people say and why, questions that relate to the "creative aspect of language use," are surely of great intrinsic interest, and are also invested with some mystery, in a sense in which the principles of rule ordering in phonology are not. Analogously, we might say that questions of human behavior are intrinsically interesting to us in ways in which the behavior of inanimate objects is not—but we would not therefore conclude that physics is superficial, in that it confines itself to inanimate matter and abstracts away from human acts (say, from the fact that the predictions of physical experiments can be falsified by human intervention, a fact that cannot be accommodated within physical theory, so far as we know). The significance of physics does not derive from the intrinsic interest of its subject matter; no one cares what happens under the exotic conditions of physical experiments, apart from the relation to physical theory. Physics is significant, applications aside, because of its intellectual depth, and if it were to turn out that the principles of phonology are considerably more sophisticated and intricate than those of semantics, that they enter into nontrivial arguments to explain surprising facts, that they give us much more insight into the nature of the organism, then phonology will be a far deeper theory than semantics, despite the more limited intrinsic interest of the phenomena with which it deals.[10]

Suppose it is a fact, as I now tend to believe, that a suitably enriched notion of surface structure suffices to determine the meaning of sentences under interpretive rules (insofar as grammar is involved in determining semantic properties; cf. chapter 2). It may still be the case—I think it is—that initial phrase markers generated by the base have significant and revealing properties. It also remains true that they enter, though now indirectly, into determining the structures that undergo semantic interpretation, and that they play a role in the theory of performance. The thesis of surface-structure interpretation, if true, would constitute a significant empirical discovery, which would in no way diminish the general interest of the results of linguistic inquiry. Under this thesis, the structures called "deep structures" in the standard theory do not play the role formerly attributed to them, but we may still agree with Strawson that "the central thesis of the transformational grammarians, the step which conditions the whole character of their theories, is the insistence that any adequate grammatical theory must recognize a distinction between the superficial syntactic structure of a sentence and its basic structure, between its deep grammar and its surface grammar" (Strawson, 1972). But we must now understand the terms "basic structure" and "deep grammar" to refer to nonsuperficial aspects of surface structure, the rules that generate surface structures, the abstract level of initial phrase markers, the principles that govern the organization of grammar and that relate surface structure to semantic representations, and so on.

I have so far briefly discussed the base component of the syntax and the initial phrase markers that it generates, omitting a host of important matters. Consider now the transformational component and the surface structures formed by its operation. I have mentioned, so far, only one transformational rule, namely, the rule that forms yes-or-no questions such as "is the man who is tall here?" from (1). This rule has the interesting property that it does not apply to embedded sentences, but only to the full sentence structure. Following Emonds, we call it a "root transformation," and the structure to which it applies, a "root sentence" (cf. Emonds, forthcoming). Indirect questions appear in embedded constructions: for example, "I wonder *who John is visiting*," and "the question *whether deep structures exist* is much debated." In this case, however, the root transformation does not apply. We do not say "I wonder *who is John visiting*," with inversion of "is."

Nonroot transformations apply at any depth of embedding. Consider, for example, the rule that preposes "*wh*-words," such as "who" or "where." The initial phrase marker underlying "who is John visiting?" is something like "John is visiting *wh*-someone," omitting bracketing.[11] Applying the rule of *wh*-movement, we derive "who John is visiting."[12] If the sentence is embedded, no further rules apply, and we have, for example, "I wonder who John is visiting." If the sentence is not embedded, we apply the additional rule of inversion, deriving the direct question "who is John visiting?"

Root and nonroot transformations have very different properties, a matter explored in depth by Emonds and others (Emonds, forthcoming). The domain of a nonroot transformation may be other than a sentence. Thus, the rule of extraposition that gives (2) applies to the underlying subject noun phrase of (3):

(2) the only one of Tolstoy's novels that I like is out of print
(3) [NP the only one that I like of Tolstoy's novels] is out of print

Let us refer to a category that can serve as the domain of a transformation as a "cyclic category."[13] There is, I think, good evidence that the transformational component applies to an initial phrase marker with more than one cyclic category in a definite and regular manner, namely, cyclically (hence the term). The transformations first apply to the most deeply embedded cyclic categories, then to the cyclic categories that immediately contain these, and so on, until the full structure is reached, at which point root transformations also apply.

Suppose further that transformations meet a condition of "subjacency," which requires that they apply to positions at the same level of the cycle or in adjacent levels (cf. Chomsky, 1973a). Thus a transformation may not, say, move an item within the cyclic category A to a position within the cyclic category C that includes A if there is a cyclic category B including A and included in C. For example, in the structure (4), where A, B, and C are cyclic, a rule may not move an item from the position X to either position Y, where $[_A \ldots X \ldots]$ is distinct from $[_A X]$:

(4) $[_C \ldots Y \ldots [_B \ldots [_A \ldots X \ldots] \ldots] \ldots Y \ldots]$

In the case mentioned earlier, from the underlying structure (3) we may derive (2), but there can be no rule (or rule application) forming (5) from (3):

(5) $[_{NP}[_{NP}$ the only one $t]$ of Tolstoy's novels] is out of print that I like

The reason is that to form (5), it is necessary to move the sentence "that I like" from the position X of (4) (marked by t in (5); thus the NP "the only one that I like" is A of (4)) to the rightmost position Y of (4), where it appears in (5).[14] In the representation (5), I inserted the symbol t (read "trace") to indicate the position from which the extraposed subject was moved (illegitimately, violating subjacency). As we will see later, this is more than a notational device.

There are examples that appear, *prima facie*, to violate the subjacency condition. Thus consider (6):

(6) John seems to be a nice fellow

There is good evidence that (6) derives from the underlying structure (6'):

(6') Y seems $[_S$ John to be a nice fellow $]$ [15]

The rule in question—call it "NP-preposing"—raises "John" from its position as subject in the embedded sentence to the subject position marked Y in the main clause. The same rule gives (7) from (7'), where the trace t again marks the position in (7) from which "John" was raised.

(7) John is certain $[_S t$ to win$]$

(7') $[_S Y$ is certain $[_S$ John to win$]]$

But now consider sentence (8), deriving from the initial phrase marker (8'):

(8) John seems to be certain to win

(8') Y_2 seems [s Y_1 to be certain [s John to win]]

Here it seems that the rule has moved "John" from the position in which it appears in (8') to the position marked by Y_2 in (8'). Taking the initial position of "John" to be X of (4), and Y_2 to be Y of (4), we have a violation of the subjacency principle. The solution is of course obvious. (8) is not derived from (8') directly, but from (8''):

(8'') Y_2 seems [s John to be certain [s t to win]],

where (8'') is derived from (8') by the rule of NP-preposing just as (7) is derived from (7'). The rule of NP-preposing applies cyclically, first to (8') giving (8''), then to (8'') giving (8), each application governed by the principle of subjacency. If we were to replace "certain" in (8) by a word that does not permit NP-preposing on the first cycle, say "probable," [16] then we could not derive the sentence analogous to (8), namely, "John seems to be probable to win." Similarly, if we were to replace "seem" by a word that does not permit NP-preposing, no sentence analogous to (8) would be derivable.[17]

The same considerations apply to certain other examples that might appear to violate the subjacency condition. Consider, for example, the slightly awkward sentences (9) and (10), where the trace t marks the position in the initial phrase marker from which *who* was moved: [18]

(9) who do the police think [s that the FBI discovered [s that Bill shot t]]

(10) who did John believe [s that Mary said [s that Tom saw t]]

The operation of *wh*-movement appears to violate subjacency in these cases. But, as we already know, the rule of *wh*-movement is a cyclic, not a root transformation. Applying the rule cyclically to the form underlying (9), we derive the intermediate forms (9'), (9''), and finally (9), just as cyclic application of NP-preposing gave (8):

(9') the police think [$_S$ that the FBI discovered [$_S$ who Bill shot t]]

(9'') the police think [$_S$ who the FBI discovered [$_S$ t that Bill shot t]]

In the same way, we derive (10).

We thus have three applications of *wh*-movement in the derivation of (9). The first application gives the grammatical sentence (9') and the third gives the grammatical sentence (9), but the structure (9'') derived from (9') is not a grammatical sentence. We could have had a grammatical sentence on the second application if we had chosen the verb "know" instead of "think" in the underlying initial structure; thus, (11):

(11) the police know who the FBI discovered that Bill shot

The distinction between (9'') and (11) lies in the properties of the verbs "think" and "know"; the verb "know" takes an indirect-question complement, but not the verb "think."

Let us now consider a slightly more complex example involving subjacency. In the examples that preceded I have been playing rather fast-and-loose with the item "that," which has vanished and reappeared several times without explanation.[19] Call this word a "complementizer." Thus the sentential structure "that Bill shot someone," which may be taken as the most deeply embedded sentence within the structures underlying (9) and (11), consists of a complementizer followed by a structure containing all the other elements of a sentence. Following Bresnan (1972), let us assume that the initial rule of the categorial component of the base states that the sentence S consists of a complementizer and a "reduced sentence": thus the initial rule is (12):

$$(12) \quad S \longrightarrow COMP \ S_{red}$$

So far, I have not been distinguishing between S and S$_{red}$, and I will also ignore the distinction, where irrelevant, in later discussion. Let us assume further that *wh*-movement does not simply prepose the *wh*-word but rather places it in the complementizer position. The reasons for this would take us rather far afield, but I think that the proposal is well motivated.[20] There are rules, which I will not discuss here, that introduce "that" into the COMP position under certain conditions when this position is not filled by a *wh*-word. On this theory, it follows that there can be no *wh*-movement within phrases that have no complementizers, for example, noun phrases. Compare the two structures (13) and (14):

(13) COMP John discovered [$_S$ COMP Bill had seen who]

(14) COMP John discovered [$_{NP}$ pictures of who]

From (13) we can derive (13′) and then (13″) by repeated cyclic *wh*-movement:

(13′) COMP John discovered who Bill had seen

(13″) who did John discover that Bill had seen?[21]

But from (14) we can derive only (14″), not (14′):

(14′) COMP John discovered who pictures of

(14″) who did John discover pictures of?

In the case of (14″), the acceptability of the sentence depends in part on the main verb; thus some people find it more natural with "find" in place of "discover."[22] But no change in verb will help (14′), which has an entirely different status. It is simply ungrammatical, and remains so under any interchange of lexical items. It is the *structure* that is impossible. The fundamental difference between (13′) and (14′) results from the fact that noun phrases do not have complementizers. Note that there is no violation of subjacency in the formation of (14″) from (14) by a single application of *wh*-movement. (Cf. note 21.)

Compare now the initial phrase markers (15) and (16):

(15) COMP John believed [$_s$ COMP Mary said [$_s$ COMP Tom saw *wh*-someone]]

(16) COMP John believed [$_{NP}$ the claim [$_s$ COMP Tom saw *wh*-someone]]

From (15) we can derive the sentence (10), repeated here as (15′), by repeated cyclic *wh*-movement, observing the principle of subjacency:

(15′) who did John believe that Mary said that Tom saw?

From (16), however, we cannot analogously derive (16′):

(16′) who did John believe the claim that Tom saw?

The sentences are analogous in structure except for the fact that (15) has a sentence with a COMP where (16) has an NP without a COMP. As we know, *wh*-movement moves a *wh*-word into a COMP position, so that (15′) can be derived step by step just as (9) was derived (cf. (9′), (9″)). But it is impossible to derive (16′) cyclically in a parallel way since there is no COMP position to receive the *wh*-word in the intermediate structure NP. Furthermore, by the principle of subjacency, (16′) cannot be derived directly from (16). Therefore, it cannot be derived at all. There is no grammatical sentence corresponding to the initial phrase marker (16),[23] though from such structures as (15) we can derive three well-formed surface structures, depending on the choice of lexical items.

Plainly, there is no semantic problem in the case of (16′). If the sentence were syntactically well formed, it would have a definite and unambiguous meaning, and there is no choice of lexical items that will improve matters, as there was in the case of (9)–(11).[24] The principle of subjacency, along with other assumptions that entered into the preceding argument, provides an explanation for the ungrammaticalness of (16′). In turn, such examples as (16′) provide empirical support for the principle of subjacency.

In the first chapter, I argued that the principle of structure-dependence must be attributed to universal grammar, since it is used correctly in the cases illustrated there even in the absence of relevant experience. The same is true in this case. It is difficult to imagine that every speaker of English who is capable of the discriminations on which this argument is based has been given instruction, or even relevant evidence, to establish the fact. A far more reasonable assumption is that the general principles that exclude (16′) (among others, the principle of subjacency, if the argument just sketched is correct) are simply innate to the language faculty, as part of the schematism that determines admissible grammars and the ways in which their rules apply, thus determining the class of languages accessible to humans by application of the language faculty.

Against such a conclusion, two arguments might be adduced (and often have been, in comparable cases). First, we know of no genetic mechanisms adequate to account for the innate structures postulated. Second, it is improper (or perhaps "question-begging") to assign such complexity to the mind as an innate property. As for the first argument, it is correct, but irrelevant. The genetic mechanisms are unknown, just like the mechanisms responsible for such learning as takes place or for the development of physical organs. The argument just presented is essentially an argument in theoretical psychology. Studying the use and understanding of language, we reach certain conclusions about the cognitive structure (grammar) that is being put to use, thus setting a certain problem for the neurologist, whose task it is to discover the mechanisms involved in linguistic competence and performance. Noting that the mechanisms appear to function in the absence of relevant experience and quite uniformly for individuals of vastly differing experience, we draw the natural conclusion that they are not learned, but are part of the system that makes learning possible. This conclusion sets a further task for human biology, which will attempt to find the genetic mechanisms that guarantee that the mental organ, language, will have the required character. There is nothing further to say, on this score.

The second argument has even less merit. It is a dogmatic assumption, and not a particularly plausible one, that the principles in question must have been developed in a few years of experience rather than through tens of thousands of years of evolution or perhaps by the operation of physical laws yet unknown. No questions are begged when we reach the natural conclusion that the mind is comparable in complexity to physical organs of the body that are not involved directly in higher mental functions. The argument merely reiterates empiricist prejudice. It is no more interesting than the claim that man must have an immortal soul.

Returning again to the technical discussion, I think that the subjacency principle is reasonably well motivated, and thus can be proposed as a principle of universal grammar, alongside of the other assumptions that we have been considering, subject to further investigation. Applying this and other principles of comparable generality, we can explain quite a number of the phenomena noted by Ross in his very illuminating study of "island constraints." [25]

Ross suggested in his work that rightward-movement rules are "bounded"—in our terms, constrained by the principle of subjacency—while leftward-movement rules need not be. Thus leftward-movement rules fall into two categories, those subject to subjacency and those that are unbounded. The distinction has persisted through subsequent work, with such rules as *wh*-movement given as examples of unboundedness, but not NP-preposing, which has been taken to be bounded and cyclic. Under the present analysis, *wh*-movement is also bounded and cyclic. The apparent asymmetry between leftward-movement and rightward-movement rules reduces to an independent left-right asymmetry in the position of complementizer. Several interesting constraints on rules fall out as special cases. If all examples of allegedly unbounded rules are subject to a similar analysis, then we may considerably improve the general theory of transformations, eliminating the category of unbounded rules. While not all problems that arise when this approach is pursued have been solved, my own feeling is that it is probably correct.

In addition to rules governed by subjacency and unbounded rules, it has been generally assumed that there are rules governed by a "clause-mate constraint" that requires that they cannot relate an item in an embedded sentence to anything outside that sentence. In terms of the abstract formula (4), modified here as (4′) to avoid the issue of subjacency, a rule that is governed by the clause-mate condition cannot, say, move an item from position X to position Y or conversely, or modify an item in position X by virtue of its relation to an item in position Y, if $B = S$:

$$(4') \; [_C \ldots Y \ldots [_B \ldots [_A X] \ldots] \ldots Y \ldots]$$

I have argued elsewhere that there is no evidence for such a constraint. The examples that have been used to motivate it are explained by independently motivated general principles.[26] If this is correct, then there is only one category of transformational rules: all such rules are governed by the subjacency principle. It is an interesting question whether (or to what extent) rules of semantic interpretation are also governed by this or some similar principle.[27]

Instead of pursuing these matters further, let us return to the examples (9″) and (11), repeated here:

(9″) the police think who the FBI discovered that
　　　Bill shot

(11) the police know who the FBI discovered that
　　　Bill shot

We may think of the *wh*-word in a question (direct or indirect) as a kind of quantifier. Thus, the "logical form" of (9″) and (11) can be taken to be (17) and (18), respectively:

> (17) the police think for which person x, the FBI
> discovered that Bill shot x
>
> (18) the police know for which person x, the FBI
> discovered that Bill shot x

In these logical forms, there is a variable x and a quantifier, "for which x," binding it. Suppose that we were to identify the variable x with the trace t left by the movement rule. Recall that the surface structure of (11), under the present theory, is something like (19):

> (19) [s the police know [s who the FBI discovered [s that
> Bill shot t]]

To convert (19) to its logical form, all that is required is the information that "who" is a quantifier binding t and meaning "for which person t." [28] With only notational modifications of the theory of transformations we can guarantee that the item "who" is identified in surface structure as the item that binds t. With a further principle that interprets "who" as "for which person x," we derive the logical form (18) from the surface structure (19).

We have not yet settled the question of the basis for the distinction in grammaticalness between (9″) and (11). Is it a difference of syntax or semantics? Is it determined at the level of base structure or surface structure? One possibility is that questions, direct or indirect, have a complementizer distinct from the one that appears with declarative structures, and that verbs are marked in the lexicon as to whether they may or may not appear with sentential complements containing this complementizer. Semantic interpretation will involve the position of this complementizer relative to other items in surface structure. I have elaborated a version of this position elsewhere, and shown how some fairly complex examples can be handled from this point of view in what seems a rather natural way. (See Chomsky, 1973a, for some discussion.)

This proposal still leaves open the status of the distinction: syntactic or semantic? I am not persuaded that the question makes very much sense, or that any reasonably clear criteria exist to settle it. Suppose that someone claims to have a very refined sort of "grammatical intuition" that tells him whether the deviance of (9″) is "syntactic" or "semantic." Such a person, then, will have an answer to the question left open here. Personally, I have no such intuitions. I can make the judgment that certain sentences are fine and others deviant (say, (11) and (9″), respectively), but have no further intuitions that provide me, in such cases as these, with the basis for these judgments. I am therefore skeptical that others have such intuitions. I suspect that they are adhering to certain traditional explanations, which may or may not be correct. (See Chomsky, 1965, chap. 4.) It remains, I think, an open and perhaps interesting question to establish sharper criteria that will help to make the question "syntactic or semantic?" more precise in such cases as these.

However these questions are resolved, we do have a simple way to derive the "logical form" of the sentences in question from surface structures in which trace appears. Let us now stipulate explicitly what we have been tacitly assuming: when a transformation moves a phrase P from position X to position Y it leaves in position X a trace bound by P. As we will see directly, this "trace theory of movement rules" has considerable justification from several independent points of view.

Notice that what we have been developing is a theory of semantic interpretation of surface structures. The position of the "quantifier" in surface structure relative to verbs determines whether the sentence has a meaning and what this meaning is. But a problem arises. Thus, to understand the sentences we have been discussing we must surely also know the position in the initial phrase marker of the phrase that has been moved. Thus consider again (6), derived by NP-preposing from (6'):

(6) John seems [$_s$ t to be a nice fellow]

(6') Y seems [$_s$ John to be a nice fellow]

To understand the sentence (6) we must know that "John" is the subject of the embedded sentence. The initial phrase marker provides this information, but the surface structure (it appears) does not. The same is true of the other examples we have been discussing. In fact, it was precisely such considerations as these that motivated the principle of the standard theory that deep structures (our "initial phrase markers") determine semantic interpretation.

But notice that under the trace theory of movement rules, the motivation disappears. The position of the bound trace in surface structure allows us to determine the grammatical relation of "John" in (6) as subject of the embedded sentence. Similarly, in the other cases. Thus, such examples as these do not choose between the standard theory and the theory that interpretation is determined by surface structure, given the trace theory of movement rules. We have, however, found some reason to suppose that surface structure does play a role in semantic interpretation; namely, the position of the quantifier "who" in surface structure is relevant to the interpretation of such sentences as (9)–(11). There is a great deal more evidence that surface-structure information contributes to the determination of meaning. Thus, it seems reasonable to postulate that *only* surface structures undergo semantic interpretation, though our "surface structures" are no longer those of the standard theory, by virtue of the trace theory of movement rules.

Objections come to mind, and I will return to some of them a little later. Let us put them aside for the moment and continue to explore the possibility that with the trace theory of movement rules, it is possible to unify the theory of semantic interpretation, restricting it to surface structures.

The original motivation for the trace theory was in part that it facilitated semantic interpretation along the lines just indicated. But there were also independent considerations that led to the same theory. (Cf. Chomsky, 1973a.) Before turning to these, let us consider some further applications of the trace theory in semantic interpretation.

Consider active-passive pairs such as (20)–(21):

> (20) beavers build dams
>
> (21) dams are built by beavers

There are various problems as to how the passive construction should be analyzed, but all approaches within the framework of transformational grammar agree that one component of the passive is a rule that moves the noun phrase "dams" from its underlying position as the object, as in (20), to the subject position, where it appears in (21). Thus, under the trace theory, the surface structure of (21) will be something like (22):

> (22) dams are [$_{VP}$ built t by beavers]

Sentences (20) and (21) plainly differ in range of meaning. Sentence (21), in its most natural interpretation, states that it is a property of dams that they are built by beavers. Under this interpretation, the sentence is false, since some dams are not built by beavers. But there is no interpretation of sentence (20), under normal intonation at least, in which it asserts that dams have the property that they are built by beavers; (20) cannot be understood as referring to all dams. Sentence (20) states that beavers have a certain property, namely, that they are dam builders, but does not imply (under any interpretation) that their activities in dam building account for all dams; in fact, (20) might be true if beavers never exhibit their species characteristic, say, if all beavers are in zoos.

Thus the position of the word "dams" in surface structure plays a role in determining the meaning of the sentences (20) and (21). In particular, to understand (21), it is important to know that the noun phrase "dams" is the subject of the sentence.

However, to understand (21) it is also important to know that the noun phrase "dams" bears the grammatical relation of direct object to the verb "build," as in the initial phrase marker. Thus, we must know that "dams" is the subject of (21) in one sense, but is the object of the verb of (21), and hence not the subject, in another sense. The necessary information is conveyed in the surface structure (22). We may assume that the subject-predicate relation is defined on surface structures, so that "dams" is the subject of (21). But the position of the trace bound by "dams" serves to indicate that it bears the appropriate semantic relation to the verb "build." We return to some further discussion. For the present, I simply want to note that two kinds of "grammatical relation" seem to be involved in the interpretation of sentences such as (20) and (21): one, the relation verb-object of the initial phrase marker, accounting for the similarity in meaning between these sentences; and another, the relation subject-predicate of the surface structure, accounting for the difference in meaning. Both relations are represented appropriately in surface structure.

Note that in these examples a question of quantification seems to be involved. We have already observed that in some cases, a kind of "quantification" of an unconventional sort is determined by surface structure. There is considerable evidence that this is true quite generally, and that the same is true of the scope of logical particles, and other aspects of what might be called "logical form." [29]

Consider now some relations between the rule of *wh-*

movement and interpretation of pronouns noted originally by Paul Postal (1971). I adapt here a reanalysis of this and related material by Thomas Wasow (forthcoming). Compare the sentences (23) and (24):

> (23) *who* said Mary kissed *him*?
> (24) *who* did *he* say Mary kissed?

In the case of sentence (23), we may understand the pronoun ("him") to refer to the person whose name answers the query "who?" But in the case of (24) this interpretation is inappropriate. To put it very misleadingly, there can be a relation of anaphora or coreference between the italicized expressions of (23) but not those of (24). But the structure of (24) is a possible anaphora structure; compare (25), which is analogous in categorial structure to (24), though the pronoun "he" in (25) can be taken as referring to John:

> (25) *John* said *he* thought Mary left

What is the explanation for this curious fact?

With trace introduced into the surface structures, we have (23') and (24') corresponding to (23) and (24), respectively: [30]

> (23') who [$_{S_{red}}$ *t* said Mary kissed him]
> (24') who [$_{S_{red}}$ he said Mary kissed *t*]

In both cases, the *wh*-movement rule has raised the *wh*-word "who" to the complementizer position, leaving trace in the position in which the *wh*-word appeared in the initial phrase marker. Applying the method of semantic interpretation outlined earlier, we have the "logical forms" (23'') and (24''):

> (23'') for which person x, x said Mary kissed him?
> (24'') for which person x, he said Mary kissed x?

The bound variable x functions roughly as a name. Thus

we would expect (23″) and (24″) to have interpretations
analogous to (26) and (27), respectively:

(26) *John* said Mary kissed *him*

(27) *he* said Mary kissed *John*

In sentence (26), the pronoun can refer to John, but in (27)
it cannot. The relevant principle again involves surface
structure. (Cf. Wasow, 1972, forthcoming; Lasnik, 1974.)
We may assume it without further discussion here. Applying the principle governing (26) and (27) to the analogous
examples (23″) and (24″), we see that in (23″) the pronoun "him" can bear an anaphoric relation to the bound
variable x (as in (26)), whereas in (24″) the pronoun "he"
cannot bear an anaphoric relation to x (as in (27)). Thus
we can understand (23″) as having essentially the meaning
represented in (28):

(28) for which person x, x said Mary kissed x?

In the case of (24″), no such interpretation is possible, any
more than it is in the analogous construction (27). The
pronoun "he" must therefore be taken to be referring to
someone whose identity is fixed elsewhere in the discourse
or context of utterance.

Thus the distinction between (23) and (24) is readily
explained by available mechanisms, given the trace theory
and the principles of semantic interpretation of surface
structure suggested earlier. Furthermore, we can now dispense with such notions as "coreference between *he* and
who" or "anaphoric relations" between these terms—notions which are, strictly speaking, without sense, since
"who" is not a referential expression but rather a kind of
quantifier in these cases, and therefore cannot enter into
relations of anaphora.

Certain qualifications must be added to extend this account to a broader class of cases, and, as in the cases discussed earlier, some problems remain unsolved. But this
does, I think, capture the essence of the matter. Pursuing

this approach, we will develop the theory of anaphora so as to apply to "logical forms" derived from surface structure, making essential use of trace as analogous to a bound variable.[31]

Let us now turn to some independent lines of argument that lead, again, to the trace theory of movement rules. Consider the sentences (29)–(32):

(29) it seems to us that Bill likes each other

(30) we expected Bill to like each other

(31) we were shocked by Bill's hatred of each other

(32) Tom seems to us to like each other

None of these are grammatical. They have something of the character of such violations of the subjacency condition as (16′). That is, the sentences are not senseless. There is no semantic reason why they should not have the same meanings as (29′)–(32′), respectively, just as (33) and (33′) are close to synonymous:

(29′) it seems to each of us that Bill likes the other(s)

(30′) each of us expected Bill to like the other(s)

(31′) each of us was shocked by Bill's hatred of the other(s)

(32′) Tom seems to each of us to like the other(s)

(33) we seem to like each other

(33′) each of us seems to like the other(s)

In general, the structures *each of us . . . the other(s)*, *we each . . . the other(s)*, and *we . . . each other* have very similar if not the same meanings. Thus, there is no warrant for ruling out sentences (29)–(32) on grounds of senselessness.

These and many other examples exemplify the "specified-subject condition," still another general condition on rules. The condition, which I will not attempt to state precisely here,[32] implies that no rule can relate X and Y in a structure such as (34), where α is a cyclic category subjacent to X and Z is its subject:

$$(34) \quad \ldots X \ldots [_a \, Z - \ldots Y \ldots]$$

Consider now the reciprocal rule that relates the phrase "each other" to its noun-phrase antecedent; we may put aside the interesting question whether there is a rule that moves "each" from the antecedent noun phrase to form the phrase "each other" in addition to the interpretive rule relating the antecedent and the reciprocal phrase. Taking X of (34) to be "we" (or "us"), Z to be "Bill," and Y to be "each other," the reciprocal rule is blocked in (29) and (30) (with $\alpha = S$),[33] and in (31) (with $\alpha = NP$),[34] by virtue of the specified subject condition.

Still unexplained, however, is the example (32). Here, there is no embedded subject Z, as in the other three cases. There is no phrase corresponding to the subject noun phrase "Bill" of (29)–(31). The last comment must be qualified. There is no subject noun phrase *physically present* in the position corresponding to that of "Bill" in (29)–(31), namely, before "to like each other." But there is a subject noun phrase "mentally present" in this position, namely, "Tom," which we understand to be the subject of "like," just as the (physically present) "Bill" is the subject of "like" in (30). Evidently, in interpreting these sentences we are concerned not with the physical position of subjects in sentences, but with their "mental position," that is, their position in the abstract structures that we are postulating in the subpart of theoretical psychology (called "linguistics") that we are developing. Our theory must account for the fact that a person who knows English operates appropriately with abstract mental structures, whatever the physical form of the sentence may be. And at a deeper level, our general theory must account for the fact that the speaker comes to know that it is abstract rather than physical structures that are relevant in interpreting (29)–(32).

Note again that, as in the case of the principle of structure-dependence, it is difficult to believe that the person developing knowledge of English as a "mental organ" is *taught* the relevant principles. People are not trained or conditioned to treat (32) "on the analogy" of (29)–(31). Rather, they just know that they are to do so, quite without training or even presentation of relevant experience that might determine this conclusion. Our theoretical psychology must account for these facts.

Recall that (32) is derived from an abstract structure (35) by NP-preposing, just as (6) was formed from (6'):

(35) Y seems to us [$_s$ Tom to like each other]

The surface structure corresponding to (32), under the trace theory, is therefore (36):

(36) Tom seems to us [$_s$ t to like each other]

Thus under the trace theory, there *is* a subject Z in the embedded sentence in the surface structure in exactly the position filled by "Bill" in the embedded cyclic categories of (29)–(31). Assuming as before that the specified-subject condition applies to surface structures, determining the relation of the reciprocal phrase "each other" to its antecedent, we have an explanation for the ungrammatical status of (32). Namely, the specified-subject condition rules it ungrammatical, exactly as in the case of (29)–(31). A speaker who is forming and interpreting sentences by the postulated means (specifically, making use of the specified-subject condition and the trace theory) will regard (32) as analogous, in the relevant respects, to (29)–(31). If, furthermore, the specified-subject condition and the trace theory are part of universal grammar, part of the biologically necessary schematism that determines the "essence of human language," the speaker will know all of this without instruction or even relevant evidence, as appears to be the case.

Thus, we have an entirely independent motivation for the trace theory.

Summarizing these remarks, we seem to have the following general structure for grammar. The rules of the categorial component and the lexicon provide initial phrase markers. Applying transformations to these, we derive surface structures (including traces), which undergo semantic interpretation. The rules of semantic interpretation assign the scope of logical operators ("not," "each," "who," etc.) and fix their meaning, assign antecedents to such anaphoric expressions as reciprocals ("each other") and necessarily bound anaphors (e.g., "his" in "John lost his way," where "his" must refer to John, as contrasted with the unbound anaphor "his" in "John found his book," where "his" may refer to any male, including John).[35] The result of application of these rules we may call a "logical form."

It would be reasonable to say that the theory of grammar—or more precisely, "sentence grammar"—ends at this point. The conditions on grammar so far discussed—the specified-subject condition, subjacency, and so on—apply to the rules of sentence grammar. Sentence grammar involves such rules as NP-preposing, *wh*-movement, scope assignment, assignment of antecedents to bound anaphors, and also rules determining thematic relations and other aspects of semantic structure that may be properly assigned to the abstract system of language, depending on how the questions raised in the preceding chapter are answered.

What we have been calling "grammar" in the preceding discussion is actually sentence grammar, in this sense. Given the logical forms generated by sentence grammar, further rules may apply. Pronouns not yet assigned antecedents may be taken to refer to entities designated elsewhere in the sentence, though this is never necessary and is not permitted under certain conditions, for example, in (27). These further rules of reference determination may involve discourse properties as well, in some manner; and they interact with considerations relating to situation, communicative intention, and the like. Similarly, though the reciprocal "each other" in (29)–(31) must be assigned an

antecedent by a rule of sentence grammar, the corresponding phrase "the others" in (29')–(31') need not be taken to
refer to members of a class designated (namely, by "each
of us") elsewhere within the same sentence. As noted before, the rules of sentence grammar obey quite different
conditions from those that apply beyond. The former, for
example, are governed by the specified-subject condition;
the latter are not (see also note 27). Other semantic rules
apply, interacting with rules belonging to other cognitive
structures, to form fuller representations of "meaning" (in
some sense).

Schematically, this seems to me a reasonable picture of
the general nature of grammar and its place within the
system of cognitive structures. To recapitulate in a dia-
gram, we may have a system of roughly the following
structure:

$$(37)\ \text{Sentence grammar:} \xrightarrow{\text{B}} \text{IPM} \xrightarrow{\text{T}} \text{SS} \xrightarrow{\text{SR–1}} \text{LF}$$

$$\left\{ \begin{matrix} \text{SR–2} \\ \text{other systems} \end{matrix} \right\} : \quad \text{LF} \longrightarrow \text{``meaning''}$$

Thus, the rules of the base (B), including the rules of
the categorial component and the lexicon, form initial
phrase markers (IPM). The rules of the transformational
component (T) convert these to surface structures (SS),
which are converted to logical forms (LF) by certain rules
of semantic interpretation (SR–1; namely, the rules involving bound anaphora, scope, thematic relations, etc.). This
much constitutes sentence grammar; certain general conditions on rules appear to apply throughout this system.
The logical forms so generated are subject to further interpretation by other semantic rules (SR–2) interacting
with other cognitive structures, giving fuller representations of meaning.

Examples of the sort just discussed provide empirical support for the trace theory on grounds of the functioning of grammatical rules, syntactic and semantic. There is another independent line of argument of a more abstract sort. Consider the effect of the rule of NP-preposing on phrase markers. In the case of such examples as (6) and (36), this rule takes the subject of an embedded sentence and raises it to the subject position in a "higher clause." The effect, then, is as illustrated in (38):

$$(38) \quad Y \dots [_s NP \dots] \longrightarrow NP \dots [_s t \dots]$$

In contrast, there are no rules that "lower" a noun phrase to the subject position (or, I believe, any position) in the embedded sentence. We might stipulate this asymmetry as a new condition on transformations.

Let us return now to the passive construction, and in particular, the rule that moves the noun phrase following the verb to the subject position, to give such forms as (22):

$$(22) \quad \text{dams are } [_{VP} \text{ built } t \text{ by beavers}]$$

This too is a rule of NP-preposing. In fact, though this is debatable, I think it is the same rule of NP-preposing as the subject-to-subject rule of (38). The effect of NP-preposing, in the case of (22) and many other passives, is as indicated in (39):

$$(39) \quad Y [_{VP} V NP] \longrightarrow NP [_{VP} V t]$$

Again, there is an asymmetry. There are rules that raise objects to subject position, but none, it appears, that move subjects to object position. Again we might stipulate this asymmetry as still another condition on rules.

Clearly, there is something similar about these two asymmetries involving the rule of NP-preposing. How can we capture it? We might stipulate that there is a hierarchy of positions, with subjects having precedence over objects [36] and subjects of higher clauses having precedence over subjects of embedded clauses. Rules are permitted to move elements only to positions that precede in the hierarchy. But this is no real improvement. It is only a notational convention, and we might ask why we set up this hierarchy, rather than some other one, say, in which subjects precede objects and there is no relation (or the converse relation) between elements that are not in the same clause. There is no logical connection between the principles illustrated in (38) and (39) that determines the structure of the hierarchy.

A considerably better approach would be to exploit the fact that in both cases the permissible rules are rules of "upgrading" which move a noun phrase closer to the "root of the sentence," that is, to a less embedded position; the impermissible rules are rules of "downgrading," which increase the embeddedness of the noun phrase. We might stipulate, then, that upgrading rules are permitted, but not downgrading rules. Thus the two principles fall together.

This is an improvement, but there are two problems. First, there are counterexamples to the proposal, as it stands. Second, we might still want to find an explanation for the upgrading principle to the extent that it is true. That is, we might hope to account for it in terms of some independent principle.

To illustrate the falsity of the upgrading conjecture, consider the sentences (40)–(42):

    (40) there is a book on the table
    (41) the city was destroyed by the enemy
    (42) the candidates have each indicated their
           willingness to debate

There are familiar analyses—not without competitors, but at least quite plausible—that postulate that in these cases a rule of downgrading applies. In the case of (40), we might argue that the source is (43), and that a transformational rule forms (43′), which in turn becomes (40) by a rule of *there*-insertion, which erases (replaces) the trace:

(43) a book $[_{VP}$ is on the table]

$(43')$ t $[_{VP}$ is a book on the table]

In the case of (41), we might assume the derivation (44):

(44) (i) the enemy $[_{VP}$ destroyed the city]
(initial phrase marker)

(ii) t $[_{VP}$ destroyed the city by the enemy]
(by NP-postposing)

(iii) the city $[_{VP}$ was destroyed t by the enemy]
(by NP-preposing)

We omit here some interesting questions about the status of the agent *by*-phrase, the auxiliary and the verbal inflection; see page 114 and note 46. The rule of NP-preposing erases the trace left by NP-postposing.

The sentence (42) might be formed by a rule of *each*-movement from (45):

(45) the candidates each $[_{VP}$ have indicated their willingness to debate]

These are all plausible analyses. In each case, a rule of downgrading applies.

Robert Fiengo has observed that the trace theory of movement rules permits us to formulate our conjecture with regard to the two asymmetries (38) and (39) in such a way as to avoid the counterexamples and at the same time to reduce the conjecture to an independent principle, thus overcoming both of the problems that arise.[37] Consider again the permissible rule of NP-preposing as in (38) and (39) and the impermissible rule of downgrading NP, which reverses the direction of the arrows in (38) and (39). The permissible rule gives the structures (46), and the impermissible rule gives the structures (47):

(46) (i) NP ... $[_{S}$ t ...]   (right-hand side of (38))

(ii) NP $[_{VP}$ V t]   (right-hand side of (39))

(47) (i) $t \ldots [_S \mathrm{NP} \ldots]$

(ii) $t [_{VP} \mathrm{V} \mathrm{NP}]$

Taking t, as before, to be a variable bound by NP as antecedent, notice that the permissible cases are instances of permissible relations between an antecedent noun phrase and an "anaphoric" element that it controls, whereas the impermissible cases are instances of impermissible anaphoric relations.[38] Thus, the examples (46′) are of the form (46) and are grammatical, whereas the examples (47′) are of the form (47) and are ungrammatical:

(46′) (i) *the candidates* expected [$_S$ *each other* to win][39]

(ii) *the candidates* [$_{VP}$ hated *each other*]

(47′) (i) *each other* expected [$_S$ *the candidates* to win]

(ii) *each other* [$_{VP}$ hated *the candidates*]

An antecedent must be "superior" in the phrase marker to the anaphor it controls, in such cases as these. Assuming the relation between noun phrase and trace to be analogous to that between antecedent and anaphor, as is entirely natural, we can reduce the upgrading principle to an independently motivated condition on the antecedent-anaphor relation.

This is a substantial step forward. We have now provided an explanation for the upgrading convention, insofar as it holds. Given the trace theory, it follows as a consequence of an independent principle of language. Under this analysis, the problem with the impermissible examples of the type (47) is that, in effect, they have a free variable not within the scope of a binding quantifier or noun phrase in their semantic interpretation, and thus are not sentences.

But the same analysis also overcomes the difficulty that the upgrading principle was falsified by the counterexamples (40)–(42). In cases (40) and (41), the offending trace has been erased by a later rule; thus the surface structure does not violate the antecedent-anaphor principle. In case

(42) there is no antecedent-anaphor relation between the phrase moved and its trace; it is senseless, in this case, to regard the trace as a bound variable, though it makes good sense to do so when the phrase moved is a noun phrase. Thus, we can interpret (6) along the lines indicated earlier, as having the logical form (48):

> (6) John seems [$_S$ t to be a nice fellow]

> (48) for x = John, x seems [$_S$ x to be a nice fellow]

But no such analysis is possible in the case of *each*-movement, since "each" is not a referential expression, nor does it bind a variable as a quantifier except in association with a noun phrase that gives the type of the variable, as in "the candidates each," which can be interpreted as "for each x, x a candidate." But in the latter case, it is the full noun phrase "the candidates each" and not the word "each" which binds the variable, which is thus crucially distinct from the trace left by *each*-movement.

The upgrading principle would have had to be stated in the form (49) to avoid the counterexamples noted:

(49) Movement rules may upgrade, but they cannot downgrade unless the position that they vacate is filled by a later rule, or unless the item downgraded is not a noun phrase.

So formulated, the convention overcomes the counterexamples, but is too *ad hoc* to have any real credibility; and it is, furthermore, without explanation or significant analogue elsewhere in the theory. But under the trace theory, (49) follows as an immediate consequence of independent principles of anaphora.

The general principle that emerges from this discussion, once again, is that since the trace is being interpreted as in effect a variable, surface structures with traces must meet the general conditions on expressions with variable-like expressions such as the reciprocal phrase "each other." Nothing further need be said, in these cases at least, to distinguish permissible from impermissible rule applications.

These considerations again make essential use of the trace theory, and thus provide an independent motivation for this theory at an entirely different and more abstract level of discussion.

Principles of the sort that we have just been discussing are of considerable importance. They restrict the class of possible rules, and also, the possible application of established rules. Therefore, they contribute to solving the fundamental problem of linguistic theory, hence of "learning theory" as this was construed in the first chapter, namely: to constrain the class of "learnable systems" so that it becomes possible to explain the rapidity, uniformity, and richness of learning within cognitive capacity. The same is true of the argument, given earlier, that we can eliminate the notions "unbounded" and "clause-mate" from the theory of transformations. In general, the same is true of all the conditions on organization of grammar and application of rules that we have been describing. These are all steps towards what has been called "explanatory adequacy." [40] From one point of view, we can properly say that these principles provide explanations for the fact that the data are such-and-such, and thus go well beyond the descriptions of such facts in particular grammars. From another point of view, the same principles serve to account for an important aspect of human learning, that is, for the construction of certain cognitive structures that play an essential role in thought and its expression (and derivatively, in communication).

If these principles can be substantiated or improved, the class of potential grammars is vastly reduced. Many potential rules are eliminated outright. Furthermore, by limiting the possible application of rules, principles of the sort discussed make it unnecessary to make available in the theory of transformations as rich an apparatus as would otherwise be needed to delimit the application of particular rules. Thus, the principles constrain the variety of grammars by reducing the "expressive power" of grammatical rules.

We might even set ourselves the goal, still distant but perhaps attainable, of so restricting the apparatus of the theory of transformations that rules can only be given in the form "move NP," with other conditions on their application expressed either as general conditions on rules, or as properties of initial phrase markers, or as properties of surface structures. In all three cases, we will try, of course, to abstract properties of universal grammar from particular conditions on rules, initial phrase markers, and surface structures. As a case in point, recall the conditions on anaphora in surface structures, to which appeal was made in the analysis of the upgrading convention.

If this goal can be reached, not only will the various cases of NP-preposing fall together, but further, these will fall together with the rule of NP-postposing that gave (44ii). Restrictions on the "expressive power" of rules, even if not as dramatic as these speculations suggest, contribute to the dual goal of attaining explanatory adequacy and accounting for the acquisition of cognitive structures, that is, for human learning.

Principles such as subjacency, the trace theory, and the specified-subject condition contribute to this end, along with other principles, among them the principle of structure-dependence and the conditions on the organization of grammar and the various types of rules that can appear in the several components of grammar. Insofar as these proposals are correct, they are contributions to universal grammar, hence to the characterization of the language faculty that is one essential component of innate mental structure.

Pursuing the discussion of possible rules a step further, consider again the derivation (44) suggested for passives.

An analogous derivation might be proposed for "passives" of nominal constructions. Thus, (50):

(50) (i)   the enemy—destruction of the city
            (initial phrase marker)

      (ii) t—destruction of the city by the enemy
            (by NP-postposing)

      (iii) the city's—destruction t by the enemy
            (by NP-preposing)

There is, however, a striking difference between the derivations (44) and (50).[41] Namely, in the case of the passive of the sentence, (44), the rule of NP-preposing must apply if the rule of NP-postposing has applied. There is no such sentence as (51), corresponding to (44ii):

(51) t destroyed the city by the enemy

But in the case of the "passive" of the nominal, (50), NP-postposing may apply without a subsequent application of NP-preposing, giving such sentences as (52), corresponding to (50ii):

(52) the destruction of the city by the enemy

The distinction is explicable in our terms. In the case of (51), there is an offending trace, violating anaphora conditions, standing as a free variable in the logical form derived from surface structure. But in (52) the trace has been erased by a rule spelling out the determiner.[42] It may be, then, that the same rules are involved, with differences in applicability that are reducible to other properties of the constructions involved.

We have noted a number of cases that seem to fall together under a rule of NP-preposing, without, however, going into a number of difficulties that arise when these phenomena are unified or the possible solutions to these difficulties. We have discussed such cases as these:

(53) John seems $[_S\ t$ to be a nice fellow]

(54) John is certain $[_S\ t$ to win the election]

(55) the city [$_{VP}$ was destroyed t by the enemy]

(56) the city's [$_{NP}$ destruction t by the enemy]

Other examples fall within the same rubric, e.g.:

(57) John [$_{VP}$ was believed [$_S$ t to be a suitable candidate]]

(58) the bed [$_{VP}$ was slept in t] [43]

Others of quite different types also come to mind as possible candidates for a similar analysis.[44] The rule of NP-preposing applies over quite an array of possible constructions; as we would expect, if the speculations of the preceding discussion prove to be justified.

Notice that if there were no passives such as (57), (58), and those of note 43, we might be hesitant to postulate a rule of passive formation in the first place. Many languages lack such constructions, restricting the "passive" to reduced passives such as (59), with no agent phrase and with the subject serving as the direct object in related transitive constructions, where "pass" indicates some passive inflection:

(59) John kill-pass   (analogous to "John was killed")

In such cases, there is no motivation for postulating a rule to form passives from actives; the facts can be described with no less (I think greater) facility within the lexicon, under rules of word formation.[45]

The theory of grammar makes a variety of devices available, and languages may differ as to their choice among them. We would expect these choices to have certain consequences both in the syntax and the semantics. Thus, it can hardly be accidental that the English passive makes use of the copula and that the verb morphology is so clearly analogous to certain adjectival constructions, so that the rules forming passives map initial phrase markers into independently existing structures of the subject-predicate form.[46] This fact may well find its place within a theory of surface-structure semantic interpretation, making essential use of the subject-predicate construction in surface structure, the theory of traces, and other related ideas. Further discussion would carry us too far afield, into areas that have so far barely been explored in a systematic way within the theory of generative grammar.

We have been operating so far on the assumption that surface structures alone undergo semantic interpretation. But there are some obvious objections to this conjecture. Thus, we have come across several rules that erase the trace left by earlier movement rules. In such cases, the position of a phrase in initial phrase markers will no longer be marked in surface structure. But in some cases at least, this initial position seemed essential for semantic interpretation. Thus, consider the passives (44iii) and (50iii):

(44) (iii) the city was destroyed *t* by the enemy

(50) (iii) the city's destruction *t* by the enemy

The surface forms contain no trace for the phrase "the enemy." But to understand the sentences, we must know that this phrase bears the semantic relation of "agent" to the verb "destroy," as is indicated in the initial phrase markers (44i) and (50i). Thus it seems that contrary to our conjecture, initial phrase markers must enter into semantic interpretation. It was for such reasons as these that formulations of the extended standard theory have in the past postulated that semantic interpretation applies to paired deep and surface structures (initial and surface phrase markers).

John Goldsmith has observed that in the derived forms (44iii) and (50iii) there is a formal structure that indicates the semantic relation of the phrase "the enemy" to the verb, namely, the *by*-phrase. Similarly, in the "there is" constructions (cf. (40)), though the trace is erased, the surface structure suffices to determine the relations of the moved noun phrase to the verb. He proposes, then, that a rule may erase a trace only if the element binding the trace appears in surface structure in a position that identifies the semantic relation it bears. Thus, the rule of NP-preposing may apply to give the passives, erasing a trace, but there could be no rule, for example, that erases the trace in (53) (= "John seems t to be a nice fellow"), and no derivation such as (60), giving (62) from the initial phrase marker (61):

(60) (i) NP_1 V NP_2 [$_S$ X VP] (initial phrase marker)

(ii) t V NP_2 [$_S$ NP_1 VP]   (by NP-postposing)

(iii) NP_2 V t [$_S$ NP_1 VP]   (by NP-preposing)

(61) John persuaded Bill [$_S$ X to stay awhile]

(62) Bill persuaded t [$_S$ John to stay awhile]

The structure (60iii) does not violate anaphora conditions, so that the derivation (60) cannot be ruled out along the lines of our earlier discussion of downgrading. But the derivation violates Goldsmith's principle.

In many well-known cases, this principle seems to suffice. It also, again, has the important property that it substantially restricts possible rule applications, an important desideratum, for reasons already explained.

Accepting Goldsmith's principle of recoverability of semantic relations, it seems that we can tentatively postulate that only surface structures undergo semantic interpretation. With this step, we can unify a considerable amount of quite fruitful research of the past few years that has shown that many aspects of semantic interpretation are best expressed in terms of properties of surface structure. In general, this is true of what might be called "logical properties" of sentences, properties involving scope of quantifiers and logical particles, anaphora, presupposition, and the like. In earlier versions of the extended standard theory, it was proposed that surface structure determines all semantic properties apart from "thematic relations" such as agency, goal, and instrument, these being determined by the interaction of lexical properties and the grammatical relations of initial phrase markers (deep structures).[47] If the argument presented here is correct, we can improve this picture, taking surface structures (now enriched by the trace theory) to be the sole elements that enter into semantic interpretation.

The trace theory permits us, in effect, to carry over to surface structures certain properties of phrase markers that initiate derivations or that appear at an intermediate stage of derivation.[48] It might be argued that this is a rather far-reaching and undesirable modification of earlier theory, rather like the introduction of "global rules": rules that apply, not to the last phrase marker of a derivation so far constructed, but to a set of phrase markers already derived, including the last of these. But this would be a misunderstanding. There is, indeed, a serious objection to global rules. This device enormously increases the class of admissible grammars and thus moves us a long step away from our goal of attaining explanatory adequacy in linguistic theory and accounting for the possibility of language learning.[49] Thus one would accept global rules only under the pressure of powerful evidence, which, I believe, has so far not been forthcoming. But the trace theory does not extend the class of admissible grammars. Nor does it restrict this class. Rather, it changes the class and is thus immune to the methodological objections that are rightly raised against the introduction of global rules. The structures generated are enriched, but the class of grammars is not.

It is quite true that the trace theory allows properties of earlier stages of derivation to appear in surface structure, but this in itself is nothing new. One might imagine a theory of transformations postulating operations that disregard the categories of the initial phrase markers (the labels on the brackets, in the notation we have been using here). In comparison, the conventional theory carries categorial information over to derived structure. One would not therefore argue that the conventional theory already contains global rules, since properties of initial phrase markers (namely, the categories that appear within them) are carried over to surface structures. The conventional theory generates richer surface structures than an alternative that disregards categories in transformational derivations, and in much the same sense, the trace theory enriches the class of derived structures as compared with the conventional theory, requiring that additional properties of earlier stages of derivation appear at later stages (including surface structures) with all the consequences that follow for rule application. The issue of globality does not arise.

This discussion by no means exhausts the arguments pro and con, and avoids serious questions that arise under more careful formulation and more extensive application. I hope that the discussion is, nevertheless, sufficient to give some indication of the kinds of principles that it seems reasonable to postulate as general properties of human language.

This discussion has been restricted to English, a serious limitation. Nevertheless, I have not hesitated to suggest that the principles that appear to have explanatory power for English are principles of universal grammar. On the assumption that the language faculty is a common human possession, the inference is plausible (though, obviously, nondemonstrative). The logic of the argument has already been outlined. On the assumption of uniformity of language capacity across the species, if a general principle is confirmed empirically for a given language and if, furthermore, there is reason to believe that it is not learned (and surely not taught), then it is proper to postulate that the principle belongs to universal grammar, as part of the system of "pre-existent knowledge" that makes learning possible.

Under the simplifying assumptions of chapter 1, then, it it reasonable to propose that principles of the sort outlined here find their place in the component of the innate language faculty that determines what kind of system can be learned. Recall that there were two major simplifying assumptions: first, that individual differences can be ignored; and second, that learning is "instantaneous." As noted before, the first assumption is true to a very good approximation, so far as is known. Apart from gross abnormalities, there is no known reason to suppose that individuals differ in ways relevant to the present discussion, though there are no doubt differences in fluency, talent, and knowledge that would appear at a finer level of detail.

But the assumption that learning is instantaneous is obviously false. We might, more realistically, say that children proceed through a sequence of cognitive states S_0, $S_1, \ldots, S_f$, where S_0 is the "initial state," prior to any language learning, and S_f is the "final state," a "steady state" attained fairly early in life and not changing in significant respects from that point on. When the child has attained this steady state, we say that he has learned the language. Attainment of a steady state at some not-too-delayed stage of intellectual development is presumably characteristic of "learning" within the range of cognitive capacity.

Consider now the transition from one state to the next, say, from state S_5 to state S_6.

We may ask various questions about this transition. First, what is the input to the learning theory available to the child at this stage, call it LT_5? To be realistic, it is surely not at all the data available up to stage S_5, considered as a cumulative record. No one remembers which sentences he has heard in the past. Rather, the input to LT_5 consists of two parts: (i) the grammar attained at state S_5; and (ii) new data available at S_5. Thus, LT_5 will operate on the tentative theory constructed so far by the child, the theory that organizes past experience, not on a list of all data so far utilized.[50] We may ask, then, whether we would seriously falsify the account of learning (and if so, in what respects) by assuming that the input to LT_5 is the data so far utilized rather than the grammar that represents the child's theory at this point (along with other new data).

We may also ask a slightly more subtle question. The grammar generates a system of "potential experience," including the actual experience that led to the construction of the grammar (and excluding parts of actual experience that have been ruled out as wrong or irrelevant in the course of learning), but also including far more, in fact, infinitely more. Furthermore, as already noted, no one can recall which sentences he has heard (with insignificant exceptions). The notion of "familiarity" does not apply in any relevant way to sentences of a language. Ideas expressed may be unfamiliar, and so may turns of phrase. But over a vast range sentences are "familiar" to us if they are part of the language generated by our grammar, subject to qualifications relating to length, complexity, absurdity, insight, and so on, which are not to the point in the present context. We may now ask whether we falsify the account of learning by assuming that the input to LT_5 is the language generated by the grammar available at stage S_5 rather than the grammar itself; the two possibilities differ, since different grammars may generate the same language.

Without pursuing such complications any further, let us distinguish two approaches to the question of the input to LT_5: an *extensional* approach, which takes the input to be "experience" (say, sentences with formal and semantic properties), either the finite record of experience so far or the infinite set generated by the grammar available at state S_5; and an *intensional* approach, which assumes the input to LT_5 to be the grammar itself. In either case, a second input is the new data available.

We might ask some further questions. Is LT_5 different

from LT_6? More generally, is LT_i different from LT_j, for i distinct from j? Are the child's learning capacities different at different stages of development? Does he handle evidence differently at these various stages? Are there well-defined stages, marked by different modes of learning, or do "learning strategies" mature more or less continuously, or do they remain constant (with changes only in other systems, such as memory or attention span), or do they decay? Are there "critical periods" for various phases of language learning? Does LT_i depend in part on theories already constructed, or is it fixed in some maturational sequence? These are all serious questions, the kinds of questions that arise in developmental psychology.[51] To my knowledge, there are no answers that are very informative at the level required to pursue the investigation into language learning beyond the earliest stages, which involve very little of the specific structure of language.

If there were answers to such questions as these, we might develop a more realistic theory of language learning. It might reveal that our simplifying assumption, namely, that the mechanism for language learning is extensional and instantaneous, was far off the mark. It would follow, then, that the conclusions suggested with regard to universal grammar would also have to be modified.

Frankly, I doubt that the simplifying assumption, though obviously false, significantly affects the validity of the analysis based on it. If our initial assumption does indeed seriously falsify the situation, if there are substantially different stages with fundamentally different LT_i's, if these are in an important way intensional, and if furthermore the character of LT_i depends significantly on grammars (or other cognitive structures) already attained, then we would expect to find substantial differences in the result of language learning depending on such factors as order of presentation of data, time of presentation, and so on. But we do not find this, at least at the level of precision of currently available analytic tools. Nor does ordinary experience suggest that this is so. Despite considerable variety in learning experience, people can communicate readily (at the level of communication relevant to this discussion), with no indication that they are speaking fundamentally different languages. It seems that the cognitive structure attained—the grammar—does not vary much, if at all significantly, on the basis of the factors that should lead to enormous differences, were the possibilities just sketched in fact realized. This seems true within rather broad limits. Such principles of universal grammar as structure-dependence and others more intricate seem immune to variability in these factors.

There are, it appears, striking uniformities in steady state attained, through wide variation in conditions of learning. These facts suggest that the initial idealization, with its falsifying assumption about instantaneous extensional learning, was nevertheless a legitimate one and provides a proper basis for pursuing a serious inquiry into human cognitive capacity. At some stage in the progress of inquiry it will no doubt have to be qualified, but one may seriously question whether this stage has been reached in the study of linguistic competence and universal grammar.

These are imprecise and qualitative conclusions, based on evidence that is hardly compelling. They surely might be called into question. To me, these conclusions seem nevertheless quite reasonable, given what is now known. To the extent that the simplifying assumption about instantaneous extensional learning must be revised, we must accordingly complicate the "innateness hypothesis" formulated earlier, namely, that the theory of universal grammar is an innate property of the mind. I will drop the matter with these inconclusive remarks. Further substantive proposals are unfortunately rather limited, though not entirely lacking (see note 50).

I have been attempting to locate language, conceptually at least, within a general system of cognitive capacity that is determined by the innate faculties of mind, and to show how one particular line of empirical inquiry might lead towards a better understanding of the innate faculty of language. Whether or not the proposals outlined here, under more precise formulation, stand the test of time and further research, it seems to me that the questions raised point to the more serious issues in the field that is sometimes labeled, misleadingly, "the theory of learning."

The study of language falls naturally within human biology. The language faculty, which somehow evolved in human prehistory, makes possible the amazing feat of language learning, while inevitably setting limits on the kinds of language that can be acquired in the normal way. Interacting with other faculties of mind, it makes possible the coherent and creative use of language in ways that we can sometimes describe, but hardly even begin to understand.

If we undertake the study of humans as organisms in the natural world, the approach I have outlined seems entirely reasonable. Given the role of language in human life and probably human evolution, and given its intimate relations to what I have been calling "common-sense understanding," it would not be very surprising to discover that other systems within cognitive capacity have something of the character of the language faculty and its products. We should anticipate that these other cognitive systems too set limits on human intellectual achievement, by virtue of the very structure that makes it possible to acquire rich and comprehensive systems of belief and knowledge, insight and understanding. I have already discussed this matter briefly in connection with the "science-forming capacity" (whatever it may be).

I would like to stress again that these conjectures should not seem in any way surprising to the natural scientist.

Rather, they conform reasonably well to what is known about how the brain works in other domains, say, the construction of visual space, or more generally, our concept of physical space and the objects in it. Furthermore, as a number of biologists have pointed out, something of the sort is to be expected on simple evolutionary grounds. Citing Lorenz,[52] Gunther Stent points out that Darwinian considerations offer a "biological underpinning" to a kind of Kantian epistemology, but in addition, these considerations concerning the evolutionary origin of the brain explain "not only why our innate concepts match the world but also why these concepts no longer work so well when we attempt to fathom the world in its deepest scientific aspects," thus perhaps posing a "barrier to unlimited scientific progress." [53] The reason, simply, is that there is no reason to suppose that the capacities acquired through evolution fit us to "fathom the world in its deepest scientific aspects." He also warns that "it is important to give due recognition to this fundamental epistemological limitation to the human sciences, if only as a safeguard against the psychological or sociological prescriptions put forward by those who allege that they have already managed to gain a scientifically validated understanding of man." A warning that we might well bear in mind in a period when pseudoscientific pretense serves so well the needs of dominant coercive ideologies.[54]

Notice that these quite natural views on the scope and limits of knowledge set no finite limits on human progress. The integers form an infinite set, but they do not exhaust the real numbers. Similarly, humans may develop their capacities without limit, but never escaping certain objective bounds set by their biological nature. I suspect that there is no cognitive domain to which such observations are not appropriate.

Suppose that the social and material conditions that prevent free intellectual development were relieved, at least for some substantial number of people. Then, science, mathematics, and art would flourish, pressing on towards the limits of cognitive capacity. At these limits, as noted earlier, we find various forms of intellectual play, and significant differentiation among individuals who vary little within the domain of cognitive capacity. As creative minds approach the limits of cognitive capacity, not only will the act of creation be limited to a talented few, but even the appreciation or comprehension of what has been created. If cognitive domains are roughly comparable in complexity and potential scope, such limits might be approached at more or less the same time in various domains, giving rise to a "crisis of modernism," marked by a sharp decline in the general accessibility of the products of creative minds, a blurring of the distinction between art and puzzle, and a sharp increase in "professionalism" in intellectual life, affecting not only those who produce creative work but also its potential audience. Mockery of conventions that are, ultimately, grounded in human cognitive capacity might be expected to become virtually an art form in itself, at this stage of cultural evolution. It may be that something of the sort has been happening in recent history. Even if correct, such speculations would not lead us to deny that there is surely a vast creative potential as yet unexplored, or to overlook the fact that for most of the human race, material deprivation and oppressive social structures make these questions academic, if not obscene. As Marx wrote in his early manuscripts, echoing Humboldt, animals "produce only under the compulsion of direct physical needs, while man produces when he is free from physical needs and only truly produces in freedom from such need." By this criterion, human history has barely begun for the majority of mankind.

If the approach to the study of cognitive capacity outlined earlier is a proper one, then we can hope to develop a theory of human nature in its psychological aspects. The possibility of such a theory has often been denied. This denial is implicit in the scholastic doctrine that the mind contains nothing beyond what the senses convey. One might read a similar conclusion into the various efforts in the modern period to relate human reason and the scope of human intelligence to the weakness of instinct, an idea that can be traced at least to Herder. (Cf. Chomsky, 1966, pp. 13ff.) Empiricist and later behaviorist psychology are firmly grounded in the doctrine that there is no nontrivial theory of human nature. Or more accurately, that such a theory is limited to the physical organs of the body, with the sole exception of those parts of the brain involved in higher mental functions. I will return directly to some of the ramifications of this doctrine.

I think it is fair to say that these empiricist views are most plausible where we are most ignorant. The more we learn about some aspect of human cognition, the less reasonable these views seem to be. No one would seriously argue today, for example, that our construction of perceptual space is guided by empiricist maxims. The same, I think, is true of the language faculty, which relates more closely to the essential nature of the human species. I suspect that the empiricist position with regard to higher mental functions will crumble as science advances towards an understanding of cognitive capacity and its relations to physical structures.[55]

The claims of empiricism have often been put forth, not as speculation, but as established fact, as if they must be true or have been demonstrated. Such claims must be evaluated on their merits, but if they are found to be without support, plain wrong, or seriously exaggerated, as I believe invariably proves to be the case, then it is appropriate to search elsewhere for an explanation for their appeal and power.

In part, the commitment to empiricist doctrine in the human sciences is a reaction to the speculative character of earlier work, its lack of firm empirical foundation. Surely this has been true of the study of language. There is, however, an obvious gap in reasoning. We can agree that classical rationalist and empiricist doctrines should be recast (or perhaps replaced) so as to be more directly susceptible to empirical test, and that empirical evidence should be brought to bear, as far as possible, in determining their validity. Those who fashioned the traditional doctrines would not have quarreled with this principle. Descartes and Hume and Kant were grappling with problems at the borders of scientific knowledge, problems that are both conceptual and empirical, and sought such evidence as they could muster to justify their theoretical speculations. (Cf. chapter 4, pp. 224–7.) But from a justifiable concern for empirical confirmation, we cannot argue to a commitment to empiricist doctrine. Rather, empiricist and rationalist theories alike must be cast in a form in which they are subject to confirmation, and this task seems no more difficult in one case than in the other. I have tried to suggest how these theories can be so reformulated, without doing violence to certain basic leading ideas (though others must be discarded), and have argued further that where we have any glimmerings of understanding, we are led to theories with a distinctively rationalist character.

But the conflict between rationalist and empiricist doctrines, and the grip of the latter on the modern temper, cannot be explained solely on the "intrinsic" grounds just mentioned. As Harry Bracken (1973a) has emphasized:

> The empiricist/rationalist debates of the seventeenth century *and* of today are debates between different value systems or ideologies. Hence the heat which characterizes these discussions.

The issues have changed from the seventeenth century to today, though there may well be some common threads. Complicating the matter further, the issues and conflicts can be perceived along many dimensions and in quite different ways. But the social and ideological context has always been critical, a fact often noted. Locke's epistemology, as John Yolton shows, was developed primarily for application to religious and moral debates of the period; "the vital issue between Locke and his critics [on the doctrine of innateness] was the grounds and foundations of morality and religion" (Yolton, 1956, p. 68). Throughout the modern period, not to speak of earlier eras, such questions lie in the background of seemingly arcane philosophical controversies and often help explain their issue.

Classical British empiricism arose in often healthy opposition to religious obscurantism and reactionary ideology. Its appeal, perhaps, resides in part in the belief that it offers a vision of limitless progress in contrast to the pessimistic doctrine that humans are enslaved by an unchangeable nature that condemns them to intellectual servitude, material deficit, and eternally fixed oppressive institutions. Thus, it might be understood as a doctrine of progress and enlightenment.

This may also be the reason for the appeal of empiricist ideology in Marxist thought, a commitment that has often been expressed in the most extreme forms. Gramsci went so far as to argue that "the fundamental innovation introduced by Marxism into the science of politics and history is the proof that there does not exist an abstract, fixed and immutable 'human nature' . . . but that human nature is the totality of historically determined social relations" (Gramsci, 1957, p. 140)—a statement that is surely false, in that there is no such proof, and a questionable reading of Marx. In his introduction to Jean Itard's study of the Wild Boy of Aveyron, Lucien Malson asserts categorically that "the idea that man has no nature is now beyond dispute"; the thesis that man "has or rather is a history," nothing more, "is now the explicit assumption of all the main currents of contemporary thought," not only Marxism, but also existentialism, behaviorism, and psychoanalysis. Malson too believes that it has been "proven" that the term "human nature" is "completely devoid of sense." His own critique of "psychological heredity" aims to "destroy . . . the notion of human nature" by demonstrating that there are no "mental predispositions [present in the embryo] which are common to the species or to man in general." To be sure, there are inherited biological characteristics, but not in the area in which man "displays his peculiarly human qualities." "The natural in man is due to inborn heredity, the cultural to his acquired heritage," with no contribution from "psychological heredity" (Malson, 1972, pp. 9–12, 35).

Such claims are not untypical of left-wing opinion, a fact that demands explanation, since plainly there is no compelling empirical argument to buttress them. The explanation, I think, is the one just given: it has been assumed that empiricist doctrine is fundamentally "progressive," as in certain respects it was in an earlier period.

There are quite independent issues that must be clearly distinguished in considering a doctrine put forth as a theory of human nature, or of the lack of any such distinctive nature. Is it correct, or at least plausible? What were its social and political implications at certain historical periods in fact? How were these implications perceived? To what extent (if at all) did these implications, as perceived, contribute to the reception of the doctrine? What (if anything) does this tell us about the commitments of those who defend it? All these questions arise in the case of the advocacy by the revolutionary left of empiricist principles, in particular the doctrine that human nature is nothing but a historical product and thus imposes no limits and suggests no preferred directions for social change.

I have been discussing, so far, only the question of truth and plausibility; there is, I believe, little of either. As a problem of intellectual and social history, the matter is complex. Empiricism has indeed served as a doctrine of progress and enlightenment. It is closely associated with classical liberal thought, which has been unable to survive the age of industrial capitalism.[56] What remains of value in classical liberal doctrine is, in my opinion, to be found today in its most meaningful form in libertarian socialist concepts of human rights and social organization. Empiricism rose to ascendancy in association with a doctrine of "possesive individualism" that was integral to early capitalism,[57] in an age of empire, with the concomitant growth (one might almost say "creation") of racist ideology. Bracken has argued that

> racism is easily and readily stateable if one thinks of the person in accordance with empiricist teaching because the essence of the person may be deemed to be his colour, language, religion, etc., while the Cartesian dualist model provided . . . a modest conceptual brake to the articulation of racial degradation and slavery. [1973b] . . . Empiricism provides a model of the person in which colour, sex, language, religion, etc. can be counted as essential without the logical embarrassments such suggestions as coloured minds create within Cartesianism. [1974, p. 158]

He has argued that "the relation between empiricism and racism is historical," not in that there is a logical connection, but in that empiricism facilitated the expression of the racist ideology that came naturally enough to philosophers who were involved in their professional lives in the creation of the colonial system (Bracken, 1973b). He has also developed the theme that

> the anti-abstractionism and anti-empiricism of Cartesianism are connected with concern for human freedom. More generally, the rationalist model of man is taken to support an active and creative mind which is neither impressed from "outside" to "inside" nor considered to be malleable. . . . Cartesian thought constitutes a vigorous effort to assert the dignity of the

person. . . . [In contrast] the empiricist blank tablet
account of learning is a manipulative model. . . .
[1974, pp. 16, 156; 1973b]

I think that this is an accurate perception, on both conceptual and historical grounds. As for the latter, I have
commented elsewhere on the roots in Cartesian thought of
Rousseau's opposition to tyranny, oppression, and established authority; and at a greater remove, Kant's defense
of freedom, Humboldt's precapitalist liberalism with its
emphasis on the basic human need for free creation under
conditions of voluntary association, and Marx's critique of
alienated fragmented labor that turns men into machines,
depriving them of their "species character" of "free conscious activity" and "productive life," in association with
their fellows (Chomsky, 1973b, chaps. 8, 9).

A similar line of argument has been developed by Ellen
Wood. She suggests that Kant's attack on certain aspects of
empiricist doctrine "is not simply an epistemological quib-
ble, but a far-reaching argument about the nature of human
freedom," and that Marx's work can be understood in part
as an attempt "to give concrete expression to Kant's notion
of freedom as self-activity." "The controversy over the nature of mind," she correctly observes, "has a great deal to
do with the question of man's place in the natural order."
The question whether "the human mind [is] to be regarded
simply as a responsive cog in the mechanism of nature," as
in empiricist doctrine, or as "a creative, determinative
force" is a crucial one, which arises in many forms in the
context of the debate over various models of mind (Wood,
1972, pp. 29, 28, 174).

Kant described "man's inclination and duty to *think
freely*" as "the germ on which nature has lavished most
care." [58] A concern for this "species character" lies at the
core of Cartesian thought and animates an intellectual tradition (not the only one) that derives in part from it, not
limiting itself, however, to the inclination and duty to think

freely, but also affirming the need to produce freely and creatively, to realize one's full potentialities, to revolt against oppression, and to take control of the institutions of economic, political, and social life.

The doctrine that the human mind is initially unstructured and plastic and that human nature is entirely a social product has often been associated with progressive and even revolutionary social thinking, while speculations with regard to human instinct have often had a conservative and pessimistic cast. One can easily see why reformers and revolutionaries should become radical environmentalists, and there is no doubt that concepts of immutable human nature can be and have been employed to erect barriers against social change and to defend established privilege.

But a deeper look will show that the concept of the "empty organism," plastic and unstructured, apart from being false, also serves naturally as the support for the most reactionary social doctrines. If people are, in fact, malleable and plastic beings with no essential psychological nature, then why should they not be controlled and coerced by those who claim authority, special knowledge, and a unique insight into what is best for those less enlightened? Empiricist doctrine can easily be molded into an ideology for the vanguard party that claims authority to lead the masses to a society that will be governed by the "red bureaucracy" of which Bakunin warned. And just as easily for the liberal technocrats or corporate managers who monopolize "vital decision-making" in the institutions of state capitalist democracy, beating the people with the people's stick, in Bakunin's trenchant phrase.

The principle that human nature, in its psychological aspects, is nothing more than a product of history and given social relations removes all barriers to coercion and manipulation by the powerful. This too, I think, may be a reason for its appeal to intellectual ideologists, of whatever political persuasion. I have discussed elsewhere [59] the striking similarity in the doctrines evolved by authoritarian socialists and ideologists of state capitalism, those who constitute "a secular priesthood claiming absolute authority, both spiritual and lay, in the name of unique scientific knowledge of the nature of men and things" (Berlin, 1972), the "new class" of technical intelligentsia, who hope to bring about "the reign of *scientific intelligence,* the most aristocratic, despotic, arrogant and elitist of all regimes." [60] The "empty organism" doctrine is a most natural one for them to adopt.

Creativity is predicated on a system of rules and forms, in part determined by intrinsic human capacities. Without such constraints, we have arbitrary and random behavior, not creative acts. The constructions of common sense and scientific inquiry derive no less from principles grounded in the structure of the human mind. Correspondingly, it would be an error to think of human freedom solely in terms of absence of constraint. Bakunin once remarked that "the laws of our own nature . . . constitute the very basis of our being" and provide "the real condition and the effective cause of our liberty." A libertarian social theory will try to determine these laws and to found upon them a concept of social change and its immediate and distant goals. If, indeed, human nature is governed by Bakunin's "instinct for revolt" or the "species character" on which Marx based his critique of alienated labor, then there must be continual struggle against authoritarian social forms that impose restrictions beyond those set by "the laws of our own nature," as has long been advocated by authentic revolutionary thinkers and activists.

It is reasonable to suppose that just as intrinsic structures of mind underlie the development of cognitive structures, so a "species character" provides the framework for the growth of moral consciousness, cultural achievement, and even participation in a free and just community. It is, to be sure, a great intellectual leap from observations on the basis for cognitive development to particular conclusions on the laws of our nature and the conditions for their fulfillmênt; say, to the conclusion that human needs and capacities will find their fullest expression in a society of free and creative producers, working in a system of free association in which "social bonds" will replace "all fetters in human society." [61] There is an important intellectual tradition that stakes out some interesting claims in this regard. While this tradition draws from the empiricist commitment to progress and enlightenment, I think it finds still deeper roots in rationalist efforts to establish a theory of human freedom. To investigate, deepen, and if possible substantiate the ideas developed in this tradition by the methods of science is a fundamental task for libertarian social theory. Whether further investigation will reveal problems that can be addressed or mysteries that will confound us, only the future can tell.

If this endeavor succeeds, it will refute Bertrand Russell's pessimistic speculation that man's "passions and instincts" render him incapable of enjoying the benefits of the "scientific civilization" that reason can create (Russell, 1924), at least if we understand "passions and instincts" (as Russell sometimes did) to include the "instincts" that provide the basis for the achievements of the creative intellect, as well as the "instinct of revolt" against imposed authority—in some measure, a common human attribute. Rather, success in this endeavor might reveal that these passions and instincts may yet succeed in bringing to a close what Marx called the "prehistory of human society." No longer repressed and distorted by competitive and authoritarian social structures, these passions and instincts may set the stage for a new scientific civilization in which "animal nature" is transcended and human nature can truly flourish.

PART II

CHAPTER 4

Problems and Mysteries in the Study of Human Language

I would like to distinguish roughly between two kinds of issues that arise in the study of language and mind: those that appear to be within the reach of approaches and concepts that are moderately well understood—what I will call "problems"; and others that remain as obscure to us today as when they were originally formulated—what I will call "mysteries." The distinction reflects in part a subjective evaluation of what has been achieved or might be achieved in terms of ideas now available. Others see mysteries, incoherence, and confusion where to me the issues seem rather clear and straightforward, and conversely.

Among the problems are these: What kinds of cognitive structures are developed by humans on the basis of their experience, specifically, in the case of acquisition of language? What is the basis for the acquisition of such structures and how do they develop? Without prejudicing the outcome of this investigation, we may say that humans are innately endowed with a system of intellectual organization, call it the "initial state" of the mind. Through interaction with the environment and maturational processes, the mind passes through a sequence of states in which cognitive structures are represented. In the case of language, it is fairly obvious that rapid and extensive changes take place during an early period of life, and a "steady state" is achieved which then undergoes only minor modification. Abstracting away from the latter, we can refer to this steady state as the "final state" of the mind, in which knowledge of language is somehow represented. We can construct hypotheses concerning the initial and final states, and can proceed to validate, or reject, or sharpen these hypotheses by methods of inquiry that are familiar. We might proceed, in principle, to explore the physical realizations of the initial and final states and the processes involved in the changes of state that take place.

In these domains, much is unknown. In this sense there are many mysteries here. But we have a certain grasp of the problem, and can make progress by posing and sometimes answering questions that arise along the way, with at least some degree of confidence that we know what we are doing.

On the other hand, when we turn to such matters as causation of behavior, it seems to me that no progress has been made, that we are as much in the dark as to how to proceed as in the past, and that some fundamental insights are lacking.

Roughly, where we deal with cognitive structures, either in a mature state of knowledge and belief or in the initial state, we face problems, but not mysteries. When we ask how humans make use of these cognitive structures, how and why they make choices and behave as they do, although there is much that we can say as human beings with intuition and insight, there is little, I believe, that we can say as scientists. What I have called elsewhere "the creative aspect of language use" remains as much a mystery to us as it was to the Cartesians who discussed it, in part, in the context of the problem of "other minds." Some would reject this evaluation of the state of our understanding. I do not propose to argue the point here, but rather to turn to the problems that do seem to me amenable to inquiry.

Imagine a scientist, henceforth S, who is unencumbered by the ideological baggage that forms part of our intellectual tradition and is thus prepared to study humans as organisms in the natural world. Let us consider a course of inquiry that S might undertake, sketching conclusions that he might tentatively reach along the way, and then confront S with some of the questions of methodology and principle that have been raised by a number of philosophers who have discussed the nature and goals of linguistic theory.

S might begin with the observation that people seem to act in systematic ways with respect to the objects around them and that they use and respond to expressions in organized ways. He might also conclude that humans, rather early in their lives, seem to arrive at steady states of development in these respects, states which are then modified only in detail and which provide a basis for human actions and responses. Investigation of these matters requires idealization and abstraction, but S should not be put off by this familiar contingency of rational inquiry. S might now proceed to characterize these steady states, attributing to the organism two cognitive structures: (i) a system of beliefs and expectations about the nature and behavior of objects, and (ii) a system of language. Suppose that he calls the first system "common sense" and the second "grammar." S might then proceed to try to account for what people do, perhaps in experimentally contrived situations, on the basis of these two postulated structures and further assumptions about information-processing capacities.

S might study, for example, the ability of his subjects to recognize and identify complex physical objects and predict their behavior under various circumstances. He might find that there are qualitative differences in their ability to recognize human faces and other objects of comparable complexity. This investigation might lead S to attribute to his subjects, as an element of their common sense, an abstract theory of possible faces and a system of projection which (abstracting away from the effects of memory restrictions and the like) enables the subject to predict how a face will appear under a range of empirical conditions, given a few presentations.

S might also discover that his subjects react quite differently to the expressions (1)–(4):

(1) John's friends appeared to their wives to hate one another
(2) John's friends appeared to Mary to hate one another
(3) John's friends appealed to their wives to hate one another
(4) John's friends appealed to Mary to hate one another

Asked to verify (1) and (2), the subjects might inquire whether the wives (respectively, Mary) think that each friend hates the other friends. Asked to verify (3), they might seek to determine whether each friend directed his wife to hate the other wives. The subjects would assign (4) an entirely different status, though if pressed, they could impose an interpretation—presumably, that each friend appealed to Mary to hate the other friends. In the case of (1)–(3) the problem of "imposing an interpretation" in this sense does not arise. S might contrive various experimental techniques to sharpen and clarify these results, and with luck and diligence he might arrive at a plausible theory: namely, the grammar attained by his subjects as part of their final state incorporates a system of rules that characterize (1)–(3) but not (4) as well formed, that assigns "John's friends" as the subject of "hate" in (1) and (2) but not (3) (rather "their wives" is the subject of "hate" in this case), that assigns a 1–1 correspondence to John's friends and the wives in (3), and so on.

S's conclusions about these matters would be stated in a theoretical language that he would devise, including such notions as "well formed," "subject," and others, and again it would be necessary to construct various idealizations. He would discover that when expressions become too complex in specific ways (for example, with too much "self-embedding," an abstract property of structures that S might discover if he proceeded properly), subjects respond in ways that are not predictable in terms of grammar alone, though given time and computation space under contrived experimental conditions their responses converge on those predicted in terms of the grammar. On the basis of such discoveries, S would be led to distinguish between the grammar and a system of information processing perhaps not specific to language, and to account for actual behavior in terms of the interaction of these systems.

Similarly, S might discover that grammar interacts with other systems of knowledge and belief to determine how sentences are interpreted. Thus he might conclude that the 1–1 correspondence assigned to John's friends and the wives in (3) is in part a matter of grammar and in part the result of factual knowledge. Suppose "their wives" is replaced by "their children" in (3). Then interpretations multiply; one is that each friend appealed to his children to hate one another (but not to hate the children of other friends). There is still a 1–1 correlation between John's friends and a set of sets of children, but not between the friends and the union of these sets. The 1–1 correlation between friends and wives derives in part from factual assumptions about monogamy, which also eliminate interpretations of "one another" of the sort that are possible (indeed, I believe, favored) when "their wives" is replaced by "their children."

Proceeding in this way, S might develop a general theory of cognitive structures in which grammar appears as a specific component. While S would remain properly cautious about such conclusions, he would not, if rational, shy away from them on grounds of their complexity and abstractness.

Examples such as (1)–(4) would reveal to S that such notions as "analogy" and "generalization" do not carry him very far in understanding human cognitive capacities, at least in the domain of language. Thus, although (1) and (3) are very similar—they differ only in one phonological feature, hence minimally—nevertheless, speakers of the language understand them in very different ways, ignoring the obvious analogies. Similarly, (4) can be interpreted "on the analogy" of (1), (2), or (3), and subjects, if pressed, might well impose such an interpretation. Nevertheless the status of (4) is entirely different from that of its "analogues," and the obvious generalizations are not employed by S's subjects to incorporate (4) within their grammatical system. These are typical examples that would lead S to reject the idea that an account of language can be based on notions of analogy and generalization as these have often been employed in the intellectual tradition of his subjects. Noting further the persistence of the contrary belief in the face of disconfirming evidence [1] that is quite easy to come by, S might try to discover ideological or social factors that lead his subjects to reject theories that seem to offer some hope of success, while clinging to beliefs that appear to be inconsistent with even the most elementary observations.

Putting the sociological investigation to the side, S might continue to investigate the hypothesis that the final state of his subjects incorporates a generative grammar embedded among and interacting with other cognitive structures. He might take the grammar to be a system of rules and principles that assigns to each of an infinite set of expressions a semantic, phonetic, and syntactic representation, each of these being a representation in some universal system. There are, of course, alternative hypotheses to be considered; in other words, S is engaged in empirical science. Given the suggested approach, various qualifications are possible, and many questions arise about the nature of these rules and representations. These are the questions that S would pursue in attempting to refine and elaborate his theory of the final state.

Thus S's analyses would proceed at two levels of abstraction. He would be concerned with relations between particular stimuli and particular percepts—the relation, for example, between (1) and an abstract characterization of it that serves as a basis for S's explanation of how his subjects deal with it. S's analysis would proceed to a still higher level of abstraction, at which he would consider the general system of rules (grammar) that determines these particular relationships. This grammar is an explanatory theory, going far beyond the evidence at hand, and easily falsifiable by new investigations. S might conclude that his subjects attribute "knowledge of a language" to their fellows when he, S, is attributing a corresponding grammar to these subjects as part of their final state (again, under appropriate idealizations).

Pursuing his efforts to map out the cognitive structures of his subjects, S might conclude that each of them possesses an unconscious theory of humans in accordance with which they attribute knowledge of language to other humans. S might also proceed to investigate the physical representation of grammars, theories of humans, common sense, information-processing systems, other systems of factual knowledge and belief, and other cognitive structures that appear to be components of the attained steady states. In this way, he would develop a science of human cognitive structures and, perhaps, their physical basis. His inquiry might take various turns and face innumerable problems, but again, there seems no reason to expect that in this domain he would run up against impenetrable mysteries.

Suppose that among the people that S is investigating

some happen to be physicists. Observing their behavior in prediction, inquiry, exposition, and so forth, S might attribute to these individuals still another cognitive structure, call it "knowledge of physics." S would now be postulating, *inter alia*, three cognitive systems, each somehow represented in the human mind: grammar, common sense, and knowledge of physics. He might notice that there are striking differences between these systems. Knowledge of physics is conscious knowledge; the physicist can expound and articulate it and convey it to others. In contrast, the other two systems are quite unconscious for the most part and beyond the bounds of introspective report. Furthermore, knowledge of physics is qualitatively distinct from the other two cognitive structures in the manner of its acquisition and development. Grammar and common sense are acquired by virtually everyone, effortlessly, rapidly, in a uniform manner, merely by living in a community under minimal conditions of interaction, exposure, and care. There need be no explicit teaching or training, and when the latter does take place, it has only marginal effects on the final state achieved. To a very good first approximation, individuals are indistinguishable (apart from gross deficits and abnormalities) in their ability to acquire grammar and common sense. Individuals of a given community each acquire a cognitive structure that is rich and comprehensive and essentially the same as the systems acquired by others. Knowledge of physics, on the other hand, is acquired selectively and often painfully, through generations of labor and careful experiment, with the intervention of individual genius and generally through careful instruction. It is not quickly and uniformly attained as a steady state, but is transmitted and modified continually on the basis of controlled inquiry and an explicit record that provides the basis for the next stage of construction.

Having discovered this much, S should realize that humans are somehow specifically adapted to acquire grammar and common sense, as they are adapted to walk and not to fly. Proceeding to a still higher level of abstraction in his inquiries, S would attempt to characterize this specific adaptation. Thus returning to the postulated theory of faces, he might ask how this theory, with a characterization of possible faces and a system of projection, arises in the organism. Why is it, specifically, that there is no comparable theory, as part of common sense, for certain other objects of comparable complexity? What assumptions about the initial state of the organism and its biologically determined maturational processes might account for the construction of this aspect of common sense within empirically given conditions of time and access to data? Investigation of this problem might lead S to the hypothesis that basic elements of the theory of human faces are represented in the initial state, as a biologically determined innate property. Knowing something about the evolution of organisms, S would not regard this as a strange or unexpected conclusion. Notice, incidentally, that biologically determined systems might begin to function only at a particular level of maturation, or after appropriate triggering experience. Thus the theory of faces (like language) might be innate, though fully functional only at a particular stage of development.

To test these hypotheses and other related ones, S might try to vary conditions of exposure and to study the variety of systems of common sense that result. To the extent that there is concomitant and systematic variation, S would adjust his postulates concerning innate structure. In this way, he would develop a theory of learning of common sense in the only rational way, namely, by characterizing as closely as possible the states achieved by the organism—steady states, in the case of common sense—and then specifying a function that assigns the attained steady state as a value given a characterization of the data available. The resulting theory of learning of common sense might involve complex assumptions as to the interaction of maturation and experience, with regular succession of states of determinate kinds (in the sense, say, of Piagetian theory). Whatever the complexity of the problem, it seems to pose no special mysteries, and we can see how it would be investigated.

There are various approaches that S might explore in attempting to construct a theory of learning of common sense. To mention two, he might postulate a schematism, innate to the mind, that is refined and further articulated by experience. Thus he might conclude that the visual system contains analyzing mechanisms that interpret sensory presentations in terms of line, angle, and motion, and that these mechanisms are simply put into operation on exposure to appropriate experience, so that, as Descartes and Cudworth proposed, we see a presented figure as a (perhaps distorted) regular geometrical figure because of the mind's initial adaptation to produce such figures as "exemplars" for the interpretation of experience. Similar ideas might be developed to explain recognition of faces, and much else.

Alternatively, S might suppose that the mind is a blank tablet, equipped only with the ability to record impressions and retain faded impressions, to construct associations among presented impressions, to match impressions (perhaps along certain innately given dimensions), to generalize along dimensions that are innate or constructed, to modify the probability of response in terms of contingencies of reinforcement defined in terms of the stimulus space, and so on. Let us call these two quite different approaches R and E, respectively. I mean to suggest, by this terminology, that they reflect leading ideas of rationalism and empiricism. I have discussed the historical question elsewhere, and will return to it below; for the moment, I will only restate my belief that these formulations, as presented,[2] were quite appropriate, and that they offer an illuminating framework for the investigation of problems of learning. As just noted, S is not bound to a strict version of R or E, but might develop a more complex approach, with successive stages based on the interplay of maturation and experience, and so on.

In the case of grammar, similar remarks apply. S would discover that there is considerable variety in attained grammars, but that individuals are not specifically adapted to acquiring one or another of these systems. Rather they will, with essentially equal facility, acquire knowledge of the language of the community in which they live, given minimal conditions of exposure and care.[3] Investigating this problem, S might make another quite appropriate idealization to a hypothetical uniform and homogeneous speech community, now abstracting away from the observed variety within given societies. He would try to discover the property of the mind P that enables a child endowed with P to acquire the grammar of the language spoken under this idealization. As in the case of any empirical hypothesis, the legitimacy of the idealization might be challenged, but in this case S would do well to proceed with the idealization, attempting to explain the complex real-life situation in terms of P and other human capacities. S would not thereby be ignoring the intriguing problems of variation of dialect and individual style, as sometimes alleged. Rather, he would be approaching these questions in terms of a specific theory, devised for the idealization. If indeed there is such a property P, and if, as seems likely, it is a fundamental factor in acquisition of language in the complex situations of real life, then S would now be in a position to undertake a serious investigation of the more complex problems with some hope of success.

Having gotten this far, S would now proceed to investigate the property P. Again, he might proceed in the manner of R, formulating a general schematism (call it "universal grammar") and an evaluation procedure which, he would postulate, jointly constitute P, or an essential element in it. Endowed with these systems in its initial state,[4] the child develops a grammar by employing the evaluation procedure to select among grammars that conform to universal grammar. If the latter is sufficiently restrictive, a small amount of evidence might lead quickly to the selection of a grammar that is very rich and complex and that goes well beyond this evidence; in particular, a grammar that provides representations for sentences that are not related by any useful notion of "analogy" or "generalization"[5] to the evidence available. Another approach, along the lines of E, would be to formulate certain analytic procedures, again attributed to the organism as an innate property, which can be applied to the data of sense to produce a grammar. If we interpret the methods of structural linguistics based on segmentation and classification as a "learning theory" (contrary to the intentions of those who developed these methods, so far as I know), then it would be reasonable to regard these as an instance of E, perhaps the most complex version that has yet been developed.

Adopting an approach of the character of R or E, or some combination of the two, S would now be trying to develop a theory of language learning, again in the only rational way. Namely, he would first characterize as closely as he could the states achieved, and then, having made certain assumptions about what is learned, he would attempt to specify a function that assigns appropriate constituents of the achieved final state as a value given the characterization of the data available to the learner. This function would constitute his theory of language learning.

To make the discussion a bit more concrete, consider again examples (1)–(4). Let us suppose that S has moved from the study of the relation between particular stimuli and particular percepts to a study of the grammar that

determines an infinite class of such relations by assigning
a structural description to each expression, in particular, a
representation in terms of phonetic, semantic, and syntactic properties. In the case of (1)–(4), let us say that the
grammar he postulates is a familiar transformational grammar of the sort described in chapter 3, which derives the
surface structures of (1)–(4) from the initial phrase markers
("deep structures") (1′)–(4′) respectively (omitting details):

(1′) $[_s [_{NP} X] [_{VP}$ appeared [to their wives]
       $[_s [_{NP}$ John's friends] $[_{VP}$ to hate one another]]]]

(2′) Same as (1′), with "Mary" in place of "their wives"

(3′) $[_s [_{NP}$ John's friends] $[_{VP}$ appealed [to their wives]
       $[_s [_{NP}X] [_{VP}$ to hate one another]]]]

(4′) Same as (3′), with "Mary" in place of "their wives"

We may take X to be an initial phrase marker variable
(an abstract *proform*) which is either replaced in a derivation or placed by an interpretive rule within the scope of
a controlling NP. (1) (respectively, (2)) is derived from (1′)
(respectively, (2′)) by the rule of NP-preposing which replaces the matrix subject X by the embedded NP "John's
friends." We might think of this operation as leaving a
"trace," t, interpreted (by convention) as controlled by the
NP that has been moved from this position. In the case
of (3), an interpretive rule assigns X to the control of the
NP "their wives." The mode of application of this rule is
a property of the verb "appeal"; compare (5), where "they"
refers to the wives, and (6), where it refers to John's friends:

(5) John's friends made an appeal to their wives that they
    (should) hate one another

(6) John's friends made a promise to their wives that they
    would hate one another

Suppose we now assume that "thematic relations" such
as agent, instrument, and so on are assigned in a general
way in terms of relations expressed in initial phrase mark-

ers and lexical properties, and that other aspects of semantic representation (scope, anaphora, etc.) are determined by surface structure.[6] Suppose we also have a *reciprocal rule* that gives the meaning of structures of the form . . . *NP* . . . *one another* . . . , when the two phrases in question are "anaphorically related." This rule is not without its complications. Thus, compare "John's parents hate one another," "John's grandparents hate one another."[7] In the case of (3) and (4) the anaphoric relation cannot hold between "John's friends" and "one another," though it can hold between "their wives" and "one another," and between "Mary" and "one another." (In the latter case, the reciprocal rule gives gibberish, accounting for the status of (4).) The condition that determines how this anaphoric relation may apply is of considerable generality. One might propose various formulations. I will call it the "specified-subject condition" (henceforth SSC) and formulate it as follows:

(7) In a structure of the form [. . . X . . . [Z – WYV] . . .], no rule can relate X and Y if Z is the subject of WYV and is not controlled by X.

For discussion of the condition and related matters, see Chomsky (1971, 1973a); also chapter 3, pages 101–3. This condition prevents an anaphoric relation from holding in the unwanted cases discussed above. It also applies in many other cases. Consider the following:

(8) Mary appeared to John's friends to hate one another

(9) (a) John's friends appeared to me to hate us
     (b) John's friends appealed to me to kill us
     (c) I appeared to John's friends to hate us
     (d) I appealed to John's friends to kill us

(10) (a) John's friends saw pictures of one another (themselves)
     (b) John's friends saw Mary's pictures of one another (themselves)

(11) (a) who did you see pictures of?

    (b) who did you see Mary's pictures of?

(12) (a) I didn't see pictures of many of the children

    (b) I didn't see John's pictures of many of the children

(13) (a) Latin is a waste of time for us—to study

    (b) Latin is a waste of time for us—for them to teach us

    (c) it is a waste of time for us—to study Latin

    (d) it is a waste of time for us—for them to teach us Latin

(8) has no interpretation. "John's friends" cannot be related anaphorically to "one another" because of SSC, since the trace left by NP-preposing is controlled by "Mary"; and the reciprocal rule cannot assign an interpretation to the pair *Mary, one another*. (9a) and (9d) are fully grammatical, but (9b) and (9c) have the same oddity as do "I hate us" and "I'll kill us." A rule called by Postal the "unlike-person constraint" (UP) requires that a pair (NP, pronoun) have disjoint reference.[8] UP does not apply in cases (9a) and (9d), being blocked by SSC. If we replace "us" by "them" in (9a–d), grammaticality is reversed throughout for the same reasons, if "them" is interpreted as anaphoric. In the case of (10b), but not (10a), SSC blocks the reciprocal and reflexive rule (under an appropriate definition of "subject," discussed in Chomsky [1972b, 1973a]); thus (10a) is grammatical, but not (10b). The same is true of (11a,b). (12a) may be interpreted as meaning that I saw pictures of few (=not many) of the children, but (12b) cannot be interpreted analogously as meaning that I saw John's pictures of few (not many) of the children The reason is that SSC blocks the rule assigning the meaning *few* to *not . . . many*. Thus, if (12b) is interpretable at all, it can only be understood as meaning that John's pictures of many of the children are such that I didn't see them. (13a) is a paraphrase of (13c), but (13b) is not well formed, and in particular, is not a paraphrase of the well-

formed (13d). Again SSC explains the difference, if we take the abstract phrase structure to be as indicated by "—" in (13), a conclusion for which there is independent evidence. Thus once again, analogies are blocked by the general condition SSC.

It is worth emphasizing that each of these examples adds further support to the conclusion that approaches of the character of E, which assigns a fundamental role to segmentation, classification, analogy, and generalization, are mistaken in principle. Furthermore, in these examples at least, "semantic explanations" seem beside the point. Thus there is no semantic consideration that blocks the interpretation (13d) for (13b), or that prevents (8) from having the perfectly sensible interpretation "it appears to each of John's friends that Mary hates the other(s)," just as (2) has the interpretation "it appeared to Mary that each of John's friends hates the other(s)." In such cases, we might trivialize the notion "analogy" by building into it some condition equivalent to SSC, but this is clearly beside the point. (Cf. note 5.) Notice that SSC itself might well have a functional or semantic explanation, but this is a different matter. (Cf. Chomsky [1973a] for some discussion.)

Such examples might lead our scientist S to postulate a grammar containing such rules as NP-preposing, reciprocal interpretation, UP, a rule giving the meaning of *not . . . many*, and so on. The rules would be governed by such principles as SSC, and by the general principles of interpretation of initial phrase markers and surface structure mentioned earlier (cf. note 6, and chapter 3, pp. 94–117). If S is inclined to believe that the theory of language learning is of the character of E, he will attempt to design procedures of association, habit formation, induction, or analysis by segmentation and classification that will give this grammar as "output" on the basis of a record of data. A system of procedures will be tested for adequacy in terms of its success in this task. As just noted, an analysis of properties of the grammar suggests that no such approach is feasible and that a theory of the character of R is much more likely to be successful.

Following this line of thinking, S might ask what elements of the grammar might be candidates for universal grammar, the schematism that constitutes an element of the initial state (the property P). The empirical conditions of his problem are plain enough. The variety of languages provides an upper bound on the richness and specificity of the properties that he may assign to universal grammar. The necessity of accounting for acquisition of particular grammars provides a lower bound. Between these bounds lies the theory of language learning, what we have called "LT(H,L)" in chapter 1.

S might propose, for example, that SSC, some of the principles of interpretation of initial phrase markers and surface structures (cf. note 6), the conditions on permissible grammatical rules, and so on are elements of universal grammar, whereas such rules as NP-preposing are specific to English or have properties specific to English. Thus he might conclude that a child must learn the rule of NP-preposing or some of its properties, but need not learn SSC, or the general properties of grammar. Rather, he would have this information available as an element of P, a property of his initial state (though, as noted earlier, this genetically determined property may, as in other familiar cases, function only at a certain maturational stage or under appropriate triggering conditions). The child will thus select a grammar meeting these conditions and containing the rule of NP-preposing with its particular properties. Evidence for the latter rule is considerable, as noted in chapter 3 and references cited there.

Since there has been much confusion about these matters, perhaps it may be useful to recall a still simpler case that illustrates the general point. Consider again the discussion of the principle of structure-dependence of rules discussed in chapter 1, pp. 30–3. For reasons explained there, S would naturally conclude that some feature of the child's initial state leads him to reject the structure-independent hypothesis 1 to account for question formation, selecting instead the more abstract and complex structure-dependent hypothesis 2, on the basis of evidence compatible with both.[9] S might conclude that universal grammar provides a notation for rules that simply does not permit the formulation of structure-independent rules, despite the advantages that they would have for some different organism or device. This conclusion would constitute one part of S's theory of language learning. The example again supports the more general conclusion that a theory of language learning is of the character of R rather than E.

If we sufficiently enrich the system of universal grammar, postulated as an element of the innate property P, it may be possible to account for acquisition of grammar on the basis of the limited evidence available. At least, this seems a feasible prospect (but see note 4).

Suppose that S succeeds in developing a tentative theory of learning for common sense and for language. If my guess is right, these would be of the character of R; that is, they would involve fixed and highly restrictive schemata which come into operation under limited conditions of exposure to data, determine the interpretation of these data as experience, and lead to the selection of systems of rules (grammar, common sense) which are put to use in human action and interaction. It is not excluded that the schematisms for grammar and for common sense have nontrivial common elements, and S will naturally search for these.[10] There may be "generalized learning strategies" that form part of both of these empirical theories. On the other hand, it seems likely that these schematisms will have unique elements as well, just as common sense may well have special devices to distinguish faces from other geometrical objects. There is no reason to expect to find in the property P significant analogues to the analyzing mechanisms for identification of faces or determination of line, angle, and motion.[11] There is no reason to expect that the principle of structure-dependence or SSC will appear in the theory of common sense. At some sufficiently abstract level, one may find analogies; S might ask whether the system for identifying faces involves an abstract representation or model and a "transformational system" of projection. But as a scientist, S would have no dogmatic beliefs as to the character of the various systems of learning and their interrelation. Rather, this would be an empirical problem that he would hope to solve.

To the extent that S succeeds in characterizing the innate properties of mind that make possible the learning of grammar and common sense, he would be able to explain why these systems are qualitatively so different from the third cognitive structure mentioned earlier, knowledge of physics. That is, he would now regard the properties of mind that underlie the acquisition of language and common sense as biological properties of the organism, on a par in this respect with those that enable a bird to build a nest or reproduce a characteristic song; or, for that matter, comparable to the properties that account for the development of particular organs of the body. (Cf. chapter 1.) Humans are not specially adapted, in the same way, to the learning of physics.

Parenthetically, S might conclude that something similar is true of physics as well. The human mind is a biologically given system with certain powers and limits. As Charles Sanders Peirce argued, "Man's mind has a natural adaptation to imagining correct theories of some kinds. . . . If man had not the gift of a mind adapted to his requirements, he could not have acquired any knowledge" (ed. Tomas, 1957). The fact that "admissible hypotheses" are available to this specific biological system accounts for its ability to construct rich and complex explanatory theories. But the same properties of mind that provide admissible hypotheses may well exclude other successful theories as unintelligible to humans. Some theories might simply not be among the admissible hypotheses determined by the specific properties of mind that adapt us "to imagining correct theories of some kinds," though these theories might be accessible to a differently organized intelligence. Or these theories might be so remote in an accessibility ordering of admissible hypotheses that they cannot be constructed under actual empirical conditions, though for a differently structured mind they might be easily accessible.

If S regards humans as part of the natural world, such speculations will seem by no means strange or incomprehensible to him, and he might in fact attempt to investigate them and establish specific conclusions about these matters through scientific inquiry. In pursuing this effort, he would note that while man's mind is no doubt adapted to his requirements, there is no reason to suppose that discovery of scientific theories in particular domains is among the requirements met through natural selection. S might go on to develop a theory of problems and mysteries for the human organism. There would be problems in domains where admissible (or readily accessible) hypotheses are close to correct, and mysteries elsewhere—for this organism. To take a specific case, consider the question of causation of behavior discussed briefly in chapter 1. It might be that our inability to deal with this question reflects a temporary condition of ignorance, a defect that can be overcome, in principle, as science progresses. But S might discover that this optimistic view is incorrect and that the human mind is inherently incapable of developing scientific understanding of the processes by which it itself functions in certain domains. Kant suggested that the "schematism of our understanding, in its application to appearances and their mere form, is an art concealed in the depths of the human soul, whose real modes of activity nature is hardly likely ever to allow us to discover, and to have open to our gaze" (trans. Kemp,

1958). Perhaps this is true, in some respects at least. There is nothing contradictory in the belief that investigation of the inherent intellectual capacities of a specific biological organism, humans, might lead S—even if S is human himself—to a scientific demonstration that some possible sciences lie beyond human grasp, perhaps the science of causation of behavior among them. I am not urging this conclusion, but merely noting that it is not ruled out *a priori*.

Returning to the more comfortable matter of problems that do not seem to be mysteries, let us suppose that S has now established the basis for the fundamental distinction between grammar and common sense, on the one hand, and knowledge of physics, on the other. Though the latter, too, is derived on the basis of specific properties of mind, it does not reflect these properties in the same way as language and common sense do. Hence the vast qualitative difference in relative accessibility.

S could not, I believe, determine that common sense and grammar are qualitatively different in this respect from physics merely by inspecting the three cognitive structures that he has been led to attribute to humans within his comprehensive theory of their attained intellectual organization. If our present beliefs are near correct, the grammar of language is a highly intricate system of rules and principles. There is no absolute sense of the notion "simplicity" in terms of which grammar is "simpler" than, say, atomic physics, and although common sense has not been investigated in a comparable way, much the same may well be true in this case. The qualitative differences that S would discover in his investigation of humans doubtless reflect the structure of the mind as a contingent biological system. This is the only rational conclusion, I believe.

This Peircean view of acquisition of cognitive structures should not be strange to physiological psychologists, at least. (Cf. chapter 1, pp. 8–9.) It might be suggested that much of learning theory has been investigating an artifact—"unnatural" learning under experimental conditions devised so as to be outside the organism's inherent capacities, conditions which thus provide smooth learning curves and the like, but perhaps tell us very little about the organisms studied.[12]

When a learning theory is formulated with sufficient precision, it becomes possible to ask whether it is capable in principle of accounting for the attainment of a state of intellectual organization or a cognitive structure that we have reason to postulate for the mature organism. Suppose, for example, that a specific learning theory can be demonstrated to have the following property: an otherwise unstructured system that can be modified in accordance with the mechanisms of this theory can approach, in the limit, any finite-state device that produces strings left to right as it shifts from state to state, but nothing other than such a device. Since it is well known that even the syntax of extremely simple systems (e.g., propositional calculus) cannot be represented by such a device and that the syntax of language surely cannot, we can conclude at once that the learning theory is inadequate as a theory of language learning.[13] Thus a theory which predicts convergence towards demonstrably inadequate systems must obviously be rejected as a theory of the actual attainment of systems that are far richer. In this case, then, S could go beyond the conclusion that general learning theories of known sorts are completely implausible.

In fact, the scientist S, if indeed unencumbered by our intellectual tradition, would, I think, be unlikely ever to have considered the notion that there is a "theory of learning" in any interesting sense. Thus, suppose that there is a general theory of learning that applies to rats as well as humans, and that humans differ from rats simply in that they make use of its mechanisms more rapidly, fully, and effectively, and can thus attain more complex states by means of the devices postulated in this theory. We would then conclude that humans must be as far superior to rats in maze-running ability as they are in ability to acquire language. But this is grossly false. Similar observations would lead a rational scientist to conclude at once that the human ability to learn language involves a special faculty or cognitive system of some sort, distinct from the cognitive system that underlies the ability to learn how to run a maze, and unavailable to rats or, as far as we know, any other organism.[14] For if language were simply acquired by a "generalized learning strategy" that applies as well in other domains (say, maze running), we would expect other organisms that are comparable to humans in these other domains (and thus, by assumption, use strategies similar to those employed by humans in these domains) to have comparable language-acquisition ability as well. (Cf. pp. 18, 19.)

The properties of common sense that are involved in the special human ability (if such exists) to deal with faces as compared with other geometrical figures, the properties of universal grammar, the properties that distinguish grammar and common sense from knowledge of physics, would also lead S to reject the hypothesis that there is a general learning theory, common to all organisms, undifferentiated in a single organism with respect to cognitive domain. These observations would lead S to the natural conclusion that the intellectual organization of a mature human is a complex integrated system that includes cognitive structures that are acquired on the basis of rather specific initial adaptations. The nontrivial content of the "theory of learning" would be given by specifying these initial adaptations and the ways in which they change through maturation and experience. The steady states that are attained uniformly and rapidly should give particular insight into the nature of the organism. These steady states might well reflect quite different physiological properties and structures. There is little reason to suppose that there are "laws of learning" of any substance and generality that account for the acquisition of these complex and specific steady states, or for the integration of cognitive structures that constitute the mature mind.

Problems of acquisition of knowledge and belief have generally been investigated in a way that to a natural scientist might seem rather perverse. There has been little attention to the problem of characterizing "what is learned." Rather, certain *a priori* assumptions have been presented as to how learning takes place: principles of association, habit formation, and the like. These *a priori* assumptions have been pursued with speculative and experimental studies of the systems that might be acquired by these methods, with virtually no effort to establish that the systems that can be acquired are those that are acquired. A more natural approach, it seems to me, is the one sketched above: analysis of the states attained, followed by attempts to determine the nature of systems capable of attaining these states under given conditions of time and access to data, and investigation of the physical basis for these achievements, whatever it may be.

Psychologists sometimes go so far as to define their discipline so as to exclude consideration of the states attained. Thus it is common to distinguish "linguistics," taken as the study of grammar, from "psychology," which is concerned with behavior and learning.[15] To a scientist following the course outlined for S, this would seem a senseless distinction. Linguistics is simply that part of psychology that is concerned with one specific class of steady states, the cognitive structures that are employed in speaking and understanding. The study of language learning is concerned with the acquisition of such cognitive structures, and the study of behavior is concerned with the ways in which they are put to use. It is self-defeating to construct a discipline that is concerned with use and attainment of some cognitive structure, but that excludes consideration of the structure itself.

Equally misleading, I think, is the tendency in philosophical discussion to speculate on the ways in which language and its use might be taught. Language is not really taught, for the most part. Rather, it is learned, by mere exposure to the data. No one has been taught the principle of structure-dependence of rules, or SSC, or language-specific properties of such rules as NP-preposing. Nor is there any reason to suppose that people are taught the meaning of words. It may be true that "teaching someone how to use an expression is the native soil from which talk about meaning has grown," [16] but this historical comment gives little reason to suppose that explanations of meaning are exhausted, or even advanced, by an account of teaching. The study of how a system is learned cannot be identified with the study of how it is taught; nor can we assume that what is learned has been taught.

To consider an analogy that is perhaps not too remote, consider what happens when I turn on the ignition in my automobile. A change of state takes place. We might investigate the characteristics of the new state by examining fumes from the exhaust, the vibration level, the motion of the car when I press the accelerator, and so on. A careful study of the interaction between me and the car that led to the attainment of this new state would not be very illuminating. Similarly, certain interactions between me and my child result in his learning (hence knowing) English. We can learn something about this new state in ways outlined earlier.[17] But a careful study of the interactions between me and my child that result in his attaining this new state might give little insight into what it is that he has learned or what kind of an organism he is.

No doubt John Austin (1940) is correct in saying that when we are asked, "What is the meaning of (the word) rat?" we can reply in words or get the questioner to imagine an experience or situation in which the word would or would not be used. But from this observation we cannot go on to conclude, as he does, that this description tells us all that we might reasonably want to know about the meaning of the word. It seems that he is relying on the implicit assumption that when we have described how we might teach, we need no longer ask what is learned. Austin is thus limiting himself to a description of turning on the ignition, whereas the model of language that he is condemning in these remarks is concerned rather to give an account of the state of the system that is activated by these manipulations.

Let us ask finally how S might go about describing the results of his inquiries. Specifically, consider the much-debated question whether the cognitive structures S is attributing to the organism constitute some kind of belief or knowledge.

Consider first the case of common sense. S is attributing to his subject a system of rules and principles concerning the organization and behavior of objects. S claims that his subject differs from a rock or a bird in that this cognitive structure is an element of his final state. Since the subject is a physical organism, the system attributed to him must have a finite representation. Evidently, there a e many conceivable finite representations of the system, however much we know about it, but S will not therefore conclude that there is no way to choose among these on empirical grounds. The empirical evidence is never exhausted. Furthermore, discoveries now unanticipated may reveal the relevance of certain types of evidence that seem now to have no bearing on the issue. S might arrive at a general principle of organization that excludes some finite representations but not others, and he might show that acquisition of cognitive structures in this and other cases can be explained on the assumption that this general principle is operative as an innate schematism. Such a demonstration would provide evidence in support of a finite representation that observes the principle, and against another finite representation that violates it. In this and innumerable other ways S might try to determine which of the various imaginable finite representations of the cognitive system are plausible candidates for a theory of the final state of his subject. On the basis of a postulated representation of a cognitive system, and other assumptions about information processing, S will try to explain many phenomena, such as why it is that his subject takes two presentations to be the same face but not two others. S will thus try to account for the fact that his subject believes he is seeing the same face twice. One might imagine various direct or indirect ways in which such specific beliefs and expectations could be tested.

S might refer to the postulated cognitive structure as a "system of beliefs." The finite representation postulated as the subject's characterization of his system of beliefs and many beliefs that are implied by it will be unconscious, no doubt, and inaccessible to introspection. In many instances, the subject does express beliefs. S will explain this fact by showing how these expressed beliefs follow from the finite representation. Suppose that the subject expresses beliefs that do not follow, or rejects beliefs that do, or neither accepts nor rejects beliefs that are assigned a definite status under this characterization, or acts in such a way that S must attribute to him beliefs that are inconsistent with the characterization. Then S will try to explain this result in terms of the interaction of other systems with the cognitive system of belief; failing in this effort, he will have to revise the finite representation.[18]

It may be expected that conscious beliefs will form a scattered and probably uninteresting subpart of the full cognitive structure. At least, if this is so, there should be no reason for surprise. Nor do I see any objection to S's practice in referring to the cognitive structure attributed to the subject as a system of beliefs.

Consider now the case of grammar. If S speaks English, he will say that some of his subjects have "learned French" and now "know French." Furthermore, in many specific instances, they can articulate their knowledge, as knowledge that so-and-so. Again, the set of such cases is unlikely to be of much interest in itself. S will attempt to explain these instances by showing how they follow from the grammar of French, interacting with other cognitive structures. In this way, he will try to account for facts analogous (for French) to those mentioned earlier (cf. (1)–(13)). The problems of confirmation and choice of theories are analogous to those that arise in the case of investigation of common sense.

Obviously, the grammar is not in itself a theory of performance (behavior). It is, however, proper for S to propose that the grammar is a component of such a theory and to proceed at this point to construct a theory of interaction of structures that would serve as a theory of performance for his subjects.[19] S might refer to the grammar attributed to the speaker as a representation (or model) of his knowledge of his language. S might also want to say that the subject who knows the language knows the grammar, and that in his initial state he knew universal grammar. Thus S's subject differs from an English speaker, a rock, or a bird in that he knows the grammar of French (to use the suggested terminology). He is like an English speaker, and different from a rock or a bird, in that in his initial state he knew universal grammar.

Since some might object to this terminology, S might prefer to invent some technical terms. Let us say that if a speaker knows the language L then he *cognizes* L. Furthermore, he cognizes the linguistic facts that he knows (in any uncontroversial sense of "know") and he cognizes the principles and rules of his internalized grammar, both those that might be brought to awareness and those that are forever hidden from consciousness. Furthermore, he cognizes the principles that underlie the acquisition of language in the first place, the principles of universal grammar (assuming that the approach outlined earlier is correct). Thus a person who knows English cognizes certain facts, for example, that necessarily bachelors are unmarried and that "is" goes with singular subjects. He also cognizes that specific rules are ordered in a certain way relative to one another. Furthermore, the person cognizes that transformations apply in a cyclic ordering and obey SSC, that initial phrase markers and surface structures contribute to semantic interpretation in ways described earlier, and that transformations are structure-dependent. The latter examples constitute part of "innate cognization" (assuming that the theory suggested earlier is correct).

If we decide to use the word "know" in a narrow sense, restricting it to conscious "knowledge of" or to "knowing how" ("why, who . . . ," and so on) as this notion is often construed, then "knowledge of" as in "knowledge of language" will have to be explicated in terms of the new technical vocabulary, so it appears.[20] In this usage, what is "known" will be a rather ill-defined and, perhaps, a scattered and chaotic subpart of the coherent and important systems and structures that are cognized. For psychology, the important notion will be "cognize," not "know."

Or, we might make the decision to sharpen and perhaps extend the term "know" so that it has just the properties of "cognize," thus eliminating the new terminology. Then we will be able to explain explicit knowledge of certain facts by showing how these cases are related to the system of "tacit knowledge." [21]

I doubt that this question can be settled by consideration of "ordinary usage," which seems to me vague and inexplicit at just the crucial points. The philosophical tradition is varied. Leibniz, for one, spoke of unconscious knowledge, though he seems to have regarded all knowledge as accessible to consciousness. Hume described instincts as those parts of an animal's "knowledge" that it "derive[s] from the original hand of nature," in contrast to the "parts of knowledge" that it learns from observation.

It seems to me that the principles that determine our systems of knowledge and belief interact so completely and inseparably with "our knowledge," in anyone's sense of this term, that it would be difficult to develop a coherent account that would isolate "true knowledge." However, it is unclear that more than terminology is at stake here. Thus S might choose to abandon the terms "knowledge" and even "knowledge of language" (if some find that offensive), while noting that there is little warrant in ordinary usage for these decisions. If so, he will speak of acquiring, cognizing, and competence, instead of learning, knowing, and knowledge.

As long as we are clear about what we are doing, either approach seems to me quite all right. "Provided we agree about the thing, it is needless to dispute about the terms" (Hume).

Consider now some of the objections that have been raised to the approach sketched above. I cannot survey the literature here, but will mention a few cases that I think are typical. I will not consider further the question that some philosophers seem to feel is crucial, namely, whether the term "knowledge" is properly used in these accounts.

Robert Schwartz argues that "the fact that we can specify [a subject's] competence in terms of a formal system of generative rules does not in itself imply that [he] has represented a *corresponding* system in him." [22] This observation is surely correct. No nontrivial theory is ever "implied" by the evidence available. But Schwartz apparently wants to say something beyond this truism. He suggests the following example to illustrate the "messy issue" that he thinks arises. Suppose a certain device, D, labels spheres "+" if their density is greater than 1 and "−" if their density is less. Suppose that a system of equations E is proposed, involving relations between volume, density, weight, and so on, which describes the output of D. But, Schwartz notes, D "might not employ a set of principles anything like [E]." Thus it might never consider weight, volume, and so on, but might contain a liquid of density 1 and label "+" any sphere that sinks, and "−" any sphere that floats. "Would it be reasonable to claim that our equations [E] are internally represented in this machine?" His answer is that it would not, even though "in some sense the liquid in the machine could be held to 'stand for' the equations [E]."

Suppose that S, observing D, concluded that its "cognitive state" involves calculations of the sort expressed in E. Further investigation might convince S that this conclusion is wrong and that a very different principle is employed, namely, the one Schwartz suggests. It would not, of course, be "reasonable" to persist in maintaining that D "employ[s] a set of principles anything like [E]," since this conclusion has been refuted. The fact that E continues to describe input-output relations correctly is uninteresting to S, once he has discovered the actual principles employed. There is no "messy issue" here.

Of course, if S were simply satisfied to say that E describes input-output relations, he would not have proceeded with further investigation to determine whether D actually employs principles like E. But as a scientist, S would have been interested to discover what it is about D that makes E an accurate description. To determine this, he might put forth the working hypothesis that D actually calculates in accordance with E, or that E enters in some important way into the actual performance of D. And he would then seek evidence bearing on this hypothesis. He would be interested to discover that this hypothesis is false. No such inquiry would occur to someone who was so lacking in curiosity as to leave the matter with the statement that E correctly describes regularities in D's behavior. But there seems no problem of principle here.

Schwartz observes that in the case of a person riding a bicycle, any specific proposal as to the organization of the system of habits and skills involved "is subject to doubt, and as long as such doubt remains, care must be taken in interpreting the assertion that the laws of physics [internally represented in some specific fashion] model [the subject's] bicycle skills." Again, the observation is correct. Since nontrivial theories are not "implied" by data, care must always be taken when they are proposed. I see absolutely no interest in this observation, nor should S pay the least attention to it. He already knew that he was engaged in empirical research. Schwartz seems to feel that something more is at stake, but he gives no indication of what it may be, and gives no reference to any work to which these strictures seem at all relevant.

The preceding example has to do with S's theory of common sense, but Schwartz applies the argument as well to his theory of grammar. He notes that "any true description of regularities of or within the set of grammatical sentences will tautologically be true of the output of [the subject's] competence." If we find a specific regularity in the subject's language, then he "might be said to 'know' this regularity but only in the sense that he will consider strings that violate this rule ungrammatical." "These regularities then are regularities true of what [the subject] knows (the class of grammatical sentences) and not regularities he knows." Insofar as Schwartz is simply proposing a usage for the term "know," I see no interest in pursuing the discussion, except to point out that it seems curious to accept "X knows the class of grammatical sentences" (and, I suppose, "X has learned rules that specify this class," i.e., "X has learned a grammar") but not "X knows the rules of his grammar."

Let us replace "know" by "cognize" in the preceding discussion, to avoid the terminological issue. Should we say, then, that the subject cognizes the rules and regularities only in the sense that he considers strings that violate them ungrammatical? Only if we are so lacking in curiosity as to be unwilling to try to determine whether a particular theory about the subject is in fact correct. If S were satisfied to say only that some theory describes regularities true of the class of sentences that the subject cognizes, he would not conduct further investigation to choose between this theory and some other theory describing the class of sentences in terms of some different system of rules. But, there surely are ways of investigating alternative theories. Thus consider the theory of English sketched earlier. S might propose that the reciprocal rule is a transformational rule moving "each" and "one" to give "each other" and "one another" from initial phrase markers of the form *each of NP . . . the other, one of NP . . . the other.* His colleague S' might propose rather that "each other" and "one another" are base-derived and interpreted by a semantic rule. S" might propose that the underlying structures are conjunctions.[23] If S, S', and S" are satisfied to observe that their theories describe correctly certain regularities, then further investigation stops. If they proceed, in the manner of any scientist, to attribute cognitive structures differing in these respects to their subjects, they will then proceed to seek other data to choose among these hypotheses.

The evidence might be quite varied. For example, it might derive from other languages. Thus suppose that postulating a transformational rule violates a certain principle U, and that by taking U (which, say, is otherwise confirmed) to be part of universal grammar, we can explain certain facts in other languages just as SSC serves to explain certain facts in English. On the empirical assumption of uniformity among humans with respect to language acquisition, this evidence would serve to counter S's assumption that the English-speaking subjects are, in fact, making use of a cognitive structure that involves a transformational movement rule. Thus the contrary theories of S' and perhaps S" receive some indirect, but valuable, empirical confirmation. Many other kinds of evidence can be sought.

S, S', and S" have every reason to take their hypotheses to be working hypotheses concerning the steady state attained by their subject and thus subject to further confirmation or disconfirmation. Surely there can be no general objection to the normal "realist" assumptions of any scientist in this case (though, obviously, care must be taken, etc.).

Perhaps what Schwartz has in mind is something different. Perhaps he has in mind a case in which two theories are compatible with all the evidence that might in principle be obtained. If so, S should simply dismiss this consideration, as any working scientist would. The notion "all the evidence that might in principle be obtained" surely requires some explanation. I doubt that any sense can be made of it. Furthermore, even if we accept it as meaningful, nothing follows with regard to S's enterprise. In the real world, he will never have exhausted the evidence, and with diligence and imagination can seek new evidence to select between empirically distinguishable theories.

Suppose that S comes up with several theories as the best ones he can devise without examination of the internal structure of his subjects. Then he will say, regretfully, that he cannot determine on the basis of the evidence available to him which (if any) of these theories correctly characterizes the actual internal structure. In Schwartz's sphere example, S will not be able to determine whether E or rather the account in terms of a liquid of density 1 is the

correct theory. As in the case of the spheres, so in the case
of language: S will not be perplexed about the nature of
the theories he is proposing and their relation to fact;
rather, he will be annoyed that he cannot (by hypothesis)
proceed to choose among theories that seem plausible. In
any event, there seems no reason for S to abandon the
standard procedure of any scientist, with its conventional
realist assumptions, in such cases as these.

Schwartz then proceeds to raise certain objections to the
study of language learning as pursued by S. He feels that
"the psychologically interesting question is whether the
factors that shape the learning of language are specific to
language or whether they are general features of the learning apparatus." He argues that "the child develops many
skills and competences, acquires knowledge of relationships and regularities in his environment, learns games and
complex patterns of social behavior, etc., in essentially the
same 'untaught' manner he learns language," and in these
cases too standard behavioral theories seem inadequate.
Yet it would, he believes, "seem implausible to claim distinct innate schemata responsible for each." He further
suspects that there will be "no *interesting* version" of the
claim that children "would encounter enormous . . . difficulty learning a language not of the predestined form,"
since children acquire complex symbol systems that "do
not fit the natural language mold." It would, he argues, be
"circular" to claim simply that "any symbol system that
violates the Chomskian canons is not a language and thus
outside the scope of the claim."

These remarks are offered in criticism of "Chomsky's approach to language-learning," namely, the one sketched
earlier. Taking his comments in turn, it would surely be
interesting to determine whether the factors that shape
language learning are specific or general, though it is
curious to insist that this is "*the* psychologically interesting question." Thus suppose the question to be resolved by

elementary observations such as those noted earlier (cf. pp. 18–19, 158–9), which suggest that the factors that shape language learning are specific. Are there no psychologically interesting questions left? Perhaps this is true for someone wedded to traditional dogma, but surely many questions remain for a scientist, who would be interested to discover the detailed character of the factors that are involved in acquiring various cognitive structures.

The failure of familiar learning theories to account for cognitive structures apart from language is repeatedly emphasized in the work that Schwartz is criticizing. Noting that other systems are learned "untaught" and have complex properties, uniform among learners, one would naturally proceed as outlined earlier in each such domain: determine the character of the system acquired, the evidence on the basis of which it was acquired, and the innate factors that make possible the acquisition of this system on the basis of the available evidence. Thus, if the principles of structure-dependence, SSC, and so on appear to be properties of the acquired system of language, we will attempt to account for this fact by postulating an innate mechanism capable of determining these principles on the basis of the available data; for reasons already discussed, it seems plausible to regard these principles as comparable to those that determine the nature and function of organs. In other domains, we find quite different properties and will proceed in a comparable way, postulating whatever innate structures are required to explain the facts. Schwartz believes that it is "implausible" to postulate distinct innate schemata for different "skills and competences," but since he offers no arguments, we may disregard the judgment. It has no more weight than the unargued belief that embryos learn to have eyes or that people learn to organize perceptual space by the mechanisms involved in word association. There is no place for such dogmatic claims. Schwartz never considers any of the ob-

vious reasons for doubting that there is an undifferentiated
learning theory, nor does he give any argument for his
beliefs apart from the observation that many skills and
competences are learned untaught, from which we can
conclude only that a theory that presupposes teaching is
wrong.

Schwartz's claim of "circularity" is obviously in error.
When S proposes that universal grammar has certain
properties, he is advancing an empirical hypothesis. We
may test it by studying the facts of language. In principle,
we might test the proposal by asking whether a child will
use language in accordance with the principles put forth
even in the absence of evidence that these principles apply, as in the cases discussed earlier. Thus, observing that
no child ever makes the mistake of producing (14) instead
of (15), corresponding to the declarative (16), S might
postulate that a property of the child's initial state excludes the structure-independent hypothesis 1 of chapter
1 (p. 31) as unformulable.

(14) is the man who tall is in the room?

(15) is the man who is tall in the room?

(16) the man who is tall is in the room

S might then proceed to ask whether other phenomena
obey the principle advanced, or he might proceed in principle to construct an appropriate experimental situation in
which such examples as (14) and (15) are never presented,
and ask whether subjects invariably use the structure-dependent rule that gives (15) rather than (14). If so, he will
have gained confirming evidence for the empirical hypothesis that the principle of structure-dependence is part of
universal grammar, since that assumption provides an explanation for the facts. Similar remarks apply in the case of
the more complex examples discussed earlier. In practice,
because of conditions of time and feasibility, more indirect
tests must be sought, but the logic of the situation is clear

enough, and even the existence of tests that could be used in principle suffices to refute the charge of circularity.

There is good reason to anticipate that further research will support the conclusion that principles of the sort discussed earlier do constitute part of the innate schematism for language acquisition. Thus it is surely implausible to suppose that in the cases in question (e.g., (14) and (15)), every child has had sufficient relevant experience with appropriate examples. On the contrary, it is often a difficult problem even to discover examples that bear on the hypotheses in question (cf. SSC.) Yet if we find that people observe these principles, we must seek an explanation for this fact. The only explanation that has been proposed, to my knowledge, is the one suggested before: the principles belong to universal grammar, which is an element of the "initial state." But whether this proposal is right or wrong, there can be no doubt that the project outlined is an empirical one, at every step. Hence the charge of circularity is surely false. If it were justified, there would be no point in testing specific proposals, say, that SSC or the principle of structure-dependence belongs to universal grammar. Being tautological, the proposals could not be false.

For similar reasons, we can readily see why there might be—and indeed, already is—an "interesting version" of the hypothesis that children would encounter considerable difficulty in learning languages that violated postulated universals, contrary to Schwartz's contention. At least this is true if we take an "interesting version" of the hypothesis to be one that has far-reaching empirical consequences and considerable explanatory value.

It is easy to see where Schwartz's argument goes astray. In the first place, he is overlooking the fact that we have certain antecedently clear cases of language, as distinct from maze running, basket weaving, topographical orientation, recognition of faces or melodies, use of maps, and so on. We cannot arbitrarily decide that "language" is whatever meets some canons we propose. Thus we cannot simply stipulate that rules are structure-independent, then concluding that examples such as (14) and (15) are not relevant to "language" as determined by this stipulation. Of course, there are unclear cases as well, and there is the constant problem of determining when a theory must be abandoned in the face of apparent counterevidence (see note 18), or when cognitive domains have been improperly delimited in the first place. But these are hardly new problems unique to this enterprise. On the contrary, they arise constantly in any rational inquiry.

Furthermore, quite apart from the matter of antecedently clear cases, recall that S is attempting to map out the full system of cognitive structures for his subject, determining their character and interaction, at each step making certain idealizations and advancing empirical hypotheses, hence taking steps that are not "implied" by his data, naturally. If he finds that other symbol systems "do not fit the natural language mold," he will try to determine what mold they do fit. He will study their character and the basis for their acquisition, proceeding in the same manner as in his study of language, untroubled by dogmatic beliefs about the "uniformity" of learning.

Ultimately, S will hope to find that symbol systems that fit different molds also have different neural representations, and that the various innate factors postulated to account for the facts will also, where distinct, have different physical representations. Little is known as yet, but there is at least evidence that essential linguistic structures and functions are normally represented in the left hemisphere, and that some of the other "symbol systems" that Schwartz (following Goodman) irrelevantly introduces into the discussion are primarily controlled by the right hemisphere, perhaps in areas homologous to the language centers (nonspeech sounds, speech sounds not used in the context of speech, melodies, etc.); cf. chapter 2, note 8. There also appear to be some differences in the stage of maturation at which various centers are established in their function (recent work on face recognition reported by Susan Carey is suggestive in this regard). Whether or not these tentative proposals prove correct on further investigation, clearly they are of the sort that a scientist concerned with symbol systems, their character, interaction, and acquisition, should explore. Schwartz seems to believe that any departure from the "natural language mold" in the case of other symbol systems must be accidental—that is that any innate schematism for language learning must simply be a general schematism for learning. But he has offered no argument whatsoever for this contention, and he simply ignores the many obvious problems it faces, some mentioned earlier.

The concerns about theory and evidence that Schwartz expresses and his objections to the program outlined earlier are typical of much recent discussion. But the objections have no foundation and the concerns, where justified at all, have no bearing on the issues, so far as I can see, in that they apply in a comparable way to any variety of empirical inquiry. They are worth considering in detail only because of the insight they provide into empiricist assumptions.

If Schwartz's claims on these matters had any merit, they should apply as well to the study of physical organs. Suppose that S develops a theory T dealing with the structure and function of the human eye, and postulates the innate factors F to account for the growth of an organ satisfying T. Suppose now that he turns his attention to the liver. Paraphrasing Schwartz, we might argue that it is "implausible" to postulate distinct innate factors F' (which, along with F and others, constitute the genetic coding that determines the nature of the organism) to account for the growth of the liver. After all, the eye and the liver are both organs, and it would be "circular" to claim that any organ not satisfying T is not an eye "and thus outside the scope of the claim" embodied in F. Or, suppose that S decides to study the eyes of mammals and insects, postulating different genetic mechanisms to account for the striking differences in the final states attained and the pattern of development. Following Schwartz, we counter that he has committed a logical error, since the insect eye is also an eye and it would be circular to claim that an organ that violates the theory of the mammalian eye is not a mammalian eye "and thus outside the scope of the claim" concerning the basis for its development. Plainly, none of this can be taken seriously.

It is a question of fact whether map reading and language use involve the same or similar mechanisms (e.g., SSC, the principle of the transformational cycle, etc.), and whether the cognitive structures involved develop on the basis of the same or similar innate factors. The observation that we call both language and maps "symbol systems" contributes no more to an inquiry into their nature, function, and origin than the observation that the mammalian and the insect eye are called "eyes" or that the eye and the liver are called "organs." Similarly, the observation that both symbol systems are learned is as informative as the observation that both organs develop. No conceptual argument can establish that a scientist is wrong to postulate fundamentally different cognitive or physical structures, or to attempt to explain these differences on the basis of distinct innate factors. An empirical argument must be brought to bear. This Schwartz entirely fails to do. Consequently, his discussion is simply beside the point.

Similar arguments are developed in Atherton and Schwartz (1974). Much of their discussion is devoted to refutation of positions on "innateness" that have never appeared in the literature, to my knowledge. At the very end, they point out that the psychologist "must postulate

the existence of whatever capacities can be shown necessary for language mastery." But, they assert, "to argue
that the features responsible for natural language are so
highly task-specific that they can be separated from cognitive life in general would be to strip the claim that natural language is innately *species*-specific of most of its
metaphysical as well as its theoretical and philosophical
interest." This remark, which ends the paper, is the only
observation they make which has any real bearing on S's
program (or familiar variants of it in earlier discussion),
apart from points already discussed.

But there is a crucial logical slip in their formulation.
They assume without argument that if the features responsible for natural language are "highly task-specific"
then these features "can be separated from cognitive life
in general." But this does not follow. Correspondingly, the
assumption that the eye involves highly specific mechanisms does not imply that "the features responsible for
[the eye]" can be separated from the general (physical or
cognitive) functioning of the organism. Given empiricist
prejudice, the argument is perhaps comprehensible. Thus,
on these assumptions, "cognitive life in general" is a system developed incrementally by means of association, conditioning, habit formation, generalization, induction, abstraction of certain specific kinds that have been proposed
(I omit, again, vacuous formulations of empiricist theory).
Any highly specific system developed on the basis of other
principles will therefore be "separated from cognitive life
in general." Abandoning empiricist prejudice, we will explore various cognitive domains, attempting to map out
their structures, interaction, and function and to determine the "features responsible" for the cognitive structures that develop. As in the case of the physical structure
of an organism, so in the case of its cognitive organization,
the discovery that some cognitive structure develops on
the basis of highly specific features implies nothing about

its relations, however intimate, to other structures that enter into the organism's cognitive state.

As for the notion of metaphysical, theoretical, or philosophical interest, since Atherton and Schwartz do not explain what they mean, I will drop the matter.

W. V. O. Quine argues along somewhat similar lines in his discussion of methodological problems of linguistics in Quine (1972). In a familiar terminology, grammars are said to be "weakly equivalent" if they generate the same set of sentences and "strongly equivalent" if they generate as well the same set of structural descriptions. Quine asks us to consider the following situation. Suppose that two grammars are "extensionally equivalent" over the class of sentences, that is, weakly equivalent. Suppose further that "both systems fit the behavior . . . of all us native speakers of English." Plainly these systems do not "guide" behavior in the sense that "the behaver knows the rule and can state it" and this knowledge "causes" the behavior ("guiding is a matter of cause and effect").[24] But it would be wrong, Quine holds, to suggest that English speech might be "rule-guided" in some other sense, that is, unconsciously. In his view, it is senseless to say that "two extensionally equivalent [weakly equivalent] systems of grammatical rules need not be equally correct" and that "the right rules are the rules that the native speakers themselves have somehow implicitly in mind." What he rejects is the doctrine that "imputes to the natives an unconscious preference for one system of rules over another, equally unconscious, which is extensionally equivalent to it." Quine accepts the notion of

> implicit and unconscious conformity to a rule, when this is merely a question of fitting. Bodies obey, in this sense, the law of falling bodies, and English speakers obey, in this sense, any and all of the extensionally equivalent systems of grammar that demarcate the right totality of well-formed English sentences. These

are acceptably clear dispositions on the part of bodies
and English speakers.

What Quine questions is my "intermediate notion of rules
as heeded inarticulately."

The same considerations, Quine argues, bear on the doctrine of linguistic universals. "Timely reflection on method
and evidence should tend to stifle much of the talk of
linguistic universals," he suggests, since such reflection will
reveal that there are distinct but extensionally equivalent
grammars and it may be impossible to determine un-
equivocally when apparent uniformities are simply an artifact of the translation process.

Quine believes that there is considerable "folly" in the
proposals he criticizes, though it can be cured in time by
"conscientious reflection on method and evidence." He is
willing to concede that some course of inquiry might "convince us that there is indeed an unarticulated system of
grammatical rules which is somehow implicit in the native
mind in a way that an extensionally equivalent system is
not." But he feels that "clarification of criteria" has not
been given sufficiently for this "enigmatic doctrine."

One can certainly sympathize with Quine's "plea against
absolutism" and his desire for clarification of criteria. But
nothing in his account suggests that there is any problem
here that has so far gone unrecognized, or that there is any
folly to be cured. Specifically, I find no argument against
S's procedure (which, of course, is familiar from earlier accounts), or, for that matter, against any account that appears in the literature.

Consider one of the few relevant concrete cases that
Quine discusses, namely, the problem of choosing between
two extensionally equivalent grammars, one of which assigns to the sentence *ABC* the immediate constituents
AB–C and the other, *A–BC*. Is there some "enigma" here?
I think not, though there are surely problems. Proposals
for resolving the problems have been advanced in the lit-

erature of generative grammar since the outset, and I think that they are right in principle, though sometimes difficult to apply in practice.

Suppose that S faces this problem, and does not think much of Quine's "unimaginative suggestion": Ask the natives. Suppose that S has evidence to suggest that intonation patterns are determined by grammatical structure.[25] The evidence might come from the language in question or from other languages, which are relevant for reasons already discussed. Such evidence might bear on the choice between the two proposed grammars; thus we might discover that the rules needed for other cases give the correct intonation if we take the constituents to be $A-BC$ but not $AB-C$. Or suppose that S has reason to postulate that transformations are structure-dependent in this sense: a transformation applies to a string partitioned into a sequence of strings each of which is either arbitrary or is a string of a single constant category. Suppose that specific transformations—say, coordination—observe constituent structure in this sense. These principles, which might be supported by all sorts of evidence, might lead to a choice between the two grammars in this case (say, if we found that where ABC and ADE are well formed, then so is $A-BC$ and DE; though where ABC and FGC are well formed, still AB and $FG-C$ is not). Other evidence might be derived by application of the principle that contextual features of lexical items are internal to constituents, or from semantic considerations of varied sorts. Given a rich general theory of universal grammar, S might bring many kinds of evidence to bear on the question. Examples abound in the literature.

Is there anything enigmatic in all of this, apart from the inescapable problems of empirical uncertainty? I think not. At least, Quine suggests nothing, here or elsewhere.

Quine's sole point reduces to the observation that there will always be distinct theories that are compatible with all the evidence at hand. That is true if we restrict our-selves, as he sometimes unreasonably suggests, to consider-ation of weak generation of sentences; and it will remain true if we consider as well a variety of other evidence. But this observation is without interest. Again, S already knew that his nontrivial theories were underdetermined by evidence. Quine has offered no reason to suppose that S's investigation of language is subject to some problem that does not arise in his investigation of common sense, or in any scientific investigation of any subject matter. Hence his strictures on method and on linguistic universals, and his general charge of "folly," are entirely without force.

Though Quine does not explicitly invoke his principle of "indeterminacy of translation" in this connection, it seems that his discussion here is related to that principle. I have argued elsewhere [26] that this principle amounts to nothing more than the observation that empirical theories are underdetermined by evidence. Quine gives a counter-argument in Quine (1969a). He asserts that "the indeter-minacy of translation is not just inherited as a special case of the under-determination of our theory of nature. It is parallel but additional." His argument is as follows:

> (17) Consider from this realistic point of view, the totality of truths of nature, known and unknown, observable and unobservable, past and future. The point about indeterminacy of translation is that it withstands even all this truth, the whole truth about nature. This is what I mean by say-ing that, where indeterminacy of translation ap-plies, there is no real question of right choice; there is no fact of the matter even to *within* the acknowledged under-determination of a theory of nature.

The remarks of (17) constitute Quine's full answer to my query: In what respect does the problem of determining truth in the study of language differ from the problem of determining truth in the study of physics?

Quine's "realistic point of view" takes theory in physics as "an ultimate parameter"; that is, "we go on reasoning and affirming as best we can within our ever under-determined and evolving theory of nature," which includes "ourselves as natural objects." With this, our scientist S of course agrees, and he studies language exactly as he studies physics, taking humans to be "natural objects." Quine's formulation (17) merely reiterates his belief that somehow indeterminacy of "translation" (actually, what is at stake, on Quine's grounds, is the status of all propositions about language that face more than his "ordinary inductive uncertainty," hence virtually all of the nontrivial study of language) withstands all of the truth about nature. The remark (17) is false if the study of "translation" is part of the theory of nature, and true otherwise. But Quine's assertion (17) gives no reason to doubt that the theory of "translation" is part of the theory of nature, hence underdetermined by evidence only as physics is. And this was the only point at issue.

Similarly, when Quine asserts that there is no fact of the matter, no question of right choice, he is once again merely reiterating an unargued claim which does not become more persuasive on repetition. If the underdetermination of physical theory by evidence does not lead us to abandon the "realistic point of view" with regard to physical theory, then the comparable underdetermination of grammatical theory by evidence does not support Quine's claim that there is no fact of the matter in this domain to be right or wrong about: for example, in the case of the constituent analysis of the sentence *ABC*, the rule of NP-preposing, SSC, the principles of semantic interpretation discussed in chapter 3, a theory of the meaning of a word, or whatever. Neither here nor elsewhere has Quine given any argument whatsoever to justify his assertion that statements about language that go beyond his notion of "ordinary induction" (with its uncertainties) are subject to some methodological doubts that do not hold (in principle) in any nontrivial empirical study. His thesis of "indeterminacy" thus has no support beyond the truism that theory is underdetermined by evidence in empirical research.

A consistent skepticism will lead one to challenge any empirical assertion about the natural world. Thus noting the underdetermination of a theory of nature, we can pointlessly observe that given any proposed nontrivial physical theory, there are alternatives compatible with all available evidence. If we are willing to follow Quine in granting some sense to the notion "totality of evidence," the same statement can be made about a theory compatible with the totality of evidence. Correspondingly, in the case of propositions of the theory of language that are not derived by "ordinary induction," we can observe, equally pointlessly, that there are alternatives compatible with the evidence.

Quine urges "a change in prevalent attitudes toward meaning, idea, proposition." We must abandon the "conviction . . . that our sentences express ideas, and express these ideas rather than those, even when behavioral criteria can never say which." Depending on how we interpret "behavioral criteria," Quine's assertion is either indefensible, in that it imposes conditions on the study of language that cannot generally be met in empirical inquiry, or it is correct, but simply goes to show that the study of language and translation is in principle on a par with physics. Consider two theoretical propositions of the theory of language, P, which asserts that sentence s "expresses these ideas," and P', which asserts that s "expresses those ideas." Suppose we interpret the phrase "behavioral criteria" in Quine's dictum as meaning "necessary and sufficient conditions couched in terms of observation." Then we cannot expect that P and P' will be differentiated by behavioral criteria. But Quine's proposal, so understood, is unreasonable, in that theoretical concepts and propositions employing them can rarely be provided with "criteria" in this sense, and there is no justification for imposing such a requirement on this branch of empirical inquiry alone. Suppose we interpret the phrase "behavioral criteria" as meaning simply "relevant evidence." Thus what is proposed is that we abandon the conviction that P differs empirically from P' where there is no relevant evidence bearing on the choice between them. But with this proposal the scientist will readily agree. In this respect, the study of language (specifically, translation) is on a par with other branches of empirical science. To choose between P and P', we will seek relevant evidence, which might be indirect and will in general be inconclusive, that is, not logically compelling though perhaps compelling. As we will see directly, Quine vacillates between these two senses of "behavioral criteria" (see below, p. 199 and note 35). Whichever interpretation we pick, the proper conclusions are unsurprising and do not differentiate the study of language (or translation) from physics, in principle.

One might argue that such concepts as "meaning, idea, proposition" have no place in the study of language. Thus one might argue that relevant evidence will never exist for theoretical statements employing these concepts, or that there is a better theory that avoids them entirely but accounts for the relevant evidence. But this kind of critique, justified or not, rests on no novel notion of "indeterminacy." Rather, the issue is in principle just like those that arise in other branches of empirical inquiry.

Quine pursues a similar line of argument in Quine (1968). He points out correctly that whatever problems bedevil translation also appear in the case of our own language: that is, if there is some problem of principle affecting the hypothesis that the native's *gavagai* translates our term "rabbit," then the same problem arises in asking whether "our terms 'rabbit,' 'rabbit part,' 'number,' etc., really refer respectively to rabbits, rabbit parts, numbers, etc., rather than to some ingeniously permuted denotations." The question, Quine holds, is "meaningless," except "relative to some background language." Quine's solution to the dilemma is that "in practice we end the regress of background languages, in discussions of reference, by acquiescing in our mother tongue and taking its words at face value." But this is no help at all, since every question that he has raised can be raised about the "mother tongue" and the "face value" of its words. In fact, there was no interesting problem in the first place, apart from the underdetermination of theory by evidence. Quine has yet to pose any problem that should trouble a natural scientist taking the course suggested for S, a scientist who regards people as "natural objects" and their use of language a part of nature, to be studied in a familiar way.

In the same article, Quine argues that "semantics is vitiated by a pernicious mentalism as long as we regard a man's semantics as somehow determinate in his mind beyond what might be implicit in his dispositions to overt behavior." Is the problem here the reference to "mind," or is it the gap between what is regarded as determinate and what is implicit in dispositions? Suppose that we replace "mind" by "brain" in Quine's formulation. Is there something "pernicious" now? Or suppose we reformulate Quine's thesis as follows: "Science is vitiated by a pernicious physicalism so long as we regard an object's state (structure) as somehow determinate in its physical constitution (body) beyond what might be implicit in its dispositions." Is the latter thesis to be taken seriously? Surely not. But then, neither is the former, at least on any grounds that Quine suggests.

As far as I can see, Quine's thesis of indeterminacy of translation and its several variants (e.g., Quine, 1972) amount to no more than an unargued claim that the study of language faces some problem over and above the familiar underdetermination of nontrivial theory by evidence. But I think that Quine's position on this matter is not only unargued but also of doubtful consistency. Thus consider the following formulation (Quine, 1969b):

> Learning by ostension is learning by simple induction, and the mechanism of such learning is conditioning. But this method is notoriously incapable of carrying us far in language. This is why, on the translational side, we are soon driven to what I have called analytical hypotheses. The as yet unknown innate structures, additional to mere quality space, that are needed in language-learning, are needed specifically to get the child over this great hump that lies beyond ostension, or induction. If Chomsky's antiempiricism or anti-behaviorism says merely that conditioning is insufficient to explain language-learning, then the doctrine is of a piece with my doctrine of the indeterminacy of translation.

Consider the "as yet unknown innate structures" mentioned in this passage. Since they are "as yet unknown," presumably they are "knowable," or to put it more properly, hypotheses concerning these innate structures have exactly the status of propositions of natural science, and in fact are simply a part of biology. Consider, then, a set of hypotheses H_1 concerning these innate structures needed in language learning to get the child past the limitations of ostension or induction. Examining these hypotheses, the scientist S might derive a new set of hypotheses H_2 concerning the class of systems that can be attained by an organism equipped with the innate structures characterized by H_1 (he might sharpen these hypotheses H_2 by considering the nature of the available evidence, but for simplicity, let us put this consideration aside). The hypotheses H_2 also fall strictly within natural science, in principle, and raise no new questions of "indeterminacy."

Clearly we can make no *a priori* assumptions about the hypotheses H_1 and H_2; they are to be discovered, tested, refined, by the methods of the natural sciences. It is, in particular, surely possible that H_2 will have bearing on the choice of alternative phrase-structure analyses (e.g., $A-BC$ versus $AB-C$), on the principle SSC, on the theory of surface-structure semantic interpretation, on the trace theory of movement rules, or on the nature and properties of "nameable" objects (e.g., rabbits and rabbit-stages) and all sorts of other matters.

The hypotheses H_2 express properties of language that cannot be determined (by the child, by the linguist) by the methods of "ostension, or induction." But looking back at Quine's earlier account, it was precisely the hypotheses of this character that were allegedly subject to "indeterminacy of translation," [27] a new problem that does not arise in the natural sciences. Presumably it is for this reason that Quine notes that the doctrine under dicusssion is "of a piece with my [Quine's] doctrine of the indeterminacy of translation." Recall, however, that "where indeterminacy of translation applies, there is no real question of right choice; there is no fact of the matter even to *within* the acknowledged under-determination of a theory of nature." Apparently then, the hypotheses H_1 and H_2 have nothing to be right or wrong about and cannot be selected, confirmed, refined, or rejected in the manner of the natural sciences, although they are, as we have seen, perfectly ordinary hypotheses of human biology dealing with "as yet unknown" (hence knowable) innate biological structures and the restrictions and scope they entail with regard to what is learned. In short, it appears that Quine is committed to the belief that this specific part of biology is subject to some new problem of principle that does not arise elsewhere in the natural sciences, despite his earlier claim that "the whole truth about nature" was immune to this strange "indeterminacy." It is difficult to see how one might reconcile these various contentions. I return to other apparent internal contradictions in Quine's doctrines on these matters in a moment.

Consider finally Quine's claim that English speakers obey any and all extensionally equivalent systems of grammar in just the sense that bodies obey the law of falling bodies (see p. 179 above).[28] This is a singularly misleading analogy. The rules of English grammar do not determine what speakers will do in anything remotely like the sense in which the law of falling bodies determines that if people jump from a building, they will hit the ground in a specifiable time.[29] All that the rules of grammar tell us is that a person will (ideally) understand and analyze a sentence in certain ways, not others—a very different matter. But even putting this fundamental difference aside, to be consistent Quine should, I believe, reformulate his claim: English speakers obey any and all of the extensionally equivalent English grammars (whether we consider weak or strong equivalence, or some still stronger notion involving even richer empirical conditions) in just the sense in which bodies obey the law of falling bodies or the laws of some other system of physics that is extensionally equivalent (with respect to some given class of evidence). Put this way, the claim is quite uninteresting, for just the reasons already discussed. Physicists do not need to be cured of the "folly" of assuming that the laws they postulate are true, and of seeking evidence to choose among alternative systems that are (so far) compatible with evidence. Nor does S have to be cured of the analogous "folly" when he is studying a particular organism as part of the natural world.

Part of the interest of the study of language, if conducted in the manner outlined for S, is that it shows the inadequacy of Quine's notions "fitting" and "guiding" for the study of human behavior. A person's behavior is not in general consciously guided by rules in Quine's sense of the term, and we can go well beyond the assertion that it simply "fits" rules in Quine's sense. Rather, the scientist can proceed, in the normal way, to postulate that his theory of humans in fact is true, that humans have the characteristics, the mental organization, the cognitive systems attributed to them under the best theory he can devise. And on this standard "realist" assumption, just the assumption that Quine's physicist adopts, S will proceed to seek evidence that will confirm or disconfirm his theories of human nature and competence. He will try to choose among alternative theories that are compatible with the evidence so far available. Ultimately, we hope, the investigator will go on to ask whether his theory is confirmed by the study of the central nervous system, again, unperturbed by the inevitable underdetermination of theory by evidence.

Pursuing Quine's methodological discussion a step further, consider again Quine (1972). Here Quine objects to what he terms my "nihilistic attitude toward dispositions" and "rejection of dispositions." This seems to him so odd that he adds: "I'd like to think that I am missing something." Indeed he is. A look at the statements of mine that he partially cites makes it quite clear what he is missing. His belief that I "reject dispositions" is based on my criticism of his definition of language as a "complex of present dispositions to verbal behavior, in which speakers of the same language have perforce come to resemble one another" (1960, p. 27). I pointed out (Chomsky, 1969a):

> Presumably, a complex of dispositions is a structure that can be represented as a set of probabilities for utterances in certain definable "circumstances" *or "situations."* But it must be recognized that the notion "probability of a sentence" is an entirely useless one, *under any known interpretation of this term.* On em-

pirical grounds, the probability of my producing some given sentence of English . . . is indistinguishable from the probability of my producing a given sentence of Japanese. *Introduction of the notion of "probability relative to a situation" changes nothing, at least if "situations" are characterized on any known objective grounds.* . . .

Quine quotes these remarks, omitting the phrases here italicized. He then says that he is "puzzled by how quickly he [Chomsky] turns his back on the crucial phrase 'in certain definable "circumstances," ' " and he adds that verbal dispositions would be idle if not defined in terms of specific circumstances. His puzzlement derives from his omission of the final sentence of the quoted section, which notes that introduction of "circumstances" helps his case not at all.

Quine further adds that he has "talked mainly of verbal dispositions in a very specific circumstance: a questionnaire circumstance, the circumstance of being offered a sentence for assent or dissent or indecision or bizarreness reaction." But as noted in Chomsky (1969a), this simply makes matters worse. Plainly, a language is not a complex of dispositions to respond under the particular set of *Gedankenexperiments* that Quine considers, nor did Quine make this patently false claim in the work I was discussing (viz., Quine, 1960).

Since Quine insists on the same point elsewhere (Quine, 1974, pp. 14 ff.), perhaps a further word is in order. Quine is concerned here to allay a "curious criticism," namely, my criticism of his characterization of a language as a complex of dispositions to verbal behavior. He cites the same comment from Chomsky (1969a), again omitting the final sentence which notes that his case is in no way improved if we consider "probability relative to a situation," and the further discussion of this point. He then makes the following comment:

Let us not forget that dispositions have their conditions. The probability that a given lump of salt will dissolve at time t is as may be, but the probability that it will dissolve if immersed in water is high. Chomsky's worry may have been a more specific difficulty: that of setting conditions for the triggering of verbal dispositions. This is an important problem, and happily it has an easy solution—a solution, indeed, that was prominent in the book that Chomsky was commenting on. It is the procedure of query and assent, which I shall take up in §12.

Section 12 is an elaboration of the procedure of query and assent of Quine (1960). In this section, Quine discusses "the continuing enterprise of ostensive learning," what he calls "statement learning." He is concerned with "the learning of assent," for example, the way that a child learns "to say 'yes' in the presence of the color red and the sound 'red.'"

Unfortunately, this procedure—even if we grant that it has the role in language learning that Quine proposes—has no bearing whatsoever on the questions that I raised. A language, Quine held, is a "complex of present dispositions to verbal behavior." If we suppose that a complex of dispositions can be represented as a set of probabilities for utterances in certain specifiable circumstances—a supposition that Quine apparently accepts—we face a series of problems that I pointed out. No way of assigning probabilities to utterances on empirical grounds relative to situations seems to offer any hope of salvaging Quine's characterization of language as a complex of dispositions to verbal behavior. I noted further that "clearly, however, a person's total 'disposition to verbal response' under arbitrary stimulus conditions is not the same as his 'dispositions to be prompted to assent or to dissent from the sentence' under the particular conditions" of Quine's query-and-assent procedure. Quine's assertion that the problem of "setting the conditions for the triggering of verbal dispositions" is solved by the query-and-assent procedure can only mean that he is failing to make this crucial distinction. Taking his proposal literally, we must conclude that a language is a complex of dispositions to assent or dissent under the conditions of the query-and-assent procedure. But this is plainly not the case. I see no other interpretation of his claim that the problems of characterizing utterance probability in situations and thus salvaging his definition of "language" as a complex of dispositions to respond (recall that this is what is at issue) "has an easy solution" in terms of his procedure of query and assent.

I suspect that Quine's failure to deal with the numerous and fundamental problems that stand in the way of his proposals derives from his continuing belief that "the child learns most of language by hearing the adults and emulating them" (Quine, 1974). If a child learns most of language by hearing and emulation, and—as Quine elsewhere insists— learning a language is a matter of learning sentences, then the child must learn most of his sentences by hearing and emulation. But this is so grossly false that one can only wonder what Quine may have in mind, particularly since elsewhere he observes correctly that a language is an infinite system characterized by a generative grammar, and further, that conditioning, induction, and ostension do not suffice for language learning. The problem of interpretation is analogous to those mentioned in note 30 below.

Perhaps what Quine means is nothing more than the truism that speakers (adults) provide the child with the data for language learning. But on this interpretation, the child learns all (not most) of language by hearing the adults (or other speakers). And the comment, so understood, loses any relevance to the discussion in which it appears.

The comments in Chomsky (1969a) apply, without modification, to Quine's more recent formulations. I also went on there to make the obvious point that "if a language is a complex of dispositions to respond under a normal set of circumstances, it would be not only finite (unless it included all languages) but also extremely small," for reasons there explained. I also pointed out that Quine avoids the multitude of problems that arise if his account is taken seriously by shifting his ground from "totality of speech dispositions" to "dispositions to be prompted to assent to or to dissent from the sentence," a set of dispositions which, he claims, constitutes all of the evidence available in principle to the linguist. Now in my remarks there is no "rejection of dispositions," but rather, of false or empty statements about dispositions, for example, the statement that a language is a complex of present dispositions to verbal behavior. Quine's response (Quine, 1969a, and elsewhere) deals with none of the issues raised. He responds that dispositions to assent or dissent are surely within the totality of speech dispositions (true, but irrelevant) and that resort to this subset does not avoid the problems but solves them (surely false); and he notes that the problem of distinguishing Japanese from English on empirical grounds does not bear on his experiments concerning dispositions to assent and dissent (true, but irrelevant). Obviously, these remarks, where accurate, have no relation to any of the points raised in my comments.[30]

In Chomsky (1969a) I pointed out that in earlier work Quine had also misused the notion "disposition," namely, in his proposal that synonymy "roughly consists in approximate likeness in the situations which evoke two forms and approximate likeness in the effect on the hearer" (Quine, 1953). This proposal is untenable. Compare the statements "watch out, you'll fall down the stairs" and "watch out, you'll fall down the sequence of steps arranged one behind and above the other, in such a way as to permit ascent or descent from one level to another." Consider the situations which evoke these two synonymous utterances and their effects on hearers. Quine is not alone in this kind of misformulation. William Alston (1963) suggests that a statement

of the form " 'x' means 'y' . . . is justified to the extent that
when 'x' is substituted for 'y' in a wide variety of sentences,
and *vice versa*, the dispositions of members of the linguistic
community with respect to employing sentences for the
performance of linguistic actions is, in each case, roughly
the same for the sentence produced by the alternation as
for the sentence which was altered." Again, the example just
cited and innumerable others like it show at once that this
statement is far from the mark. It is all very well to try to
relate comments about meaning, speech acts, and so on to
behavior, but not at the expense of factual accuracy. In
fact, to deal with these matters I believe one must pursue
the course outlined earlier for the scientist S, abstracting to
the competence that underlies language use. In the theory
of competence, it may be possible to make sense of some
notion of "synonymy," but direct analyses in terms of dispositions, so far as I can see, are quite hopeless.

Again, I stress that these remarks do not imply a "rejection of dispositions." On the contrary, I suggest that we
take the notion "disposition to respond" seriously, thus concluding that Quine's proposed formulations are quite wrong,
I believe irremediably so.

My remarks (Chomsky, 1969a) on efforts to define "language" in terms of dispositions to respond and on probability of utterances in definable circumstances are also discussed in Suppes (1973). He objects that these remarks are
"written without familiarity with the way in which probability concepts are actually used in science." His reason is
that in considering even the "simplest probabilistic phenomenon," say, coin flipping, we may be dealing with probability of outcome approaching zero, but "it in no sense
follows that the concept of probability cannot be applied
in a meaningful way to the flipping of a coin." Similarly,
"there are many probabilistic predictions about verbal behavior that can be made, ranging from trivial predictions
about whether a given speaker will utter an English or

Japanese sentence to detailed predictions about grammatical or semantic structure." Thus, "our inability to predict the unique flow of discourse no more invalidates a definition of language as a 'complex of dispositions to verbal behavior' than our inability to predict the trajectory of a single free electron for some short period of time invalidates quantum mechanics. . . ."

These remarks are completely beside the point. Suppes has failed entirely to understand the questions that were at issue in the discussion to which he refers. It is correct that given a grammar, we can develop "sophisticated applications of probability theory" untroubled by the fact that "the basic objects of investigation have either extremely small probabilities or strictly zero probabilities." Given a characterization of English and Japanese by a grammar, we can make predictions as to whether a given speaker will utter a sentence of English or Japanese, so characterized. But it is equally correct that lacking a characterization of the language by a generative system (or some approximation thereto) we can make little sense of empirical observations of the probability of utterances (whether in empirically definable circumstances, or in some corpus of utterances). In particular, we can make no sensible predictions as to whether the next utterance will be English or something else.

The analogy to quantum mechanics is quite false. Physicists do not characterize the theory of quantum mechanics as a complex of dispositions of electrons to move here or there as experimentally observed. Rather, they develop a theory of such movements and relate it to experimental observation, a totally different matter.

If a language is defined as a "complex of dispositions to verbal behavior," determined simply in terms of probability of response in given situations without reference to any postulated theory of competence, we will be faced with the mass of problems I mentioned. If, on the other hand, the "complex of dispositions" is expressed in terms of a postulated theory of competence, all of the questions at issue are begged.

In the same connection, Suppes objects to the "imperialistic ambitions . . . that many linguists seem to have for a theory of competence" *vis-à-vis* the theory of performance and claims "that the two can proceed independently." He does not explain what he has in mind in referring to these "imperialistic ambitions," but presumably he is thinking of the contention that the study of performance—use of language—can progress only to the extent that we have some understanding of the system that is used. The latter contention, however, is hardly "imperialistic." Rather, it is close to truism. Thus, if all we know about language is that it consists of words, we can study the use of words and construct probabilistic models for word sequences. On the other hand, if we know something about "grammatical or semantic structure," then we can proceed, as Suppes proposes we do, to construct probabilistic models that provide detailed predictions about these postulated structures. The probabilistic grammar that Suppes discusses makes use of a classification of questions on syntactic and semantic grounds; that is, it presupposes a partial theory of competence that provides such a classification. His own examples illustrate the truism that the theory of language use cannot sensibly proceed independently of the theory of competence. No "imperialistic ambitions" have been expressed beyond this truism.

As for Suppes's contention that neither of these theories "need precede" the other, if by "precede" he means "temporally precede," of course there can be no objection. The study of language is concerned with the system and its use. The linguist is thus concerned with the competence acquired and performance models that incorporate this competence and are concerned with its use. It is impossible to lay down *a priori* conditions as to the points in this complex system at which new insights will arise. I fail to see any issue here. (Cf. note 19.) Suppes properly endorses Quine's "plea against absolutism," but he seems to have some misconception as to the nature of the work to which he alludes.

Since Quine has been perhaps the leading critic of the project suggested earlier for the scientist S, it may be helpful to consider further his remarks on the study of language. As I read Quine, we must distinguish two different and, I believe, inconsistent doctrines. The first is that of Quine (1960). Here a theory, and also a language,[31] is "a fabric of sentences variously associated to one another and to nonverbal stimuli by the mechanism of conditioned response," and Quine goes on to specify three mechanisms by which "sentences can be learned": association of sentences with sentences, association of sentences with stimuli, and "analogic synthesis," a notion left obscure apart from a single example, namely, a case of substitution of one word for another in a given context.[32] He also defines a language here as a "complex of present dispositions to verbal behavior, in which speakers of the same language have perforce come to resemble one another," a formulation which, as already noted, is either empty or wrong, depending on how we introduce "situations."

Learning also involves a "quality space" with dimensions and a distance measure to be determined experimentally.

> In fact, the denizens of the quality space are expressly stimulations . . . , any and all, with no prior imposition of dimensions. Any irrelevant features of the stimulations will in principle disappear of themselves in the course of the experimental determination of the quality space . . . [which can be] . . . explored and plotted by behavioral tests in the differential conditioning and extinction of his responses.

"The final dimensionality of someone's quality space, if wanted, would be settled only after all the simply ordinal comparisons of distance had been got by the differential conditioning and extinction tests," by "considerations of neatest accommodation," along the lines of Goodman (1951).[33]

Now consider the proposals of Quine in the late 1960s (1969a,b). He states that the method of conditioning "is notoriously incapable of carrying us far in language" and takes his "doctrine of the indeterminacy of translation" to be "of a piece" with the doctrine that "conditioning is insufficient to explain language learning." He insists that "generative grammar is what mainly distinguishes language from subhuman communication systems," and he speaks of "the as yet unknown innate structures, additional to mere quality space, that are needed in language-learning . . . to get the child over this great hump that lies beyond ostension, or induction." He also adds "an explicit word of welcome toward any innate mechanisms of language aptitude, however elaborate," that can be made intelligible and plausible. While in 1960 Quine was following the Skinnerian pattern, as he repeatedly states, in the later work he defines "behaviorism" merely as the view that all "criteria" must be couched in observation terms and that conjectures must "eventually be made sense of in terms of external observation"—so that "behaviorism" is just another name for weak verificationism.

I see no way to reconcile the earlier and later views. If conditioning is insufficient to explain language learning (1969) then a language is not a fabric of sentences and stimuli associated by conditioned response (1960), and sentences are not "learned" by the three mechanisms of 1960. If generative grammar is the essential defining characteristic of human language, then, again, the earlier account can be dismissed, since a generative grammar can be described neither as a fabric of sentences and stimuli associated by conditioning nor as a complex of dispositions to respond. If innate mechanisms of arbitrary complexity are permissible, so long as conjectures are eventually made sense of in terms of external observations, then there is no reason to assign any special place to dimensional structures such as a "quality space," nor to structures determined by differential conditioning and extinction tests (as distinct, say, from recall or recognition tests).[34]

Quine's later views seem to me an almost complete abandonment of behaviorism and all of its trappings—in my opinion, a welcome move. I say "almost complete" because in the more recent version the notion "conditioned response" still plays a role, one that seems to me highly dubious (cf. below). But it seems to me more interesting that Quine's later views do not fall within the class of systems E (cf. pp. 146f. above), though the earlier version does insofar as it is clear. Thus, if we are prepared to welcome any innate mechanism, however elaborate, we are not bound to procedures of the character of E, but can explore richer and, I believe, more adequate theories.

Quine's discussion of this important matter obscures the central issues. Quine suggests (1969b) that by "rationalism" I mean simply the principle that innate structures must be rich enough to account for language acquisition while not so rich as to be incompatible with data, and he expresses his agreement with this "indisputable point about language." He then adds that "innate biases and dispositions are the cornerstone of behaviorism" and that beyond "qualitative spacing of stimulations," "unquestionably much additional innate structure is needed, too, to account for language learning." His "empiricism" or "behaviorism" will apparently welcome any account of these innate endowments so long as conjectures "can eventually be made sense of in terms of external observation."[35] Thus his "behaviorism" or "externalized empiricism" can certainly accommodate my "rationalist" alternative.

But I nowhere suggested that "rationalism" was to be construed in the way Quine proposes. Rather, I suggested that there are two general approaches R and E (cf. above, pp. 146f.), each of which postulates innate mechanisms, but mechanisms of very different sorts, as explained at some length. Obviously, R and E (or any rational inquiry) should satisfy the "indisputable point about language" which he cites. I suggested further that this requirement cannot be satisfied by any approach of the character of E, in particular, by the approach of Quine (1960), which, I argued (Chomsky, 1965, 1969a) can be subsumed within E insofar as it is not vacuous. Quine's response that behaviorism also postulates innate mechanisms is plainly irrelevant to any issue that was under discussion.

Consider now the roles still assigned to conditioning in Quine's more recent suggestions. These are two:

(18) A quality space is to be determined by conditioning experiments (1969a).

(19) "Conditioned response does retain a key role in language-learning. It is the entering wedge to any particular lexicon, for it is how we learn observation terms (or, better, simple observation sentences) by ostension. Learning by ostension is learning by simple induction, and the mechanism of such learning is conditioning," which is "notoriously incapable of carrying us far in language" (1969b).

As for (18), it is doubtful that a "quality space" can be determined in any sensible way in isolation from other innate cognitive structures. Conditioning experiments can be devised to show that people can associate geometrical objects by shape, by area, by position in visual space, and for all I know, by time of day when presented. Experiments can probably be devised to show that people generalize from one presentation of a face to another that does not "match" it in the sense of Goodman (1951)—for example, a right and left profile—or that they generalize in terms of dimensions determined by a notion of matching (of faces) in Goodman's sense. Furthermore, contrary to Quine's contention (cf. note 33), there is no justification for the belief that Goodman's methods, whatever their interest in their own right, have any privileged position for the investigation of a quality space.

A scientist investigating human cognitive structures might construct an abstract quality space as part of the full integrated system, but I see no reason to suppose that it has a more primitive character than other components of the system, or that it can be determined in isolation, or that a reasonable hypothesis about a quality space is less infected by theoretical considerations with their "indeterminacies" than other components of innate cognitive structure, or that relevant experiments for determining dimensionality can be selected in isolation from the general theory of innate cognitive structure. Thus both the commitment to a particular class of experiments (conditioning and extinction) and the commitment to an isolable quality space with some privileged character seem to me highly questionable.

Consider (19). In the first place, I see no way to make sense of the statement that the mechanism of learning by simple induction is conditioning. But there are more serious issues. Recall that according to the 1960 theory, induction leads to "genuine hypotheses" with "normal inductive" uncertainty, as distinct from the analytical hypotheses that "exceed anything implicit in any native's disposition to speech behavior"; and further, in using such analytical hypotheses—say, in proposing that they constitute part of a generative grammar—we "impute our sense of linguistic analogy unverifiably to the native mind." (Recall that virtually all of syntax, as well as most semantics, consists of analytical hypotheses; 1960, pp. 68ff.) The imputation is unverifiable because of the alleged problems of indeterminacy.

As already noted, Quine seems to have now implicitly rejected all or part of this doctrine. But it seems that in Quine's present view, the mechanisms (namely, conditioning) that account for learning of observation terms are still qualitatively different from those involved in other aspects of language learning. However, I see no reason to suppose that there is any fundamental difference in this regard. Putting to the side now Quine's concerns over "indeterminacy," consider what is perhaps the most "elementary" notion we have, the notion "physical object," which, I suppose, plays a role in the most elementary processes of learning through ostension, induction, or conditioning. But the notion "physical object" seems to be quite complex. At the very least, some notion of spatiotemporal contiguity seems to be involved. We do not regard a herd of cattle as a physical object, but rather as a collection, though there would be no logical incoherence in the notion of a scattered object, as Quine, Goodman, and others have made clear. But even spatiotemporal contiguity does not suffice as a general condition. One wing of an airplane is an object, but its left half, though equally continuous, is not. Clearly some *Gestalt* property or some notion of function is playing a role. Furthermore, scattered entities can be taken to be single physical objects under some conditions: consider a picket fence with breaks, or a Calder mobile. The latter is a "thing," whereas a collection of leaves on a tree is not. The reason, apparently, is that the mobile is created by an act of human will. If this is correct, then beliefs about human will and action and intention play a crucial role in determining even the most simple and elementary of concepts. Whether such factors are involved at early levels of maturation, I do not know, but it is clearly an empirical issue and dogmatic assumptions are out of place. It may be that a schematism of considerable complexity and abstractness is brought to bear in learning processes that might be regarded as very "elementary," whatever sense can be made of this notion; very little sense, I am suggesting. We are, I think, led back again to the Peircean view mentioned earlier. And I think that even Quine's newer doctrine involves empirical claims of a most dubious sort. (Cf. also chapter 2, pp. 43ff.)

I have dwelt on these matters at such length because I believe that the problem of choosing between systems of the general character of R and E, or some combined doctrine, is a very significant one. I've argued elsewhere (e.g., Chomsky, 1965), that these two approaches express leading ideas of rationalist and empiricist speculation. Quine believes that little is at stake, but for the reasons just explained, I think he is mistaken.

Others have taken a similar view. Jonathan Cohen suggests that the arguments I gave against E show only that "techniques of simple enumeration" are inadequate for language learning (or construction of scientific theories, etc.), but that these arguments do not bear on "the techniques of eliminative induction." The latter "are adequate for scientific discovery" and "may also be adequate for language learning." Thus we need not "indulge in the relatively extravagant assumption of innate linguistic universals." [36]

The problem with Cohen's proposal is that there do not exist "techniques of eliminative induction" in any relevant sense. For "eliminative induction" to proceed, we need some specification of the class of admissible hypotheses, in Peirce's sense, or at least some ordering of admissibility, perhaps partial. The theory of universal grammar, as sketched here and in the references cited, is one such specification, of the character of R. But the systems that fall within E as I outlined it fail to provide a specification of admissible hypotheses that offers any hope of accounting for the facts. [37] If the method of "eliminative induction" is supplemented with an initial schematism that limits the class of "humanly possible grammars," it will fall within R; if it is not so supplemented, it is empty. If it is supplemented in this way, it will express the "assumption of innate linguistic universals," which is not only not "extravagant" but, so far as I know, unavoidable.

Cohen presents a number of arguments against assuming innate universals. He points out analogies between language acquisition and scientific discovery, concluding that by parity of reasoning, if the assumption of innate linguistic universals is required for the first, then some analogous assumption is required for the second. This conclusion he takes to be more or less a *reductio ad absurdum*. To account for scientific discovery, he argues, it suffices to postulate the "general capacity for eliminative induction." Why not, then, assume that this capacity suffices for language learning as well?

But Cohen's argument fails for reasons already discussed. The scientist S, casting a finer net than Cohen, notes the analogies between language acquisition and scientific discovery, and also notes fundamental qualitative differences, already discussed. These would lead him, I have argued, to postulate a system of innate linguistic universals. But as S proceeds to map out the full cognitive system of his subjects, he will also try to develop principles that account for scientific discovery. Recognizing that a "general capacity for eliminative induction" is entirely vacuous and leads nowhere unless there is a specification of a class of admissible hypotheses or some ordering of admissibility, he will try to determine this specification. For reasons already noted, it is likely to be very different from the system of linguistic universals that characterizes admissible grammars; were the systems one and the same, the fundamental differences between acquisition of language and common sense on the one hand and knowledge of physics on the other would be inexplicable. It is quite possible that S would postulate a theory of the character of R, with innate universals, to account for the ability to gain scientific knowledge. In fact, I know of no coherent alternative.

Basically, Cohen's arguments fail because of their vagueness. The substantive content of a learning theory is largely determined by the specification of admissible hypotheses, if my proposal is correct. Since we know nothing about the basis for scientific discovery, we can only speculate. But insofar as "parity of reasoning" has any force, it would lead us to suspect that in this domain as well the substantive content of any adequate theory will be given by a characterization of admissible hypotheses, as Peirce argued. Surely nothing is gained by invoking the vacuous concept "eliminative induction." The emptiness of this proposal can be seen at once if we ask the simplest question: How, in principle, could we program a computer to carry out "eliminative induction," in the case of language acquisition or scientific discovery, in the absence of constraints on admissible hypotheses? Cohen's discussion of "eliminative induction" tacitly concedes this point, by presupposing, as an element of this method, "a conception of what is to count as a hypothesis," *inter alia* (p. 51).

Cohen then suggests a further line of argument. He claims that "postulating an innate ability to do x in order to explain how it is that children are able to do x allegedly without learning from experience" is a "tautological pretence," and that to avoid this "triviality" it is necessary to discover "consequences that are testable independently of the language-learning facts it purports to explain—e.g., some consequences for brain physiology or for the treatment of speech disorders" (alternatively, we must abandon the hypothesis that there are language-specific mechanisms). "But since the Chomskyan theory does lack independently testable consequences [of this kind], it seems that theoretical progress in the explanation of language-learning should not be sought in the direction of richer and richer theories of innate universals, as Chomsky suggests, but in the direction of less and less specific theories of innate endowment that will account for such linguistic universals as there appear to be."

No one doubts the importance of searching for consequences of linguistic theory beyond "the language-learning facts." But consider Cohen's argument, which rests on the assumption that postulating an innate ability to do x to explain how it is that children are able to do x is a tautological pretense. Is Cohen's assumption correct? Suppose that the scientist S postulates the structure-dependent property of rules (SDP) or the principle SSC as an element of universal grammar; thus he postulates that children do not learn these principles, but rather construct a linguistic system observing these principles. Thus S is postulating an "innate ability to observe these principles" in order to explain how it is that children observe those principles "without learning from experience." By Cohen's assumption, S's hypothesis is a tautological pretense and therefore cannot be falsified. But in fact it can be falsified all too easily, say, by further investigation that shows that SDP or SSC is violated elsewhere in the language or in some other language. In fact, proposals concerning universal grammar —hence, on the interpretation suggested earlier, proposals concerning innate capacity—have repeatedly been revised on just such grounds. Thus Cohen's initial assumption is false, and his argument collapses.[38]

The theories of universal grammar so far proposed, though not a tautological pretense as Cohen falsely alleges, are still far from sufficiently rich and restrictive to explain acquisition of language; they do not sufficiently limit the class of admissible hypotheses. Thus, contrary to what Cohen asserts, it seems that theoretical progress in the explanation of language learning should be sought in the direction of richer theories of innate universals, at least, until some other approach is suggested that has some degree of plausibility. Cohen's suggestion that we seek less

and less specific theories of innate endowment that subsume linguistic universals merely expresses, once again, the
conventional belief that the language faculty has no special
properties, that there is simply a generalized learning capacity. But like others who are committed to this belief,
he gives no plausible argument for it and does not face
the obvious problems that arise in maintaining this view.

It would be necessary, rather than simply desirable, to
search for evidence in some other domain (say, neurophysiology) only if we had reached the point of constructing
adequate theories [39] that could not be distinguished empirically without such further evidence. This remark is indeed a "triviality," but one that has no bearing on the
nontautological character of explanatory hypotheses formulated in the terms outlined earlier, that is, in terms of a
postulated schematism of universal grammar.

Notice that if experiments with humans were possible, S
could obtain evidence relevant to theories of universal
grammar in many other ways. Thus he could test his assumption that SDP and SSC form part of universal grammar by exposing children to invented systems violating
the proposed conditions and determining how or whether
they manage to acquire these systems. If acquisition of
such systems is possible but qualitatively different from
acquisition of natural language—if, say, it has the properties of scientific discovery—then S will take this as confirm-
atory evidence for his theory that SDP and SSC form
part of the language faculty, which is one of the several
faculties of mind. The fact that such experimental procedures are possible in principle again demonstrates the nontautological character of the explanatory theories in
question.

In this connection, Cohen argues that if a Martian's
language violated a proposed theory of universal grammar
but were learnable by humans, this result would show that
universal grammar does not mirror human linguistic capaci-

ties. Therefore, he concludes, if we adopt the assumption that there are innate linguistic universals, we must "scour the whole universe, not just the earth, in pursuit of intelligible exotic languages." Thus the project is unfeasible.[40]

This argument fails for two reasons. First, it is based on a fundamental misunderstanding of the nature of scientific inquiry, and second, the formulation is, once again, too imprecise to have any bearing on the issues. Consider the first failing. We note at once that there is no distinction between a "Martian language" and any invented language. Thus we need not "scour the universe" to discover possible counterexamples to a proposed theory, to be presented to human subjects in a learning test. Rather, we can freely invent such counterinstances. Given a proposed theory of universal grammar that provides a system of innate linguistic universals, we can at once construct languages that violate the postulated principles and seek to determine, in one or another way, whether they are accessible to humans in the manner of natural language. We can continue this search for disconfirming evidence indefinitely, and in many ways. If this makes the original project unfeasible, as Cohen claims (eliminating now his irrelevant reference to "scouring the universe"), then any empirical inquiry is unfeasible on exactly the same grounds. Once again, Cohen's discussion of "Martian languages" merely underscores the obvious: nontrivial empirical theory is underdetermined by evidence.

Furthermore, Cohen's discussion is crucially imprecise on the matter of "learnability." Suppose that we have a theory UG of universal grammar. Suppose that we have a system L (Martian or invented, a distinction of no account) violating the innate linguistic universals postulated in UG. Suppose we find that L is learnable by humans exactly in the manner of attested human languages, that is, under comparable conditions of time and exposure to data, with comparable success, and so on. Then we reject UG, just as we would reject it if we found evidence from attested human languages contradicting its assumptions. Suppose, however, that we find that L is "learnable" only as physics is learnable. This discovery does not refute UG, just as UG is not refuted by the observation that college students can learn theoretical physics, a theory that no doubt violates the principles of UG. Obviously, the mind has capacities beyond the language faculty, and the fact that physics (or Martian) is learnable in itself proves nothing about the language capacity.

Finally, Cohen argues that simpler approaches suffice to account for language acquisition, and he sketches a few possibilities. Unfortunately, the latter do not begin to deal with even the most elementary properties of language that have been discussed in the literature, for example, the property of structure-dependence. Consequently, his proposals cannot be taken seriously as they stand. As for the further possibility that ability to use transformations may simply be a special case of "some generic skill," this proposal is entirely empty until the "generic skill" in question is specified; and the proposal is not particularly plausible, for reasons already mentioned.

Cohen's discussion is one of the best and most accurate that I have found, but I think he has given no serious argument for any of his conclusions.[41] Cohen points out that if the approach he is criticizing is a reasonable one and if its specific conclusions do receive some confirmation, then "the case for a *de jure* approach to the semantics of natural languages is considerably strengthened," in a sense of "*de jure* approach" that he develops and rejects. Since his arguments against the general approach lack any force and since there is at least some confirmation for it, it follows that the "*de jure* approach to semantics of natural languages is considerably strengthened," contrary to his intentions, if his reasoning in this regard is correct.

Cohen's failure to confront the only interesting questions

that arise in the case of language learning is revealed still more clearly in his more elaborate discussion of the question in Cohen (1970). Here he suggests again that with a proper concept of eliminative induction, one can overcome the arguments that a language-learning system should have the character of R, as argued in Chomsky (1965) and elsewhere; and he argues further, on the same grounds, that a "general learning strategy" should be able to "do the job." His proposed method of induction presupposes "first of all a certain set of materially similar universal hypotheses, where material similarity is defined over a subject matter . . . and secondly, a set of natural variables . . . that are inductively relevant to such hypotheses" (and, further, it presupposes some method for modifying hypotheses, for moving to higher-order hypotheses, and for idealizing and rejecting certain data; these methods remain unspecified). But unfortunately for his argument, the question at issue was the nature and source of the initial set of universal hypotheses and the "natural variables," and about this question Cohen has nothing to say.[42] In Chomsky (1965) and elsewhere it was argued that the delimitation of these hypotheses must be in terms of principles of the character of R rather than E, and many specific proposals were put forth. Cohen's approach is so vague and inexplicit that we cannot tell whether it falls within R or E; nor can we discover any of its relevant properties from his account. He merely stipulates that his "general learning strategy" is based on an unspecified initial set of hypotheses, a technique (unspecified) for modifying hypotheses, a choice (unspecified) of relevant variables, an initial limitation to "relatively few concepts" (which are unspecified), and so on.

There can be no objection to "an inductive language-learning device" which is "a formulater and tester of hypotheses," with a "nisus toward generalization [that] will lead it to formulate hypotheses about relationships between [the relevant] variables which will subsume and explain, as it were, the more elementary hypotheses that have already been established." None of the questions that concern us are clarified by these remarks, or by references to "the continuity of inductive methodology from first-order, elementary generalizations, through second-order, correlational generalizations, to third-order, theoretical generalizations," or by assuming a "device [that] always hypothesizes as boldly as it can about its initially noticed data. . . ." Contrary to what Cohen asserts, no "light seems to be shed by the proposed account of inductive reasoning," for the simple reason that the proposed account reduces to hand-waving at every crucial point.

Cohen believes that "in syntax the number of relevant variables is vastly fewer, and their size vastly smaller, and hypotheses are much more easily tested, than in most fields of natural science." This, he claims, is the reason why children learn language more quickly than we solve problems in natural science. I doubt that he would maintain this thesis if he were to attempt to formulate the principles that govern language and its use. He also suggests that "the more abstract the concepts that are invoked [in linguistic theory], the more plausible it is to suppose that, if innate at all, these concepts represent certain general abilities that have indefinitely many applications," but he gives no credible argument for this thesis,[43] beyond such claims as the following: "It is certainly not obvious . . . that the structure-dependence of, say, an interrogative transformation is substantially different from the structure-dependence of an individual jump in the children's game of hopscotch." But it seems obvious that the two are "substantially different," since even the notion of "abstract phrase structure" does not appear in the children's game, so that the notion of "structure-dependence" has no nontrivial application in this case.

Cohen also observes that "one has yet to read—in the

psychological literature—of an English speaker for whom there is adequately attested evidence both that he knows some such syntactic feature and that he has never experienced any evidence for it." This is true, for quite uninteresting reasons. No one has ever collected the entire linguistic experience of any speaker; consequently, we do not know for sure that particular speakers who observe the principle of structure-dependence, for example, have not explicitly been taught that they are to produce (15) rather than (14) (see p. 173), though the belief that in every case relevant instruction or evidence has been provided surely strains credulity. Again, the issue is plainly an empirical one, and if one wished to undertake the tedious task of demonstrating that speakers observe the principle without having been instructed that (14) and similar cases are improper, he would know how to proceed.

In short, Cohen's belief that he has shown "the importance of inductive logic for an adequate theory of language" or that he has given some argument against learning theories of the form of R, or some argument in support of general learning strategies, is entirely without foundation. He has simply avoided all of the questions that have been under discussion. The arguments bearing on the choice of an approach of the character of R or E and the arguments in support of the theory that universal grammar specifies innate linguistic universals of the sort that have been extensively discussed are untouched by his discussion. We can, no doubt, define "empiricism" as an approach which includes theories of all imaginable types, in particular theories of the character of both R and E. But this terminological suggestion is of no interest. It remains true that the substantive theories discussed within the empiricist framework are of the form of E and are inadequate, for the reasons that have been discussed at length in the literature and again in earlier discussion here. Incidentally, Cohen's explicit disparagement of Hume's approach amounts to nothing more than a preference for vacuous suggestions over fairly concrete (but wrong) proposals.

Cohen argues that "the real issue" is not the issue between "Humeianism, on the one hand, and Rationalism on the other" (i.e., between E and R, in the sense outlined earlier); rather, "the real issue is about the scope and nature of general learning strategies as against specific ones." But if the latter is "the real issue," then we can only conclude that the real issue has yet to be formulated in any meaningful terms. No "general learning strategies" have been formulated that have even a remote relation to the actual problems that arise when one attempts to account for human learning in such domains as language acquisition, though there are a few "specific ones" that have been proposed that appear to have some plausibility and empirical support. For reasons already discussed, it seems doubtful that there exist general learning strategies of much interest or significance, though of course one must keep an open mind on this. Cohen's contention that the real issue is about the scope and nature of general learning strategies reflects again the dogmatic beliefs about the structure of human cognitive capacities that are enshrined in the empiricist tradition. I see nothing in his discussion to suggest that there is any cogency or plausibility in this traditional doctrine.

John Searle has also suggested that nothing much is at stake in the R-E opposition that I have suggested as a kind of "rational reconstruction" of certain traditional and modern views (Searle, 1972). Referring to a passage from Leibniz which I cited, he comments that if this is the "correct model" for innate structure, as I imply, "then at least some of the dispute between Chomsky and the empiricist learning theorists will dissolve like so much mist on a hot morning [since] many of the fiercest partisans of empiricist and behaviorist learning theories are willing to concede that the child has innate learning capacities in the sense that he has innate dispositions, inclinations, and natural potentialities."

It should be clear from preceding discussion that Searle has also missed the central point. In proposing two conflicting approaches, I explicitly stated that each postulates innate dispositions, inclinations, and natural potentialities. The two approaches differ in what they take these to be: in the case of E, the dispositions are the mechanisms of data processing I outlined, which give something akin to Quine's "genuine hypotheses"; in the case of R, the "dispositions" (et al.) specify the form of the resulting systems of knowledge and belief—roughly, they relate to "analytical hypotheses" in what seems to be Quine's sense.

The basic point seems to me fairly clear in the passages from Leibniz that I cited. As Alan Gewirth pointed out in response to Searle, "Leibniz draws two distinctions where the empiricists draw only one" (Gewirth, 1973). Namely, Leibniz distinguishes "powers," which are "passive, indeterminate, and remote," from "dispositions," which are "active, determinate, and proximate."

> Powers as such require the stimulation of external objects both in order to be activated and in order to receive their perceptual or ideational contents; hence, they have no specific contents of their own. Dispositions, on the other hand, already have determinate contents which the mind can itself activate, given appropriate external occasions. Both powers and dispositions may be called "capacities," but then they are capacities of two quite different sorts. . . . According to this [Leibnizian] model, then, for ideas to be innate as dispositions means that the mind has quite determinate contents of its own which it is itself able to activate and perceive; whereas for ideas to be innate merely as powers would mean that the mind has only diffuse mechanisms whose contents are exhaustively derived from the impact of external stimuli. As Leibniz frequently emphasizes, the latter model, un-

like the former, is unable to explain how the mind can attain the sorts of necessary and universal truths found in logic, mathematics, and other disciplines. And a comparable [44] sort of necessity and universality are attributed by Chomsky to the basic rules of grammar. . . . Far from being compatible with empiricist and behaviorist learning theories, as Searle and Quine hold that it is, Leibniz's doctrine shows how the mind can itself be the exhaustive source of its linguistic competence, for which external stimuli serve only as occasions for activating what is already dispositionally contained in the mind's own structure. Leibniz's doctrine therefore explains, as the behaviorist theory cannot, the necessity and universality of the linguistic rules for forming and interpreting sentences. . . .

Gewirth's comments are exactly to the point. The crucial question is not whether there are innate potentialities or innate structure. No rational person denies this, nor has the question been at issue. The crucial question is whether this structure is of the character of E or R; whether it is of the character of "powers" or "dispositions"; whether it is a "passive" system of incremental data processing, habit formation, and induction, or an "active" system which is the "source of linguistic competence" as well as other systems of knowledge and belief.[45]

A similar distinction is made by Descartes, in passages which I quoted (Chomsky, 1966, p. 78). He takes the "cognitive power" to be a faculty that is not purely passive and that is "properly called mind when it either forms new ideas in the fancy or attends to those already formed," acting in a way that is not completely under the control of sense or imagination or memory. There is in humans, he argues, a "passive faculty of perception" and an "active faculty capable of forming and producing . . . ideas." [46]

Searle argues that both my "historical claim that [my] views on language were prefigured by the seventeenth-century rationalists, especially Descartes" and my "theoretical claim that empiricist learning theory cannot account for the acquisition of language" are "more tenuous than [I] suggest." The theoretical claim is more tenuous because empiricist learning theorists also accept innate dispositions; he cites in particular Quine (1969a), already discussed. I hope it is now clear why Searle's argument with respect to my theoretical claim is beside the point.

As for the historical claim, Searle gives two reasons for his conclusion. First, Descartes did not suggest that "the syntax of natural languages was innate," but rather "appears to have thought that language was arbitrary." Second, "Descartes does not allow for the possibility of *unconscious* knowledge, a notion that is crucial to Chomsky's system."

But Searle has mistaken the historical claim. I nowhere suggested that Descartes's views on language "prefigured" mine in any of the respects Searle mentions.[47] Rather, I opened my discussion of Descartes by noting that he "makes only scant reference to language in his writings." My point was that Descartes's investigation of "the creative aspect of language use" prefigures current ideas (Searle agrees) and that certain Cartesian ideas were developed in the subsequent study of language by others. Furthermore, Cartesian "psychology" contributes to a coherent doctrine that can be drawn from work that I reviewed.

As for the second objection, the notion "unconscious cognization" is crucial to my system (and I am prepared to use "unconscious knowledge" in this sense; see above, pp. 162–6), but I am not at all sure that Descartes would disallow this notion, though I recall taking no stand on the matter. True, Descartes seems to insist that knowledge is accessible to consciousness, but on this entirely different point I have explained repeatedly that I think we must depart from the classical traditions. Thus Searle's objections to my "historical claim" are without any force.

Objections to these historical claims have been made by

others (cf. note 2). I will discuss only one last example, namely Barnes (1972), since it raises questions that relate to the foregoing discussion. Unfortunately, Barnes is rather careless in his references. Thus he asserts that "Chomsky frequently and emphatically maintains that his adoption of the innate hypothesis endorses the rationalism of Descartes and Leibniz and casts out the empiricism of Locke," citing sections of Chomsky (1965, 1966). My references to Descartes, Leibniz, and others are adequately qualified, so far as I know (Barnes cites no counterexample, nor have others, to my knowledge), and there is no discussion at all in the cited references of "the empiricism of Locke." In Chomsky (1966) Locke is not mentioned, and in Chomsky (1965) there are only two references to Locke, one stating that he did not refute the doctrine of innate ideas in the form in which Descartes presented it, and the other, that Locke's remarks on the origin of ideas seem similar in respects noted to Cudworth's. In fact, I have never even discussed—let alone "cast out"—"the empiricism of Locke."

The only further evidence that Barnes cites in support of his contention that I give frequent and emphatic endorsement to the rationalism of Descartes and Leibniz is my statement (Chomsky, 1968a) that "contemporary research supports a theory of psychological *a priori* principles that bears a striking resemblance to the classical doctrine of innate ideas." Barnes neglects to add that in elaborating this statement I noted explicitly that my conclusions seem to me "fully in accord" only with certain specific aspects of this doctrine, namely, Descartes's theory of perception of regular figures, and Leibniz's remarks on innate and unconscious principles and ideas and truths that are innate as inclinations, and so on. And this adequately qualified assertion is, so far as I know, accurate enough. Barnes also refers in this connection to Chomsky (1969c, p. 59), where the only comment even marginally relevant is this: "I think that a case can be made that certain well-founded conclusions about the nature of language do bear on traditional philosophical questions," specifically, "these conclusions are relevant to the problem of how knowledge is acquired and how the character of human knowledge is determined by certain general properties of the mind." Again, I find no emphatic endorsement of the sort he suggests.

Barnes also claims that I use terms "promiscuously"; thus he agrees with the conclusion that my theory is "essentially and irreparably vague." His examples of "promiscuous" use of terms are the following: Chomsky (1965, p. 25), "which glosses 'innate *grammar*' as 'innate *predisposition* to learn a language' "; Chomsky (1969c, p. 88), "which explicates 'innate *grammar*' as 'innate schematism.' " However, neither citation exists. Rather, in the first case I state that an "innate linguistic theory . . . provides the basis for language learning" and that we can use the term "theory of language" with systematic ambiguity to refer to "the child's innate predisposition to learn a language of a certain type and to the linguist's account of this." The linguistic theory "specifies the form of the grammar of a possible human language," but is not a "grammar," let alone an "innate grammar." The second reference that Barnes cites states that "the child makes use of an innate schematism that restricts the choice of grammars." Furthermore, "there is no reason why we should not suppose that the child is born with a perfect knowledge of universal grammar, that is, with a fixed schematism that he uses, in the ways described earlier, in acquiring language." Nowhere do I use the term "innate grammar."

Note that "universal grammar" is not one of the set of grammars made available by linguistic theory (cf. Chomsky, 1965, chap. 1, and elsewhere). Rather, it is a schematism that determines the form and character of grammars and the principles by which grammars operate. Barnes's references suggest that he may be confused about this point. However, when his misreading is corrected, there is—so far as I can see—no "promiscuous use" of terms, and no vagueness or confusion that arises from the thesis that an innate schematism of the sort discussed determines an innate predisposition to learn a language of a certain type.

Barnes asserts that "on occasion" I speak "the language of crude innatism, embracing innate principles and even innate grammars. . . ." But I never embrace "innate grammars" (except in the quite appropriate sense just mentioned, namely, innate universal grammar), and my use of "innate principles" and "universal grammar" as an innate schematism is, so far as I can see, subject to no criticism that Barnes develops in his discussion of "crude innatism."

Barnes then notes three alleged "major divergencies between Chomsky and his classical forebears." The first is that neither "Leibniz or any other classical innatist" had any "particular interest in declaring the principles of grammar to be innate." As for Leibniz, the remark is irrelevant since I cited him only in reference to other aspects of the general set of doctrines that I was surveying. But if Cordemoy, Arnauld, and others whom I discussed are "classical innatists," then I think a good case can be made that they did regard as innate certain principles that we would regard as principles of grammar, though I developed this view, again, in a manner which seems to me sufficiently and properly qualified. Barnes also adds that, as distinct from my "classical forebears," I am "not concerned to establish the foundations of science, religion and morality." That too is incorrect. I am much interested in establishing the foundations of science and morality, at least, though I regret that I have little of interest to say about these questions.[48]

The second of the "major divergencies" is that Leibniz uses arguments that are quite different from mine. This observation is irrelevant to the extent that it is true. I cited Leibniz where relevant to my concerns, and also cited a wide range of arguments that differ from Leibniz's though they fall within the classical rationalist traditions that I surveyed under the rubric of "Cartesian linguistics," as this is defined in Chomsky (1966, n. 3).

Barnes's third "divergence" is that the "classical innatists" take P to be "innate in x's mind if x has an innate disposition to know that P," whereas my view is that "P is innate in x's mind if x has an innate disposition to φ, and being disposed to φ is, or entails, knowing that P." He does not explain why I am committed to the latter view and reject the former. In fact, under any sensible notion of "disposition," and any nontrivial choice of φ (i.e., unless φ is taken to be something like "learn a language," with "entails" properly qualified, in his formulation), I see no reason to take either of these formulations seriously. Barnes seems impelled to offer some quasi-operationalist characterization of the concept of "innate in x's mind," but I see no reason to expect such an approach to be more successful in this domain than it is elsewhere in scientific inquiry. Furthermore, Barnes's formulation does not comprehend the range of cases discussed by "classical innatists." In particular, it does not apply to the cases I cited as particularly interesting, such as Cudworth's theory of perception. But even if there is some point buried here, I do not see its bearing on anything that I have discussed or proposed. I have repeatedly emphasized far more striking and significant departures from the views of the "classical innatists" in the reconstruction that I have suggested.

Barnes then raises the question "whether the existence of these innate mechanisms requires the ascription of innate *knowledge* to potential language learners." I have already explained why I think that his qualms in this regard are unwarranted. But he adds some new errors that perhaps merit a word of clarification. He interprets the claim that some principle (say, the principle of cyclic rules or SDP or SSC) is innate as the claim "that the child has an *innate disposition* to speak as the principle requires," and he argues that from the fact that an organism has an innate disposition to act in accordance with some rule or principle, we cannot infer that it has knowledge of the rule or principle. It is wrong, he argues, to identify "items of knowledge, or belief, with dispositions." My "dispositions," he points out, are neither "dispositions toward certain fairly elementary types of behaviour" nor "dispositions to assent to a proposition"— the only two cases in which one might conceivably identify items of knowledge or belief with dispositions, so he maintains.

Barnes's discussion of this point is vitiated by his failure throughout to distinguish competence from performance. A principle such as the one he cites (cyclic application of rules), taken as part of universal grammar, is not a disposition to speak as the principle requires, but rather a "disposition" (if one insists on this term) to acquire a certain competence (i.e., a certain cognitive structure, a grammar, knowledge of language). Having acquired this cognitive structure, a person may be disposed to speak in certain ways, although as I have indicated, there is little of substance that we can say about this matter.

It is perfectly true, as Barnes points out, that if a bird is disposed to fly in accordance with the laws of aerodynamics we need not attribute to it knowledge of these laws, for such reasons as the following: (i) we have (or believe that we can construct) an explanation for its behavior in terms of reflex structures and the like; and (ii) the structural organization that we so attribute to a bird plays no role in accounting for its knowledge of any particular things. In the case of "linguistic dispositions," neither (i) nor (ii) holds. We might regard universal grammar as a "disposition" to acquire certain competence, but not as a disposition to behave in certain ways. And universal grammar, I have argued, is intricately and inseparably interwoven in the mature system of knowledge of language; on the basis of the system of universal grammar, the organism comes to know the language and to know particular linguistic facts. Assuming the existence of this innate system, we can account for such knowledge. Barnes asks, "What, then, is there about innate *linguistic* dispositions that might exalt their status to the rank of knowledge?" Recognizing that these are dispositions to acquire a system of knowledge (knowledge of language, which underlies knowledge of particular linguistic facts), the answer seems evident, although, as I have already observed, there is vagueness and imprecision in the normal usage of "know" that might lead us to replace "know" by the technical term "cognize" throughout this discussion, a matter of little moment, so far as I can see.

Barnes is quite right in observing that my "dispositions" do not fall under either of the categories he suggests, but this fact simply illustrates once again the inadequacy of such an analysis of dispositions, with its failure to distinguish competence from performance, to recognize the intellectual component in nontrivial instances of "knowing how" (cf. Chomsky, 1975a), its limitation to the inadequate framework of "fitting" and "guiding," and related matters already discussed. When we consider "dispositions" that fall beyond Barnes's impoverished framework, for example, the "disposition" to acquire knowledge of language, then I believe reasons can be advanced for speaking of elements of these "dispositions" as "items of knowledge, or belief" (the difference being irrelevant in the case of language, for familiar reasons).

In proposing that R and E represent two fundamentally different ways of approaching the problems of learning (and correspondingly, the origin and nature of knowledge), I have always insisted that I regard the question as an empirical one: it is the problem of determining what are, in fact, the specific properties of the human mind, in particular, the properties of what may be called "the language faculty." A number of critics have argued that by formulating the issue as an empirical hypothesis, I am eliminating any "philosophical interest" and removing the whole matter from the concerns of the classical traditions that I have discussed in this effort at rational reconstruction. As for the matter of "philosophical interest," I take no stand. The term is too vague, and attitudes among those who call themselves "philosophers" are too varied. What I have argued is that the empirical hypotheses I have been investigating do have bearing on what philosophers have said, both in the past (e.g., Hume) and the present (e.g., Quine, who would surely reject any sharp distinction between "philosophical" and "scientific" issues).

What of the more interesting question, whether by formulating the matter explicitly in terms of conflicting empirical hypotheses I am removing the discussion, beyond recognition, from the concerns of traditional debate? I can only comment briefly on this, but I think that the criticism is quite mistaken. It is a mistake to read Descartes, the minor Cartesians, Hume, and others as if they accepted some modern distinction between "scientific" and "philosophical" concerns, or as if they made a distinction between "necessary" and "contingent" along the lines of much current discussion.

Consider Hume.[49] He understood "moral philosophy" to be "the science of human nature" (p. 5). His concern was to discover "the secret springs and principles, by which the human mind is actuated in its operations," and he likened this task to that of the "philosopher" who "determined the laws and forces, by which the revolutions of the planets are governed and directed" (p. 14). He wished to undertake "an accurate scrutiny into the powers and faculties of human nature" and to discover "the operations of the mind," this being "no inconsiderable part of science" (p. 13). "It cannot be doubted," Hume insisted, "that the mind is endowed with several powers and faculties, that these powers are distinct from each other, that what is really distinct to the immediate perception may be distinguished by reflexion; and consequently, that there is a truth and falsehood in all propositions on this subject, and a truth and falsehood, which lie not beyond the compass of human understanding" (pp. 13–14). He makes interesting and substantive claims concerning these empirical issues—for example, that the "creative power of the mind amounts to no more than the faculty of compounding, transposing, augmenting, or diminishing the materials afforded us by the senses and experience" (p. 19), and that the "only three principles of connexion among ideas" are "*Resemblance, Contiguity* in time or place, and *Cause* or *Effect*" (p. 24). The "reasonings from experience . . . on which almost all knowledge depends" involve a "step taken by the mind" on the basis of custom or habit, "a principle of human nature" (pp. 41–3). These operations of the mind "are a species of natural instincts," an "instinct or mechanical tendency"; thus they are "unavoidable" when the mind is placed in certain circumstances (pp. 46–7, 55).

Throughout, Hume takes himself to be studying the relation of knowledge to experience and the empirical principles that determine this relation. He observes that "though animals learn many parts of their knowledge from observation, there are also many parts of it, which they derive from the original hand of nature. . . . These we denominate Instincts." [50] Similarly, "the experimental reasoning itself, which we possess in common with beasts, and on which the whole conduct of life depends, is nothing but a species of instinct or mechanical power, that acts in us unknown to ourselves," undirected by our "intellectual faculties" (p. 108). By virtue of these instincts, experience "is the foundation of moral reasoning [which concerns "matter of fact and existence" (p. 35)], which forms the greater part of human knowledge" (p. 164).

Throughout, Hume is offering substantive proposals about questions that we surely regard as "scientific questions" (as he did too, it seems clear). He is discussing the instinctive foundations of knowledge (including unconscious and even

innate knowledge), surely an empirical matter, as he correctly understood the question.

Similarly Descartes could not have answered the question
whether he was a "scientist" or a "philosopher" in the sense
of these terms used by many contemporaries who restrict
philosophy to some kind of conceptual analysis. He was,
surely, both. His approach to innate ideas and mind is a
case in point. As a scientist, he thought he could explain
much of human behavior, and everything else, in terms of
mechanical principles. But 'he felt compelled to postulate
a second substance whose essence is thought to account for
observations about humans (himself and others). It is not
at all correct to assert, as many do, that his doctrine of innate ideas is an effort solely to account for "necessary
truths" as this notion is understood in contemporary discussion. Within the framework of a theory of innate ideas,
Descartes developed a theory of perception, for example,
but obviously his theory of perception or Cudworth's theory
of the "innate cognoscitive power," with its *Gestalt* properties and related structure, goes well beyond the domain
of necessary truths as understood at present—though it was
a different matter for the man who believed that he had
proved the existence of a God who is no deceiver and who
thus believed that he could show the necessity of all laws of
nature. Plainly Descartes's concept of "necessity" was quite
different, at least in presumed extension, from our own.

It is quite wrong to claim that the tradition was "paradigmatically philosophical" in its concerns,[51] at least if
"paradigmatically philosophical" is to be opposed to "scientific." Correspondingly, it seems to me entirely appropriate
to suggest the rational reconstructions R and E, as I have,
as expressions of some of the leading ideas of rationalist and
empiricist speculation on "the science of human nature,"
on acquisition of knowledge, on those parts of knowledge
derived from the original hand of nature, and so on. I have
repeatedly emphasized that R and E, as I have discussed

them, depart from some of the central ideas of the tradition (e.g., the belief that the contents of the mind are open to introspection); furthermore, these leading ideas often interpenetrate in the work of one person in complex ways, and we are under no compulsion to adhere strictly to one or the other framework (cf. Chomsky, 1965, 1966). But I do think that by sharpening these opposed conceptions and exploring them in the light of empirical research, we can move towards a solution to problems that can now sensibly be posed with regard to the nature and acquisition of cognitive structures. And at the same time, we can gain much insight into the reasons why earlier efforts have often gone astray.

Notes

Part I THE WHIDDEN LECTURES

Chapter 1. ON COGNITIVE CAPACITY

1. Aristotle, *Posterior Analytics* 2. 19 (ed. McKeon, 1941), pp. 184–6.
2. Cudworth (1838), p. 75. Except for those otherwise identified, quotations that follow in this paragraph are from the same source: respectively, pp. 65, 51, 49, 87, 122–3.
3. Leibniz, *Discourse on Metaphysics* (trans. Montgomery, 1902), p. 45. For a similar view, see Cudworth (1838), p. 64. For quotations and further discussion, see Chomsky (1966), § 4.
4. Cudworth, *True Intellectual System of the Universe*, cited by Lovejoy (1908).
5. Lovejoy (1908).
6. Henry More, "Antidote Against Atheism," cited by Lovejoy (1908).
7. Gregory (1970). Gregory suggests further that the grammar of language "has its roots in the brain's rules for ordering retinal patterns in terms of objects," that is, "in a take-over operation, in which man cashed in on" the development of the visual system in higher animals. This seems questionable. The structure, use, and acquisition of language seem to involve special properties that are, so far as is known, not found elsewhere. Language is based on properties of the dominant hemisphere that may also be quite specialized. There seems to be no obvious relationship to the structure of the visual cortex in relevant respects, though so little is known that one can only speculate. It is not clear why one should expect to find an evolutionary explanation of the sort that Gregory suggests. For more on these matters, see the chapters by R. W. Sperry, A. M. Liberman, H.-L. Teuber, and B. Milner in Schmitt and Worden (1974).
8. This view, popularized in recent years by B. F. Skinner, is foreign to science or any rational inquiry. The reasons for its popularity must be explained on extrascientific grounds. For

further discussion, see my "Psychology and Ideology," reprinted in Chomsky (1973b); also Chomsky (1973c); and the discussion of liberalism and empiricism in Bracken (1972, 1973a).

9. Antoine Arnauld (1964), p. 36. On the importance of considering "language as a biological phenomenon [comparable] to other biological phenomena" and some implications for epistemology and the philosophy of language and mind, see Moravcsik (1975b).

10. See, for example, the references of note 8. I return to the question in chapter 3.

11. Appropriateness is not to be confused with control, nor can the properties of language use noted here (what I have elsewhere called "the creative aspect of language use") be identified with the recursive property of grammars. Failure to keep these very different concepts separate has led to much confusion. For discussion of the creative aspect of language use in rationalist theory, see Chomsky (1966) and (1972a).

12. By LT I mean here the system of LT(O,D)'s, O fixed, D an arbitrary domain. In the terminology suggested, each LT(O,D) constructs a cognitive structure. Operating in concert and interaction, the LT(O,D)'s for given O form a cognitive state.

13. Hence I will not even raise the further question whether there is anything to say about M_2(CS, stimulus conditions), namely, a possible general mechanism ranging over cognitive states that might be called a "general theory of behavior."

14. See Eimas et al. (1971) and the references of note 7 above.

15. Thus we take cognitive capacity to be the set of such domains with whatever further structure this complex may have.

16. Consider the argument of Bourbaki that "as a matter of empirical fact, the bulk of mathematically significant notions can be analyzed profitably in terms of a few basic structures such as groups or topological spaces. They regard this fact as a discovery about our thinking . . ." (Kreisel, 1974).

17. Anthony Kenny, "The Origin of the Soul," in Kenny et al. (1973).

18. Imagine some hypothetical form of aphasia in which knowledge is unimpaired but all systems involving performance, i.e., putting knowledge to use, are destroyed. For discussion of this matter, see Stich (1972) and Chomsky and Katz (1974).

19. Thus my use of the term "cognitive capacity" (p. 21) might be misleading, though I have not found a term less likely to mislead.

20. I have discussed elsewhere why I think that modern criticisms of "Descartes's myth" by Ryle and others simply miss the point. Cf. Chomsky (1966), p. 12; (1972a), p. 13; (1975a).

21. On this matter, see chapter 4. Also, Chomsky (1972a), pp. 90ff.; (1971), pp. 20ff.

22. To avoid misunderstanding, I am not making the absurd suggestion that science should study what is familiar and commonplace rather than search for perhaps exotic data that shed light
on deeper principles. In the study of language no less than
physics, this would be a self-defeating program. Gross coverage
of familiar phenomena can be achieved by very different theories; it is generally necessary to seek unusual data to distinguish them. To cite an example, idioms in natural language
are (by definition) abnormal, but the capacity of various linguistic theories to deal with their character and peculiarities has
often proved quite relevant for distinguishing empirically
among these theories.

23. Note that the notions "fair" and "adequate" are yet to be made
precise, as biological properties of humans, though it is no great
problem to place some reasonable bounds.

Chapter 2. THE OBJECT OF INQUIRY

1. Interesting questions can be raised about just what kinds of
knowledge are involved in knowledge of language. For some
discussion, see chapter 4, pp. 162–6, and references cited there.

2. There is a valuable critical review of available evidence in
Fodor, Bever, and Garrett (1974). See also Fodor, Fodor, and
Garrett (forthcoming) for a discussion of the possible bearing of
such evidence on lexical decomposition.

   This is not the place to pursue the matter in detail, but some
of the argument in the former book relating to issues discussed
here is less than compelling. Thus, the authors consider an approach to LT(H,L) stipulating that the grammar acquired must
meet (at least) two conditions: conformity to UG and conformity to a data base consisting of phonetically represented
sentences. They argue (i) that the condition is not sufficient and
(ii) that a "paradox" prevents enrichment of the data base to
sufficiency. But (i), while perhaps true, follows only from unex-
pressed assumptions about the range of permitted grammars;
there is no difficulty in formulating constraints on UG sufficient
to rule out the alleged counterexamples cited, and they give no
general argument from which (i) follows. As for (ii), there is a
problem, but no paradox. Furthermore, the problem arises in
exactly the same form for any other theory of language learning. Hence I see no force to their strictures, apart from the observation, which is surely correct, that the theory they discuss is
far too weak as it stands.

3. Cf., e.g., Braine (1974). Braine asserts that theories of abstract

phonological representation require "assumptions about human memory and learning which are almost certainly wrong," and takes it to be "self-evident" that they impose an "extraordinary burden" on any acquisition theory. But the only thing that is certain, in this regard, is that little is known about human memory and learning that bears even remotely on the issue. Plainly, one can draw no conclusions from the lack of any substantive theory of memory or learning. As for the "extraordinary burden" imposed on a theory of acquisition, nothing can be said in the absence of significant psychological or neurological evidence on representation and acquisition of cognitive structures (apart from the abstract explanatory theories that have been offered and some suggestive experimental work of the sort discussed in Fodor, Bever, and Garrett [1974]). Braine's certainty about what is unknown reflects, once again, the dogmatism that has so impeded psychological theory in the past.

4. Cf. Kramer, Koff, and Luria (1972) for some interesting and relevant data. Furthermore, the knowledge of language attained by an individual in a real speech community is far more complex than under the idealization that we are considering, involving many styles of speech and possibly a range of interacting grammars. The real-world complexity deserves study, and it is reasonable to assume that such study will make essential use of the results obtained under the idealization. Evidently, the real-world complexity gives no reason to doubt the legitimacy of the idealization.

5. Such taxonomies can be of considerable interest, despite their limitations. See, e.g., Austin (1962), Vendler (1967), Fraser (1974), Searle (1975).

6. On some similar notions in comparative ethology, see Chomsky (1972a), pp. 05ff., chapter 0 below, pp. 120–4.

7. Antoine Le Grand, *An Entire Body of Philosophy, According to the Principles of the Famous Renate Des Cartes*, cited in Watson (1968).

8. See the references of note 7, chapter 1. Also Wood et al. (1971), where it is reported that "different neural events occur in the left hemisphere during analysis of linguistic versus nonlinguistic parameters of the same acoustic signal," and the further work reported in Wood (1973). For more on these matters, see Lenneberg (1967), Millikan and Darley (1967), and Whitaker (1971).

9. Cf. chapter 4, note 14. See also the report of experiments by E. H. Lenneberg on training of normal humans by techniques used with chimpanzees, in Ettlinger et al. (1975). Cf. Fodor, Bever, and Garrett (1974), pp. 440–62, for a review of the whole issue.

10. Assuming now that Quine's suggestive metaphor ("Two Dog-
    mas of Empiricism," reprinted in Quine [1953]) can be developed
    into a substantive theory. His own efforts in this direction seem
    to me to raise more problems than they solve. See chapter 4 and
    references cited there.
11. See Putnam (1962, 1975). Also Kripke (1972). For critical
    analysis of some of these notions, see Dummett, (1973), chap. 5,
    appendix; also Katz (1975). For criticism of the notion "seman-
    tic representation" from still other points of view, see Fodor,
    Fodor, and Garrett (forthcoming) and Harman (1973).
12. Katz (1972) and earlier work cited there.
13. That is, under idealizations that seem to me legitimate, if not es-
    sential, for serious study of the real-world problems.
14. Even if the semantic content of a lexical item is not fully spec-
    ified by the grammar, there might still be some analytic con-
    nections. Thus, it has been plausibly suggested that such lexical
    properties as abstract "cause," "becoming," "agency," and "goal"
    are drawn from a universal set of semantic markers, available
    for semantic representation in the lexicon. If so, then even if
    such words as, say, "persuade" and "intend" are not fully
    characterized by the grammar in isolation from other cognitive
    structures, it might still be true that the connection between "I
    persuaded him to leave" and "he intends to leave" (with ap-
    propriate temporal qualifications) is analytic, by virtue of the
    substructure of lexical features and their general properties.
        One might compare the lexical properties that have been
    utilized in semantic description with Leibniz's "simpler terms,"
    by which other terms can be defined. For some discussion, cf.
    Ishiguro (1972), pp. 44ff.
15. Cf. Chomsky (1965), chap. 1. As noted there, an evaluation pro-
    cedure is required in what we have been calling LT(H,L) if
    the compatibility conditions are insufficient to narrow the class
    of grammars considered to be the one (or ones) learned. If
    further devices for grammar selection can be devised, an evalu-
    ation procedure will be an essential part of LT(H,L) or not,
    depending, again, on the variability in the class of grammars
    meeting other conditions in this theory. Some have argued that
    more is at stake here, but I fail to see any issue.
16. A view of this sort is attributed to Leibniz by Ishiguro (1972),
    pp. 65ff. She argues that in Leibniz's theory, "the individuation
    of objects and the understanding of satisfaction-conditions for
    predicates already involve a great number of assumptions about
    laws of nature. . . ."
17. On this matter, see Kripke (1972).
18. Cf. Dummett (1973), p. 76: "in order to understand a proper
    name, we must know what sort or category of object it is to

be used as the name of." Cf. Kripke (1972), n. 58, for comments on a similar notion of Geach's.

19. Examples from Kripke (1972), pp. 268ff. As Kripke points out, "the question of essential properties so-called . . . is equivalent . . . to the question of identity across possible worlds," and thus enters into the question of applicability of model-theoretic semantics to the study of semantics of natural language. Kripke argues that the idea "that a property can be held to be essential or accidental to an object independently of its description" is not a philosopher's invention, but an idea that has "intuitive content" to "the ordinary man." While his examples and discussion do, surely, have intuitive force, it is less clear that they pertain to the question of properties essential to an object independently of its description or categorization. It seems to me that they do not suffice to establish the plausibility of this idea.

20. On this matter, see Quine (1969c), p. 343.

21. See the references of note 11.

22. I follow here the exposition in Moravcsik (1975a).

23. Kripke cites substance, origin, function ("being a table"—compare Aristotle's characterization of the "essence of a house" in terms of "purpose or end," as contrasted with the physicist's description in material terms; *De Anima* 403ᵇ). Cf. note 14.

24. Moravcsik argues that this is the proper generalization for the Aristotelian notion "*x* is the aitia (cause) of *y*."

25. Cf. Miller (1974). Miller contrasts some of Quine's empiricist speculations on the learning of color terms by conditioning with the actual "conceptual development," which appears to follow a very different course, involving, not conditioning at some "primitive stage," but rather the abstraction of the domain of color, the employment of an innate system of "focal colors," and the location of other colors relative to these in the linguistically determined system. There are, Miller suggests, two "lines of development": "One involves learning to abstract the appropriate attribute and to anchor color perceptions to some internal frame of reference, the other involves discovering which words are relevant to that frame and learning which location in the frame goes with which term." Miller's analysis seems quite compatible with the general account we have been considering.

26. The belief that cognitive structures must be taught as well as learned is so widespread that citation is hardly necessary. To mention only the most recent example that I happen to have seen, D. D. Weiss (1975) argues that "we are so equipped that we can *inherit* [the complex skills and achievements which constitute the entire edifice of civilization], but only by means of *communication*—through teaching, instruction." For some fur-

ther examples on teaching of language, see notes 38 and 39 below, and chapter 4, pp. 161–2.

27. Searle (1972). While I disagree with some of Searle's conclusions, as indicated below, the bulk of his account seems to me accurate and compelling, including many of the critical comments. D. M. Armstrong (1971) suggests that the theory that communication provides "*the* clue to an analysis of the notion of linguistic meaning" can be traced to Locke.

28. Cf., e.g., Chomsky (1957), chap. 9; Chomsky (1975b).

29. Cf. references of preceding note. Also Miller and Chomsky (1963); Chomsky (1965), chaps. 1, 4; and many other references. I am sure that the same observation holds of others who have sought "essential properties" of language in its structural features. Thus A. M. Liberman (1974) suggests "that the distinctive characteristic of language is not meaning, thought, communication, or vocalization, but, more specifically, a grammatical recoding that reshapes linguistic information so as to fit it to the several originally nonlinguistic components of the system." But he would no doubt agree that there are intimate connections between structure and function. How could this fail to be true? Who has ever doubted it?

30. Chomsky (1966); also Chomsky (1964), chap. 1.

31. Cf. chapter 1, note 7, for a possible example.

32. Moravcsik (1975a) argues that "for Aristotle functional differences can never be ultimate; they must be shown to be dependent on constitutive or structural differences." He suggests further that the Aristotelian principle that functional explanation is derivative in this sense "has crucial bearings on explanations" in the social sciences. "Ultimately linguistic dispositions need be explained in terms of the structure of mind and brain. This is already clear in biology. Nobody would try to account for the details of human anatomy in terms of adaptation-value or survival-value. . . ." This seems quite correct.

33. Stampe (1968). Stampe offers a general argument against "the search for the nature of meanings." He holds that a person who believes that meanings are entities of some sort is committed to the view that in the sentence "the meaning of x is obscure," the phrase "the meaning of x" is a referring expression, so that the sentence means "the y which is the meaning of x is obscure." He argues that this conclusion leads to absurdity; there is no entity y which is obscure. But the argument is not very compelling. Someone might take the phrase "the source of the earth's light" to be a referring expression, but not in the sentence "the source of the earth's light is obscure" (the sun is not obscure). Similarly, one might argue that there is a y such that y is the number of the planets, but deny that "the number of the planets" is a referring expression in "the number of the

planets is unknown" (9 is not unknown). It might be argued that such expressions as "the number of the planets" are not referring expressions in any context; for some interesting observations on this matter, see Higgins (1973), chap. 5. It would be rash to argue, on these grounds, that it is incoherent to postulate the existence of numbers. Philosophers who have postulated the existence of meanings do so in the belief that they can construct a successful explanatory theory in these terms. This belief, right or wrong, seems immune to the kinds of argument that Stampe develops.

34. Whether there is indeed a "circularity," as alleged, is another question. Searle's criticisms are really directed against Katz's semantic theory, though Katz is barely mentioned. But Katz has argued that there is no circularity (Katz 1972, 1975). Searle does not explain why he thinks that Katz's argument fails. See now Katz's critique of Searle, and his attempt to incorporate a theory of speech acts within a "semantic theory" of the sort he has developed. (Katz, forthcoming.)

35. The expectation was only partially correct. Twenty years after completion, parts of that manuscript are now in press (Chomsky, 1955–6).

36. Note that all of these are cases in which the "utterer" assumes that there is no audience. Armstrong (1971) states that an analysis of meaning in terms of communication need not require that the speaker definitely believes there is an audience (or even cares), but "clearly he cannot believe that there definitely is no audience," as in these and indefinitely many other cases. If he is correct, then the analysis of meaning in terms of communication that he outlines is impossible for this reason alone.

37. The question is taken up again by Schiffer (1972), pp. 76ff. He considers the case of someone writing with no thought of a potential audience and argues that it seems "essential" to such examples that the "utterer" has the intention "to *provide himself* with various arguments, explanations, etc." Thus, "in each case where it is both the case that we are inclined to say that S meant that p by uttering x and that S apparently had no audience-directed intention, S's utterance x will be part of some activity directed towards securing some cognitive response in himself, and that it is in virtue of this significant resemblance to the standard case that we class these cases as instances of S-meaning." But in the standard case, the "cognitive response" in the hearer is that he is to believe something about the beliefs of the speaker. Thus if we are to assimilate the present case to the standard case, as Schiffer suggests, it would seem that we would be taking "S meant that p by uttering x" to mean that S uttered x with the intention of bringing himself to believe that he believes that p. But this is surely far from

the mark. Furthermore, in perfectly normal cases, S may have no thought of his own possible later use of what he writes (and certainly need not when he speaks or thinks in words). It seems that all of this gets us nowhere.

38. For discussion of certain notions developed in the later work of Wittgenstein, which Strawson takes to be one source for the theory of communication-intention, see Chomsky (1964), p. 24, and (1969b), pp. 275ff. The latter discussion contains some explicit and important qualifications that have been ignored by several critics who argue that it gives an inaccurate account of Wittgenstein's general picture. As it stands, dealing with the particular questions it does, the discussion seems to me entirely accurate. On this matter, see also Moravcsik (1967), pp. 227–9 (which also contains some relevant remarks on speech-act theory).

39. Strawson adopts without comment the common assumption, mentioned earlier, that language must be not only learned but also taught. He writes that "it is a fact about human beings that they simply would not acquire mastery [of a language] unless they were exposed, as children, to conditioning or training by adult members of a community." He assumes that the "procedure of training" is guided by a concern for the ends and purposes of language. For the learners, it is "a matter of responding vocally to situations in a way which will earn them reward or avoid punishment rather than a matter of *expressing their beliefs*." There is no reason to believe that these factual claims are true.

40. Actually, some other arguments are offered, but they are unconvincing. Thus Strawson asks why, on the semantic theorist's grounds, a person should observe his own rules, or any rules: "Why shouldn't he express any belief he likes in any way he happens to fancy when he happens to have the urge to express it?" Suppose, Strawson argues, that the semantic theorist were to respond that the person wishes to record his beliefs for later reference. Strawson argues that "the theorist is debarred from giving this answer because it introduces, though in an attenuated form, the concept of communication-intention: the earlier man communicates with his later self." But the whole discussion is beside the point. There are two questions: (i) What is the nature of the "meaning-determining rules"? (ii) Why does a person follow the rules that he has (somehow) acquired? Conceivably the answer to (ii) involves reference to communication-intention, but it would not follow that "communication-intention" enters in any way into the explanation of meaning and how it is determined by rule (question (i)). Furthermore, it would suffice for the semantic theorist to respond to (ii) by asserting that it is simply a natural law that a person tends to follow the

rules he has learned. The answer is uninteresting, but not incorrect, for this reason.

41. Grice (1968). This is the only article by Grice that Strawson specifically cites, and it presumably is (at least a part of) what he has in mind in referring to Grice's work as giving reason to believe that a theory of communication-intention can be developed "which is proof against objection and which does not presuppose the notion of linguistic meaning."

42. For a criticism of Grice's theory along partly similar lines, see Ziff (1967).

Chapter 3. SOME GENERAL FEATURES OF LANGUAGE

1. See Chomsky (1972b), chap. 3; also several chapters in Parret (1974). Much of what I will describe here recapitulates or is an outgrowth of ideas presented in Chomsky (1973a). See Postal (1974a) for a critique of the latter, and Lightfoot (forthcoming) for an argument, which I think is correct, that the critique is beside the point, quite apart from questions of truth and falsity. The debate, of course, continues, and there is more that I would like to say about it, but this is not the place.

2. Less so than generally believed, I think. Several positions have emerged, but their proponents differ not only on some substantive issues but also on what the issues are. Consider just three positions: the "standard theory" (ST), the "extended standard theory" (EST), and "generative semantics" (GS). Proponents of GS generally take the major bifurcation to be between ST-EST and GS, and argue that a great deal is at stake. But many proponents of ST and EST, myself included, have argued that the central substantive issue of theory is the one that divides ST from EST-GS (namely, the role of surface structures in semantic interpretation), and that GS differs from EST primarily in that it relaxes some of the conditions on grammars imposed by EST. Part of the confusion of recent debate perhaps results from quite different perceptions as to what the issues are. For further discussion, see the references of the preceding note.

3. On this matter, see Aronoff (forthcoming).

4. Cf. Chomsky (1965), and for a summary, Chomsky (1972a), chap. 5. The rules that insert lexical items are "transformations" in the technical sense that they take into account global properties of the phrase markers to which they apply. But these lexical transformations have distinct properties not shared by operations of the transformational component of the grammar.

5. On the rules and principles that assign phonetic representa-

tions to syntactic structures and the phonological elements that appear in them, see Chomsky and Halle (1968), Bresnan (1973b), and many other sources.

6. Cf. Aronoff (forthcoming). On the structure of the categorial component, see Chomsky (1972), chap. 1, and further work by Dougherty, Bresnan, Jackendoff, Selkirk, Milner, Vergnaud, Halitsky, Siegel, and others.

7. Essentially, the theory outlined in Katz and Postal (1964) and Chomsky (1965). Cf. Katz (1972) for a recent version.

8. My own version of the standard theory was qualified in that I suggested that some aspects of meaning are determined by surface structure. By the time that Chomsky (1965) appeared, I had become convinced that this was true to a significant extent, in part, on the basis of work by Jackendoff.

9. On this matter, cf. Jackendoff (1972), Chomsky (1972a,b), and many other sources.

10. For some further discussion of this question, see Chomsky (1969c), reprinted in Chomsky (1972a).

11. On reasons for supposing that indefinites underlie such questions, see Chomsky (1964), Postal (1965). Note that the present discussion is misleading in that it overlooks the fact that the phrase markers in question are abstract structures ultimately mapped into sentences, and not sentences themselves.

12. Here and in subsequent discussion, I overlook distinctions between "who"–"whom," and other questions of morphology.

13. A transformation may in fact apply nonvacuously to only a subpart of a cyclic category. Williams (1974) suggests that transformations with smaller domains, in this sense, apply prior to those with larger domains, thus generalizing the notion of cyclic application. If this theory is correct, then the significance of what we are designating here "cyclic categories" lies in their role in determining conditions on application of rules (i.e., with regard to subjacency, "command" in anaphora, etc.).

14. Ross (1967) hypothesizes that rightward-movement rules are "bounded" in this sense. I will assume, with Ross, that this is correct. An apparent counterexample in Navajo is presented in Kaufman (1975). Her analysis, which deals with movement of an enclitic to what she assumes to be a complementizer position, suggests that Ross's principle and the more general condition of subjacency discussed here must be qualified somehow. One can think of various possibilities, but pending further study, I will simply leave the question open.

15. This analysis derives from Rosenbaum (1967). I follow here a reanalysis by Bresnan (1972).

16. Following Bresnan (1972), we assume that there are underlying structures corresponding to (i) "it is certain (probable) that John will win," and (ii) "Y is certain [John to win]," but not (iii)

"Y is probable [John to win]." The examples (ï) do not undergo NP-preposing for quite general reasons.

17. I omit an illustrative example, since more complex issues arise that I do not want to pursue here.

18. Examples of this sort were originally discussed in Baker (1970), in a somewhat different system.

19. For one possible explanation, see Chomsky (1973a). For others, see references cited there.

20. On this matter, see Emonds (forthcoming), Bresnan (1972), Chomsky (1973a), and Vergnaud (1974).

21. We might ask why (13″) cannot be derived directly from (13), since there would be no violation of subjacency. There are, I think, good reasons, based on other conditions on transformations. Cf. Chomsky (1973a), and also the discussion below of the specified subject condition, which guarantees that the operation will always be performed on the "minimal domain," in an appropriate sense.

22. On this matter, see Erteschik (1973).

23. Suppose that in (16) we replace "believe" by "consider" and "claim" by "question." Then we can derive "John considered the question who Tom saw." Cf. Chomsky (1973a). We omit here consideration of "echo questions" such as "John believed that Mary said that Tom saw *who*?" or "John believed the claim that Tom saw *who*?"

24. Suppose that in (16) we replace "believe" by "make." Then in place of (16′) we would have "who did John make the claim that Tom saw?" Many speakers find this much more acceptable than (16′). A plausible explanation is that "make the claim" is reanalyzed by a rule of idiom formation as a complex verb meaning, essentially, "claim," so that—after the reanalysis—subjacency is not violated by application of *wh*-movement. On the other hand, there is no such reanalysis possible in the case of "believe the claim."

25. Cf. Ross (1967). For discussion, see Chomsky (1973a). The latter assumed that subjacency is applicable only to extraction rules and does not apply to rules lowering elements into embedded cyclic categories, deletion rules, or interpretive rules. A problem in the proposed explanation for certain island constraints is that these also appear to hold, in some cases at least, for rules that might be taken to be deletion or interpretive rules. On this matter, see the discussion of "comparative deletion" in Chomsky (1973a), Vergnaud (1974), and Bresnan (1975). Also, Postal (1974b), M. Liberman (1974), Liberman and Prince (forthcoming). My own belief is that the explanation offered in Chomsky (1973a) and here will prove to be a subcase of something more general. On subjacency, see also Akmajian (1975).

26. Cf. Chomsky (1973a). See also references of note 1.

27. As noted in Chomsky (1973a), pronominal anaphora violates these principles. The violation was taken there to pose a problem, but further reflection shows that it does not. Pronominal anaphora belongs to an entirely different system of rules involving quite different conditions (e.g., command), not statable in the theory of transformations at all, and not even restricted to sentence grammar. There is, in fact, a rather natural analysis of rules into several categories in terms of their position in the system of linguistic rules and the conditions that apply to them. For some discussion, see below, pp. 104–5.

28. It remains to explain just what this phrase means, how it functions in inference, etc. This poses an interesting problem of descriptive semantics, which I will not explore further here.

29. On this matter, see Jackendoff (1972), Chomsky (1972b), and references cited there.

30. Recall that we are taking sentence to be analyzed as COMP S_{red}; cf. p. 88, above. I have eliminated from consideration the root transformation of subject-auxiliary inversion, for ease of exposition.

31. There is, I think, independent motivation for the assumption that the general principles of anaphora apply to logical forms rather than to surface structures directly, but I will not pursue this interesting question here.

32. Cf. Chomsky (1973a). Also chapter 4, p. 150, (7).

33. In (29), the rule is blocked not only by the specified-subject condition, but also (independently) by what is called the "tensed-sentence condition" in Chomsky (1973a).

34. I assume here an abstract notion of "subject" in accordance with which "Bill" is the subject of the embedded sentences of (29)–(30) and also of the noun phrase "Bill's hatred of each other" in (31). Cf. Chomsky (1972b), chaps. 1, 3.

35. A special case of bound anaphora is reflexivization, as persuasively argued by Helke (1970). For a theory of anaphora of the sort discussed imprecisely here, cf. Lasnik (1974) and Reinhart (1974). For general discussion of related problems, see Fauconnier (1974) and Wasow (1972, forthcoming), and references cited in these works, particularly Dougherty (1969).

36. Cf. Keenan and Comrie (1973), for discussion of a general notion of "precedence" of grammatical relations and its role in determining the domain of syntactic rules. Ross has discussed a related notion of "primacy" in unpublished papers.

37. Cf. Fiengo (1974), where there is also a more detailed discussion of other topics touched on here.

38. On the general notion "anaphora," see the references cf note 35.

39. To forestall an irrelevancy, there is no "clause-mate condition" on the rule that relates reciprocals to their antecedents. Cf. Chomsky (1973a). Thus the alleged existence of a rule raising

embedded subjects to the object position in the matrix sentence is beside the point. Cf. references of note 1.

40. Cf. Chomsky (1965), chap. 1, and earlier references cited there.

41. Emonds has argued that a different rule of NP-preposing is involved (cf. Emonds, forthcoming), noting that there are differences in the domain of the rule. Thus NP-preposing applies to the noun phrase "the lecture yesterday," giving "yesterday's lecture," but not to the sentence "he lectured yesterday," giving "yesterday was lectured by him." I think that in many cases, perhaps all, the discrepancies can be attributed to other factors. Thus, as noted before, the subject-predicate relation is defined on surface structures of sentences (but not noun phrases), and it might be plausibly argued that "was lectured (by NP)" is not a possible predicate of "yesterday," accounting for the ungrammaticalness. On the question whether the deviance of the sentence in question is "semantic" or "syntactic" in origin, cf. p. 95 above and the reference cited there. Note that we have not accounted for the possessive in (50iii); on this matter, see Siegel (1974).

42. I deal here only with the simplest case. For a more general discussion, see Fiengo (1974).

43. There are many similar examples in which NP-preposing applies to structures reanalyzed by idiom-formation rules, which assign phrases to the category Verb: e.g., "the argument was taken exception to," "John was taken advantage of," etc. Naturally, these vary in acceptability. See also note 24.

 In ordinary passives such as (55), the rule of NP-preposing disregards the grammatical relation between the verb and the NP following it, at least if we use the term "grammatical relation" in something like its traditional sense. Thus in (55), the rule moves the direct object, but in such cases as "John was told to leave" or "John was promised that he would get the job," it is the indirect object that is preposed (cf. "John was told a story," "a story was told to John"; "our promise to John . . . ," not "our promise of John . . ."; compare also "John was told about the accident," or simply, "John was told."). Thus, it comes as no surprise that in (57), for example, the rule of NP-preposing applies to an NP that bears no grammatical relation to the preceding verb at all. For discussion, cf. Chomsky (1973a) and references of note 1 above. Some of the discussion of this matter in recent literature is misleading in that it fails to make clear that there is general agreement that the rule in question is not limited to direct objects, where the notion "direct object" is understood in the conventional way.

44. Examples that come to mind are the (possible) rules that relate causatives to corresponding intransitives (e.g., "X broke the glass," "the glass broke"; "X melted the wax," "the wax melted";

cf. Fiengo [1974] for discussion) and the so-called rule of "tough-movement" relating "John was easy to please" and "*X* was easy to please John" (it is argued in Lasnik and Fiengo [1974] that the rule of "tough-movement" in fact deletes, rather than moves, the embedded object, but their arguments apply only to an analysis within the standard theory; cf. Jackendoff [forthcoming]).

45. Cf. Aronoff (forthcoming). Another significant phenomenon motivating a passive rule in English but not in many other languages—e.g., those of the type discussed here—is the application of NP-preposing to "idiom chunks," as in "tabs were kept on them" (for some discussion of cases where this is and is not possible, see Fiengo [1974]), and to noun phrases that do not ordinarily appear in comparable subject positions, e.g., "a man was found to do the job."

46. This fact, surely crucial in the analysis of passives, is discussed extensively in the earliest work on transformational generative grammar; cf. Chomsky (1955). See now Fiengo (1974).

47. Cf. Chomsky (1972b), chap. 3. Cf. also Katz (1972) and references cited there for discussion of thematic relations within the framework of the standard theory. On the issue in general, see Jackendoff (1969, 1972, 1974a).

48. Cf. the discussion of indirect questions in Chomsky (1973a); also Jackendoff (1975). In work within the extended standard theory in which relative clauses are derived by raising of an embedded NP to the antecedent position (eg., Vergnaud, 1974), it was necessary to assume that some grammatical relations that enter into determination of thematic relations are defined, not in deep structure, but at the point of first appearance of lexical items in the relevant position in the cycle. This and some other problems involving cyclic determination of thematic relations are overcome under the trace theory.

49. See my comments in Parret (1974). It is occasionally noted in the literature that theories that do not use global rules employ instead certain syntactic features to deal with such phenomena as agreement, and it is further argued that use of "arbitrary syntactic features" also gives an undesired extension of descriptive power, perhaps even more so than global rules. It is unclear what the relevance of these observations may be, since no one has proposed the use of "arbitrary syntactic features," but rather of narrowly restricted and quite well-motivated ones.

50. For discussion, see Wexler, Culicover, and Hamburger (1974) and work surveyed there.

51. For example, in Piaget's theory of developmental stages. The empirical status of Piaget's theories is controversial. For varying assessments, see Bergling (1974) and Bryant (1974).

52. On Lorenz's views in this connection, see Chomsky (1972a), p.

95. For some discussion of similar conclusions of Monod's, see Chomsky (1971), pp. 13ff.

53. Stent (1975). His argument is not unlike the conjecture in chapter 1, p. 25, that the study of M_{CS} might not fall within the science-forming capacity.

54. On this matter, see Chomsky (1969d) and Chomsky (1973b), chap. 7.

55. For some remarks on these relations, see Chomsky (1972a), pp. 97–8. Cf. Wang (1974), pp. 324ff., for some discussion of Gödel's views on the limitations on mechanistic explanations in biology. It is worth noting that his speculations on this matter, as Wang reports them, do not derive from his mathematical work, which has sometimes been invoked by others in an effort to establish similar conclusions.

56. On the collapse of liberal doctrine in the nineteenth century, cf. Polanyi (1957) and Rocker (1938). For a fuller discussion of my own views on the matters discussed here, cf. Chomsky (1969d), chap. 1; Chomsky (1973b), chaps. 8, 9.

57. On this matter, see Macpherson (1962).

58. Kant, "An Answer to the Question 'What is Enlightenment?' " in Reiss (1970), p. 59. Once "this germ . . . has developed within this hard shell, it gradually reacts upon the mentality of the people, who thus gradually become increasingly able to *act freely.*"

59. Cf. references of note 56 and elsewhere.

60. Bakunin, "The International and Karl Marx." Dolgoff (1972), p. 319. The other remarks of Bakunin cited will also be found here. For further discussion of such views and the various forms they have taken, and the realization of some of these prophetic insights, see Chomsky (1973b, c).

61. The terms are Humboldt's. Cf. Chomsky (1973b), chap. 9.

Part II

Chapter 4. PROBLEMS AND MYSTERIES IN THE STUDY OF HUMAN LANGUAGE

1. To be more precise, advocates of these notions often do not formulate them with sufficient clarity so that there could be disconfirming evidence, and in the face of examples such as (1)–(4) simply reiterate their hypothesis that some adequate theory can be developed along the lines they advocate. Such a "hypothesis" is not to be confused with explanatory hypotheses such as S might propose to account for certain facts; the term "prayer" might be more fitting than "hypothesis." Note that suspension

of judgment with respect to apparently intractable evidence is a reasonable, in fact necessary, stance in rational inquiry, but there comes a point when it becomes irrational, particularly when alternative and more adequate theories are available. It seems to me that in this case the point was reached long ago.

2. I emphasize, *as presented.* There are many articles in the literature discussing beliefs attributed to me that I do not hold, have never expressed, and have repeatedly rejected. For discussion of a few recent examples, see Chomsky and Katz (1974, 1975); Chomsky (1974, 1975a).

3. Care should be distinguished from training. Thus certain kinds of human interaction are no doubt necessary for innate mechanisms to operate, but it does not follow that this interaction constitutes teaching or training, or that it determines the character of the systems acquired. Cf. Chomsky (1965), chap. 1, §8, for discussion of this and related problems, and discussion of the alternatives I am referring to here as R and E.

4. Again, more complex versions are possible. S might be led to conclude that there are stages of maturation through which P develops, and perhaps that experience is necessary for this succession to take place, or perhaps even that variety of experience may affect the stages achieved. I will put aside these quite realistic possibilities and consider here the case of learning as an "instantaneous process." As contrasted with the earlier idealizations suggested, this one is distorting and illegitimate—there might be no answer to the questions raised. But at the present stage of our understanding, I think we can still continue profitably to accept it as a basis for investigation. Cf. chapter 3, pp. 119–22.

Peters (1972a) discusses this idealization, arguing that it is not illegitimate. But his discussion fails to distinguish two notions of "input data" for a "language-acquisition device." He takes these data to be structured and organized by earlier analysis—thus his "projection problem" is concerned with the moment of attainment of grammar, all preliminary hypotheses and stages being incorporated into the input data. In this formulation the idealization is not illegitimate. But in the work he is discussing, the input data were taken as an unstructured set (for reasons which I will not discuss here). Thus the idealization is illegitimate, as observed by those who proposed the idealization and those who criticized it.

5. We can, of course, trivialize the learning theory that takes these notions to be fundamental by defining "analogy" and "generalization" in terms of the postulated schematism and evaluation procedure. But I will here take this alternative theory to be a substantive one, which specifies these notions in some nontrivial way, say, in terms of similarity along certain presupposed di-

mensions or replacement in a given substitution class. There are many interesting problems here that would take the discussion too far afield, but that might be pursued with profit.

6. Cf. Jackendoff (1969, 1972) and Chomsky (1972b). Jackendoff (1972) contains a particularly interesting discussion of how control is determined by thematic relations. For a modification of this view in terms of the trace theory of movement rules, see chapter 3.

7. Recall also the effect of replacing "their wives" by "their children" in (3). Cf. Dougherty (1968, 1970, 1971, 1974) and Fiengo and Lasnik (1973) for discussion of the syntax and semantics of these constructions.

8. On the functioning of this rule, first noted by Postal, see Chomsky (1973a). It is immaterial here whether we interpret the rule as requiring disjoint reference or as assigning a preference to it. The disjoint-reference property is actually more general, as noted in Chomsky (1973a).

9. This conclusion is rejected by Beloff (1973, p. 185), on the following grounds: "No doubt one could easily think up dozens of bizarre rules about which one could confidently say that they would not be found in any known language, just as one could easily think up dozens of bizarre customs that would never be found in any known society, but does this mean that we are forced to postulate inborn universals?" Taking the answer to the latter question to be no, Beloff concludes that nothing much follows from the absence of such "bizarre rules" as the structure-independent hypothesis 1 of chapter 1, in natural languages. Analysis of his argument reveals a number of confusions that are, as will be seen below, typical of much discussion. Consider first the conclusion: We are not "forced" to postulate inborn universals. This is true, but irrelevant. Data never force us to a specific nontrivial explanatory theory. The question is whether rational inquiry leads us (not forces us) to postulate inborn universals to explain the facts in question. Second, consider his assumption that hypothesis 1 is "bizarre" as compared with the structure-dependent hypothesis 2. By what standards? Surely not any general considerations of simplicity or naturalness. As noted in chapter 1, such considerations would lead to choice of the structure-independent hypothesis 1. To say that this rule is "bizarre" for humans is simply to rephrase the observation that humans select structure-dependent rules. It is at this point that rational inquiry begins, seeking to discover what properties of the organism or its experience explain particular observations. The same would be true in the case of "bizarre" customs. Contrary to what Beloff seems to be saying, systematic absence of "bizarre" customs or rules always requires explanation. Sometimes uninteresting properties of organisms

may suffice to explain the phenomenon, in which case it will be dismissed as unimportant. The example in question cannot be dismissed in this way. To say that rules or customs are "bizarre" (even if correct, as it is not in this case) is simply to stop short of the only interesting questions. An explanation is required, if not in terms of inborn universals, then in some other way. I should add that Beloff's treatment of these questions is one of the best I know in a text of this sort.

10. Cf. Greenfield, Nelson, and Saltzman (1972) for an attempt to pursue this possibility.

11. There presumably are elements of P relating to identification of distinctive features, rhythmic and intonational features, and so on. Possibly these are analogous in their function to analyzing mechanisms of other perceptual and learning systems.

12. It is not obvious that the results of conditioning experiments in humans really do establish what they claim. In an extensive analysis of the literature, William Brewer (forthcoming) suggests that in fact they do not. Rather, where the experimental paradigm permits investigation of the question, it seems that the conditioning procedures generally amount to no more than a complicated device for providing the human subject with information that he uses, consciously, in responding to the instructions—which explains why a simple instruction may suffice for "extinction." See also Estes (1972) for rather similar suggestions, based on experiments designed to examine this question.

13. A demonstration of this sort is given, in effect, by Patrick Suppes for his theory of stimulus sampling. Cf. Suppes (1969). Suppes takes this result to be evidence in support of his theory. This curious conclusion can perhaps be traced to a serious misunderstanding of the issues that are at stake in the study of learning, discussed by Pylyshyn (1973).

14. We cannot attribute the differences between rat and human in this respect simply to sensory processing abilities; thus rats have sensory modalities that could be used, in principle, for language. Recent attempts to teach symbolic systems to apes might give insights into the differential abilities of apes and humans with respect to the language faculty. One suggestive study indicates that global aphasics with left-hemisphere damage and severely impaired language ability are trainable by the methods used in the experiments with apes (Glass, Gazzaniga, and Premack, 1973). Further work along such lines might be revealing in determining the specific properties of neural structures (e.g., lateralization) that presumably explain the qualitative differences between humans and other organisms in ability to attain cognitive structures. It is perhaps of some interest that the only known example of lateralization outside of humans is a case

of control of a song in one species of songbird (Nottebohm, 1970).

15. For an unusually sophisticated account, which nevertheless seems to me to suffer from a qualified version of this misleading formulation, see Reber (1973).

16. Alston (1963). Alston seems to accept at least this part of an argument for "use-analysis" that he discusses.

17. At this point, the analogy should not be pressed too far. Thus the relation between my pressing the accelerator and the car's moving is explicable in terms of known physical laws, and there seems no reason to doubt that attainment of knowledge of language is within the potential range of that part of natural science that is well understood. But it is an open question whether the same is true of language use.

18. Ultimately. It is never easy to tell when apparent counterevidence should lead to abandonment of a theory. S might attribute to his subject several systems of belief, which may lead to inconsistent beliefs. This raises problems that I will not attempt to explore here.

19. Again, familiar and inescapable contingencies of empirical inquiry should be noted. There is no guarantee that the best theory constructed on the basis of such data as (1)–(13) will be correct; consideration of broader data (in this case, data of performance) might indicate that what appeared to be genuine explanatory principles are spurious and that generalizations discovered are accidental. Investigation of the theory of performance might thus lead to different theories of competence. No problems of principle arise here, though the matter has sometimes been discussed as though they do. I return to examples below. For an account that seems to me generally accurate and perceptive, see Pylyshyn (1973).

20. On the possibility of an explication in terms of "knowing how," see Chomsky (1975a).

21. For argument in support of this decision, see Graves, Katz, et al. (1973).

22. Schwartz (1969). Cf. also Goodman (1969) for some similar remarks, and my comments in Chomsky (1975a). Compare Schwartz's correct but wholly irrelevant observation with Beloff's remark that the data do not "force" us to a specific conclusion (see note 9).

23. For debate over these issues, see the references of note 7. For another example, see Jackendoff (1974b).

24. Quine seems to be assuming that some existing systems of grammar might "guide" Danish speakers of English who have learned English from these rules. But Quine's statement that actual grammars "really fall short . . . at some points" is a vast understatement. Furthermore, there is no reason to believe that a

person could consciously master a grammar as a guide to behavior, in Quine's sense. Rather, people learn language from pedagogic grammars by the use of their unconscious universal grammar (and for all we know, this may be unavoidable in principle). Thus no speaker of Danish has to learn from a book that (14) is not the question associated with (16), or that English sentences such as (1)–(13) have the properties determined by SSC. And were they to be made conscious of principles that lead to these results, there is little doubt that these principles could not be consciously applied, in real time, to "guide" performance.

25. For discussion, see Chomsky, Halle, Lukoff (1956); Chomsky and Halle (1968); Bresnan (1973b).

26. Chomsky (1964, 1969a). See note 30.

27. Recall again the scope of Quine's "translation model," which is to be understood as encompassing the problem of understanding another speaker of the same language, learning a first language, the linguist's study of a new language.

28. For a similar proposal, see Hiż (1973).

29. In the latter case too there are familiar idealizations. Thus no physicist is concerned because the law of falling bodies may "fail" if someone reaches out to catch the falling person before he hits the ground, an act which physics, so far as we know, cannot predict or explain. On Schwartz's grounds, we must therefore conclude that physics is empty, since any fact that violates its principles is placed outside the scope of its predictions (paraphrasing Schwartz's remarks on language, discussed above).

30. Quine's responses to other criticisms and queries that I raised in the same article simply avoid or misrepresent the issues. Thus I pointed out that his characterization of language and language learning, if taken literally, conflicts with truisms that he accepts, e.g., that a language is infinite. In response, Quine simply reiterates what I stated explicitly, namely, that he of course accepts the truism. But this does not deal with the criticism, which is that the position he develops is inconsistent with the truism that he accepts. He also claims falsely that I attributed to him the theory that "learning sentences" involves "sentences only as unstructured wholes," but in fact my discussion included all of the devices he suggests for language learning, including the one he cites in response. I will not undertake to review the matter case by case here, but a careful comparison of his response with my criticisms and requests for clarification will show, I believe, that in each case he simply misunderstood the point or misrepresented what I said. The problems in Quine (1960) remain exactly as I stated them, so far as I can see.

31. In Chomsky (1969a) I pointed out tentatively that Quine ap-

pears to be using "theory" and "language" interchangeably in such contexts as these. In his response (Quine, 1969a, p. 310), he makes it explicit that this is so. Thus, he states, "language or theory [is] a fabric or 'network of sentences associated to one another and to external stimuli by the mechanism of conditioned response.'" It is quite impossible to characterize a theory in these terms, over and above the problems involved in the analysis of language.

32. If a language is a fabric of associated sentences and stimuli, and substitution of "hand" for "foot" in the context "my ―― hurts" by "analogic synthesis" constitutes a mode of "learning of sentences" (Quine's example), then this case of analogic synthesis must involve a mode of "association." But this conclusion deprives the notion "association" of any meaning.

33. These remarks are in response to my query as to what kind of quality space Quine had in mind. I noted that his examples suggested that he was restricting himself to certain dimensions with simple physical correlates, though he seemed willing to accept a strong version of the theory of innate ideas within this framework. Or, if these examples were not representative, we are left with no idea what the basis for learning is, since one might imagine a quality space with dimensions so abstract that, say, the concept "sentence in English" could be "learned" from one instance by "generalization." The reference to Goodman (1951) is indirect, but, I take it, intended.

34. Even if there is a coherent notion of "quality space" in the sense intended. I return to this question directly.

35. A few lines later he imposes the much narrower requirement that "talk of ideas comes to count as unsatisfactory except insofar as it can be *paraphrased into terms of dispositions to observable behavior*" (my emphasis). This latter requirement seems to me quite unreasonable, in psychology as in any other branch of science. Elsewhere Quine insists that "to make proper sense of the hypothesis that the subject-predicate construction is a linguistic universal, we need an unequivocal behavioral criterion of subject and predicate" (Quine, 1972). Again, this is an entirely unreasonable demand to impose on a theoretical concept such as "subject" or "predicate." To "make proper sense of the hypothesis" it would surely suffice to meet the requirement of Quine (1969b).

36. Cohen (1966), pp. 47–56, for these and following quotations.

37. In Chomsky (1965), I suggested that E, as outlined there, includes such approaches as Hume's theory of learning, Quine (1960), most "behavioral" theories that have been made at all clear, and theories of structural linguistics (apart from some elements of distinctive-feature theory), if interpreted as theories of learning.

38. Recall that the same false claim was advanced by Schwartz. One finds similar arguments rather commonly. Consider, e.g., the following statement by an anonymous reviewer in the *Times Literary Supplement*, October 12, 1973: "What evidence do we have that speakers have developed rules for Chomskyan deep structures? Undoubtedly the transformationalists have not provided it. Nor do they seem to seek it; to justify their grammars they regularly turn to logical criteria of simplicity and generality." (I assume that by "deep structures" the reviewer means something like "grammars.") "Transformationalists" have argued that speakers have developed specific systems of grammatical rules, and have sought to explain, on this basis, innumerable facts about the form and interpretation of utterances. They have thus provided substantial evidence for (and often against) specific hypotheses about the rules that speakers have developed. The reviewer feels that this is no evidence; something else is required. Suppose that a scientist investigating some device were to conclude that its structure is such-and-such, appealing to criteria of simplicity and generality along with the evidence he has accumulated about its behavior. By the reviewer's standards, no matter how much evidence the scientist provides, he has still produced no evidence for his hypotheses concerning the structure of the device; something else is needed. As in the case of Cohen, Quine, and Schwartz, we see here a reflection of the curious unwillingness to deal with human beings as part of the natural world, in accordance with the standards and methods of scientific inquiry. It is noteworthy that in each case, the author feels himself to be defending a scientific approach to the study of human behavior.

39. That is, theories that fall between the upper and lower bounds imposed by empirical requirements, discussed earlier; namely, those that satisfy the "indisputable point about language" that Quine quotes. Cf. pp. 200–201.

40. Notice that if the project Cohen is criticizing were merely unfeasible in that it would be necessary to "scour the universe" for relevant evidence, this would demonstrate that postulating linguistic universals is no "tautological pretence," contrary to Cohen's earlier claim, since on this assumption relevant evidence does not exist in principle.

41. Cohen asserts that my historical allusions to Descartes and Leibniz are inaccurate in that Descartes and Leibniz denied that innate ideas explain linguistic competence. Without entering into this latter question, I must nevertheless reject Cohen's criticism, since I nowhere attributed to Descartes and Leibniz the views that he claims they reject (and furthermore, I did refer to this element in the beliefs of Leibniz and others; cf. Chomsky [1966], p. 93). Rather, I discussed ideas of this sort that were developed

by many others, including Cartesians of varying degrees of ortho-
doxy. The references to Descartes and Leibniz were relevant to
other parts of my discussion and, to my knowledge, were quite
accurate, contrary to what Cohen claims without argument or
citation.

42. More accurately, he does make some specific suggestions, but
they are hopelessly inadequate, so far as we know; e.g., his
suggestion that the "multiplicity of concepts involved" in "generalizations about surface structure" can be "reduced to two
primitive ones ('sentence' and 'nominal') by assuming a mode
of derivation for the others like that used in categorial grammars." See Chomsky (1969c) for some comments on earlier proposals to the same effect.

43. He does offer an argument based on "Darwinian conceptions of
evolution," recognizing that such explanations are "rather speculative." The latter is an understatement. Contrary to what
Cohen claims, nothing we know of the mechanisms of evolution suggests that "the task of explaining the innateness of
certain specifically syntactic principles, in terms of Darwinian
evolution, is in principle a great deal more difficult than that of
explaining the innateness of certain more general abilities."
Cohen's argument is analogous to an argument that people learn
to walk (rather than, say, to roll) or learn to grow arms (rather
than arbitrary appendages) on grounds that the task of explaining the innateness of specific modes of locomotion (or
limbs) in terms of Darwinian evolution is in principle more
difficult than that of explaining the innateness of more general
abilities (tendencies). If we want to pursue such speculations,
consider Cohen's claim that scientific discovery proceeds by the
same mechanisms as language learning. But, as noted earlier,
over the past centuries or millennia there has been no selectional
advantage in an ability to discover the principles of quantum
theory, though there is an obvious selectional advantage in an
ability to discover the language of one's speech community.
Hence if one wants to give any weight to such speculations
(I do not), they would hardly seem to support Cohen's conclusions.

44. Note that "comparable" is not synonymous with "identical."

45. Searle has a response to Gewirth (Searle, 1973), but I think that
Gewirth's remarks stand.

46. *Meditations* (trans. Haldane and Ross, 1955), 1:191. Similar
ideas were expressed by others, before and after Descartes. Cf.
Chomsky (1966), pp. 79, 108, 112, and elsewhere. Cf. also
chapter 1, pp. 5–7.

47. Others have indeed made a claim rather like this. Thus Vendler
asserts that "Descartes envisions a 'generative' grammar, and
semantics, for his language, which would correspond to the

generative structure of thought," though he did not realize "that a natural language comes close to this ideal" (1972, p. 181). He bases this conclusion on remarks by Descartes concerning an invented language presupposing "true philosophy" in which an infinity of words (and thoughts) can be enumerated. In Chomsky (1966, p. 84), I cited similar discussions by Galileo and the Port-Royal grammarians, without, however, drawing Vendler's conclusion, which seems to me questionable.

48. Cf. the discussion of "foundations of science" above and in earlier references cited there; also, Chomsky (1970) and other material that is reprinted in (1973b). Cf. also chapters 1, 3.

49. All of the following quotations are from Hume's *Enquiry Concerning Human Understanding* (ed. Selby-Bigge, 1902).

50. Compare Lord Herbert's discussion of "natural instinct" and his contention that the system of common notions is "that part of knowledge with which we were endowed in the primeval plan of Nature." For discussion in a related context, see Chomsky (1966). It is, incidentally, too strong to say that the "limited empiricism" of Hume "rejects innate knowledge" (Barnes, 1972).

51. Cf. Cooper (1972), Chomsky and Katz (1975).

Bibliography

Akmajian, Adrian. 1975. "More Evidence for an NP Cycle." *Linguistic Inquiry* 6:115–30.

Alston, William P. 1963. "Meaning and Use." *Philosophical Quarterly* 13:107–24.

Anderson, Stephen R., and Paul Kiparsky, eds. 1973. *A Festschrift for Morris Halle.* New York: Holt, Rinehart & Winston.

Armstrong, D. M. 1971. "Meaning and Communication." *Philosophical Review* 80:427–47.

Arnauld, Antoine. 1964. *The Art of Thinking: Port-Royal Logic.* Trans. J. Dickoff and P. James. Indianapolis: Bobbs-Merrill Co.

Aronoff, Mark H. Forthcoming. *Word-Structure.* Cambridge, Mass.: MIT Press.

Atherton, Margaret, and Robert Schwartz. 1974. "Linguistic Innateness and Its Evidence." *Journal of Philosophy* 71:155–68.

Austin, John L. 1940. "The Meaning of a Word." In Urmson and Warnock, 1961.

———. 1962. *How to Do Things with Words.* London: Oxford University Press.

Baker, C. Leroy. 1970. "Notes on the Description of English Questions: The Role of an Abstract Question Morpheme." *Foundations of Language* 6:197–209.

Barnes, Jonathan. 1972. "Mr. Locke's Darling Notion." *Philosophical Quarterly* 22:193–214.

Beloff, John. 1973. *Psychological Sciences: A Review of Modern Psychology.* New York: Harper & Row.

Bergling, Kurt. 1974. *The Development of Hypothetico-deductive Thinking in Children.* IEA Monograph Studies no. 3. Stockholm: Almqvist & Wiksell International.

Berlin, Isaiah. 1972. "The Bent Twig." *Foreign Affairs* 51:11–30.

Bower, T. G. R. 1972. "Object Perception in Intants." *Perception* 1:15–30.

Bracken, Harry M. 1972. "Chomsky's Cartesianism." *Language Sciences*, October, pp. 11–18.

———. 1973a. "Minds and Learning: The Chomskian Revolution." *Metaphilosophy* 4:229–45.

————. 1973b. "Essence, Accident and Race." *Hermathena*, no. 116, pp. 88–95.

————. 1974. *Berkeley*. London: MacMillan & Co.

Braine, Martin D. S. 1974. "On What Might Constitute Learnable Phonology." *Language* 50:270–99.

Bresnan, Joan W. 1970. "On Complementizers: Towards a Syntactic Theory of Complement Types." *Foundations of Language* 6:297–321.

————. 1972. "The Theory of Complementation in English." Ph.D. dissertation, MIT.

————. 1973a. "Syntax of the Comparative Clause Construction in English." *Linguistic Inquiry* 4:275–344.

————. 1973b. "Sentence Stress and Syntactic Transformations." In Hintikka, Moravcsik, and Suppes, 1973.

————. 1975. "Comparative Deletion and Constraints on Transformations." *Linguistic Analysis* 1:25–74.

Brewer, William F. Forthcoming. "There Is No Convincing Evidence for Operant or Classical Conditioning in Adult Humans." In Weimer and Palermo, forthcoming.

Bruner, J. S., and Barbara Koslowski. 1972. "Visually Preadapted Constituents of Manipulatory Action." *Perception* 1:3–14.

Bryant, Peter. 1974. *Perception and Understanding in Young Children*. New York: Basic Books.

Chomsky, Noam. 1955–56. "Logical Structure of Linguistic Theory." Mimeographed. New York: Plenum Publishing Corp., 1975.

————. 1957. *Syntactic Structures*. The Hague: Mouton & Co.

————. 1964. *Current Issues in Linguistic Theory*. The Hague: Mouton & Co.

————. 1965. *Aspects of the Theory of Syntax*. Cambridge, Mass.: MIT Press.

————. 1966. *Cartesian Linguistics*. New York: Harper & Row.

————. 1968a. "Recent Contributions to the Theory of Innate Ideas." In Cohen and Wartofsky, 1968.

————. 1968b. *Language and Mind*. New York: Harcourt Brace Jovanovich. Extended edition, 1972a.

————. 1969a. "Quine's Empirical Assumptions." In Davidson and Hintikka, 1969. Excerpted from "Some Empirical Assumptions in Modern Philosophy of Language" (1969b). In Morgenbesser, Suppes, and White, 1969.

————. 1969c. "Linguistics and Philosophy." In Hook, 1969. Reprinted in Chomsky, 1972a.

————. 1969d. *American Power and the New Mandarins*. New York: Pantheon Books.

————. 1970. "Language and Freedom." *Abraxas* 1. Reprinted in Chomsky, 1973b.

————. 1971. *Problems of Knowledge and Freedom*. New York: Pantheon Books.

————. 1972a. *Language and Mind.* Extended ed. New York: Harcourt Brace Jovanovich.

————. 1972b. *Studies on Semantics in Generative Grammar.* The Hague: Mouton & Co.

————. 1973a. "Conditions on Transformations." In Anderson and Kiparsky, 1973.

————. 1973b. *For Reasons of State.* New York: Pantheon Books.

————. 1973c. "Science and Ideology." *Jawarharlal Nehru Memorial Lectures: 1967–72,* Nehru Memorial Fund, New Delhi. Bombay: Bharatiya Vidya Bhavan.

————. 1974. "Dialogue with Noam Chomsky." In Parret, 1974.

————. 1975a. "Knowledge of Language." In Gunderson and Maxwell, 1975.

————. 1975b. "Questions of Form and Interpretation." *Linguistic Analysis* 1:75–109.

————, and Morris Halle. 1968. *Sound Pattern of English.* New York: Harper & Row.

————, Morris Halle, and Fred Lukoff. 1956. "On Accent and Juncture in English." In Halle, Lunt and MacLean, 1956.

————, and J. J. Katz. 1974. "What the Linguist Is Talking About." *Journal of Philosophy,* 71:347–67.

————. 1975. "On Innateness: A Reply to Cooper." *Philosophical Review,* 84:70–87.

Cohen, L. Jonathan. 1966. *The Diversity of Meaning.* 2nd ed. London: Methuen & Co.

————. 1970. "Some Applications of Inductive Logic to the Theory of Language." *American Philosophical Quarterly,* 7:299–310.

Cohen, Robert S., and Marx Wartofsky, eds. 1968. *Boston Studies in the Philosophy of Science,* vol. 3. Dordrecht: Reidel Publishing Co.

Cooper, David E. 1972. "Innateness. Old and New." *Philosophical Review* 81:465–83.

Cudworth, Ralph. 1838. *Treatise Concerning Eternal and Immutable Morality.* New York: Andover.

Davidson, Donald, and Jaakko Hintikka, eds. 1969. *Words and Objections: Essays on the Work of W. V. Quine.* Dordrecht: Reidel Publishing Co.

Dolgoff, Sam. 1972. *Bakunin on Anarchy.* New York: Alfred A. Knopf.

Dougherty, Ray C. 1968. "A Transformational Grammar of Coordinate Conjoined Structures." Ph.D. dissertation, MIT.

————. 1969. "An Interpretive Theory of Pronominal Reference." *Foundations of Language* 5:488–519.

————. 1970. "A Grammar of Coordinate Conjunction, I." *Language* 46:850–98.

————. 1971. "A Grammar of Coordinate Conjunction II." *Language* 47:298–399.

————. 1974. "The Syntax and Semantics of *Each Other* Con-structions." *Foundations of Language* 12:1–48.

Dummett, Michael. 1973. *Frege: Philosophy of Language.* London: Duckworth & Co.

Eimas, Peter D., Einar R. Siqueland, Peter Jusczyk, and James Vigorito, 1971. "Speech Perception in Infants." *Science* 171: 303–6.

Emonds, Joseph E. Forthcoming. *Root and Structure-Preserving Transformations.*

Erteschik, Nomi. 1973. "On the Nature of Island Constraints." Ph.D. dissertation, MIT.

Estes, William K. 1972. "Reinforcement in Human Behavior." *American Scientist* 60:723–29.

Ettlinger, G., H.-L. Teuber, and B. Milner. 1975. "Report: The Seventeenth International Symposium of Neuropsychology." *Neuropsychologia* 13:125–34.

Fauconnier, Gilles R. 1974. *Coréférence: Syntaxe ou Semantique.* Paris: Editions du Seuil.

Fiengo, Robert W. 1974. "Semantic Conditions on Surface Structure." Ph.D. dissertation, MIT.

————, and Howard Lasnik. 1973. "The Logical Structure of Reciprocal Sentences in English." *Foundations of Language* 9: 447–69.

Fodor, Jerry A., Thomas G. Bever, and Merrill F. Garrett. 1974. *The Psychology of Language.* New York: McGraw-Hill Book Co.

Fodor, J. A., J. D. Fodor, and M. F. Garrett. Forthcoming. "The Psychological Unreality of Semantic Representations." *Linguistic Inquiry.*

Fraser, Bruce. 1974. "An Analysis of Vernacular Performative Verbs." In Shuy and Bailey, 1974.

Fromm, Erich. 1961. *Marx's Concept of Man.* New York: Ungar Publishing Co.

Gewirth, Alan. 1973. "The Sleeping Chess Player." *New York Review of Books,* February 22.

Glass, Andrea Velletri, Michael S. Gazzaniga, and David Premack. 1973. "Artificial Language Training in Global Aphasics." *Neuropsychologia* 11:95–104.

Goodman, Nelson. 1951. *The Structure of Appearance.* Cambridge, Mass.: Harvard University Press.

————. 1969. "The Emperor's New Ideas." In Hook, 1969.

Gramsci, Antonio. 1957. *The Modern Prince & Other Writings.* Trans. Louis Marks. New York: International Publishers.

Graves, Christina, Jerrold J. Katz, et al. 1973. "Tacit Knowledge." *Journal of Philosophy* 70:318–30.

Greenfield, Patricia M., Karen Nelson, and Elliot Saltzman. 1972. "The Development of Rulebound Strategies for Manipulating

Seriated Cups: A Parallel Between Action and Grammar." *Cognitive Psychology* 3:291–310.

Gregory, Richard. 1970. "The Grammar of Vision." *The Listener*, February 19.

Grice, H. P. 1968. "Utterer's Meaning, Sentence-Meaning, and Word-Meaning." *Foundations of Language* 4:225–42.

————. 1969. "Utterer's Meaning and Intentions." *Philosophical Review* 78:147–77.

Gunderson, Keith, and Grover Maxwell, eds. 1975. *Minnesota Studies in Philosophy of Science*, vol. 6. Minneapolis: University of Minnesota Press.

Haldane, Elizabeth S., and G. R. T. Ross, trans. 1955. *The Philosophical Works of Descartes*, vol. 1. New York: Dover Publications.

Halitsky, David. 1974. "The Syntactic Relatedness of S Extraposition and NP Postposition in English." Mimeographed, New York University.

Halle, Morris, Horace Lunt, and Hugh MacLean, eds. 1956. *For Roman Jakobson*. The Hague: Mouton & Co.

Harman, Gilbert. 1973. "Against Universal Semantic Representation." Unpublished manuscript, Princeton University.

————, and Donald Davidson, eds. 1972. *Semantics of Natural Language*. New York: Humanities Press.

Helke, Michael. 1970. "The Grammar of English Reflexives." Ph.D. dissertation, MIT.

Higgins, F. Roger. 1973. "The Pseudo-cleft Construction in English." Ph.D. dissertation, MIT.

Hintikka, Jaakko, J. M. E. Moravcsik, and Patrick Suppes, eds. 1973. *Approaches to Natural Language*. Dordrecht: Reidel Publishing Co.

Hiż, Henry. 1973. "On the Rules of Consequence for a Natural Language." *The Monist* 57:312–27.

Hook, Sidney, ed. 1969. *Language and Philosophy*. New York: New York University Press.

Hubel, D. H., and T. N. Wiesel. 1962. "Receptive Fields, Binocular Interaction and Functional Architecture in the Cat's Visual Cortex." *Journal of Physiology* 160:106–54.

Hume, David. 1902. *An Enquiry Concerning Human Understanding*. In *Enquiries Concerning the Human Understanding and Concerning the Principles of Morals*. Ed. L. A. Selby-Bigge. 2nd ed. New York: Oxford University Press.

Ishiguro, Hidé. 1972. *Leibniz's Philosophy of Logic and Language*. London: Duckworth & Co.

Jackendoff, Ray S. 1969. "Some Rules of Semantic Interpretation in English." Ph.D. dissertation, MIT.

————. 1972. *Semantic Interpretation in Generative Grammar*. Cambridge, Mass.: MIT Press.

————. 1974a. "Introduction to the $\bar{X}$ convention." Indiana University Linguistics Club, Bloomington, October 1974.

————.1974b. "A Deep Structure Projection Rule." *Linguistic Inquiry* 5:481–506.

————. Forthcoming. "Eventually, an Argument for the Trace Theory of Movement Rules." *Linguistic Inquiry*.

John, E. Roy. 1972. "Switchboard Versus Statistical Theories of Learning and Memory." *Science* 177:850–64.

Kaisse, Ellen, and Jorge Hankamer, eds. 1974. *Papers from the Fifth Annual Meeting, Northeastern Linguistic Society*, Harvard University, November.

Kant, Immanuel. 1958. *A Critique of Pure Reason*. Trans. Norman Kemp. New York: Random House, Modern Library.

Kasher, Asa, ed. Forthcoming. *Language in Focus: Foundations, Methods, and Systems*. Dordrecht: D. Riedel.

Katz, Jerrold J. 1972. *Semantic Theory*. New York: Harper & Row.

————. 1975. "Logic and Language: An Examination of Recent Criticisms of Intentionalism." In Gunderson and Maxwell, 1975.

————. Forthcoming. *Propositional Structure: A Study of the Contribution of Sentence Meaning to Speech Acts*.

————, and Paul M. Postal. 1964. *An Integrated Theory of Linguistic Description*. Cambridge, Mass.: MIT Press.

Kaufman, Ellen S. 1975. "Navajo Embedded Questions and Unbounded Movement." Ph.D. dissertation, MIT.

Keenan, Edward L., and Bernard Comrie. 1973. "Noun Phrase Accessibility and Universal Grammar." Mimeographed, Cambridge University.

Kenny, A. J. P. 1973. "The origin of the soul." In Kenny et al., 1973.

————, H. C. Longuet-Higgins, J. R. Lucas, and C. H. Waddington, 1973. *The Development of Mind: The Gifford Lectures 1972–73*. Edinburgh: Edinburgh University Press.

Keyser, S. Jay. 1975. Review of Steiner, 1974. *The New Review* 2:63–66.

Kramer, P. E., E. Koff and Z. Luria. 1972. "The Development of Competence in an Exceptional Language Structure in Older Children and Young Adults." *Child Development* 43:121–30.

Kreisel, Georg. 1974. "Review of H. Wang, 'Logic, Computation and Philosophy.'" *Journal of Symbolic Logic* 39:358–9.

Kripke, Saul. 1972. "Naming and Necessity." In Harman and Davidson, 1972.

Lasnik, Howard. 1974. "Remarks on Coreference." Mimeographed, University of Connecticut.

————, and Robert W. Fiengo. 1974. "Complement Object Deletion." *Linguistic Inquiry* 5:535–72.

Leibniz, G. W. von. 1902. *Discourse on Metaphysics*. Trans. G. R. Montgomery. La Salle, Ill.: Open Court Publishing Co.

Lenneberg, Eric H. 1967. *Biological Foundations of Language*. New York: John Wiley & Sons.

Liberman, A. M. 1974. "The Specialization of the Language Hemisphere." In Schmitt and Worden, 1974.

Liberman, Mark. 1974. "On Conditioning the Rule of Subject-Auxiliary Inversion." In Kaisse and Hankamer, 1974.

————, and Alan S. Prince. Forthcoming. "The Interpretation of Scope."

Lightfoot, David. 1975. "The Theoretical Implications of Subject Raising" (review of Postal, 1974a). *Foundations of Language* 13:115–43.

Lovejoy, Arthur O. 1908. "Kant and the English Platonists." *Essays Philosophical and Psychological, in Honor of William James*. Philosophical and psychological departments, Columbia University. New York: Longmans, Green & Co.

Luce, R. Duncan, Robert R. Bush, and Eugene Galanter, eds. 1963. *Handbook of Mathematical Psychology*, vol. 2. New York: John Wiley & Sons.

Macpherson, C. B. 1962. *The Political Theory of Possessive Individualism*. London: Oxford University Press.

Malson, Lucien. 1972. *Wolf Children and the Problem of Human Nature*. New York: Monthly Review Press. Translation of *Les Enfants sauvages*. Paris: Union Générale d'Editions, 1964.

Marx, Karl. *Economic and Philosophical Manuscripts*. Trans. T. B. Bottomore. In Fromm, 1961.

McKeon, Richard P., ed. 1941. *The Basic Works of Aristotle*. New York: Random House.

Miller, George A. 1974. "The Colors of Philosophy and Psychology." Paper for Conference of Philosophy and Psychology, MIT, October 1974.

————, and Noam Chomsky. 1963. "Finitary Models of Language Users." In Luce, Bush, and Galanter, 1963.

Millikan, C. H., and F. L. Darley, eds. 1967. *Brain Mechanisms Underlying Speech and Language*. New York: Grune & Stratton.

Milner, Brenda. 1974. "Hemispheric Specialization: Scope and Limits." In Schmitt and Worden, 1974.

Milner, Jean-Claude. 1973. *Arguments linguistiques*. Paris: Maison Mame.

Moravcsik, Julius M. E. 1967. "Linguistic Theory and the Philosophy of Language." *Foundations of Language* 3:209–33.

————. 1975a. "Aitia as Generative Factor in Aristotle's Philosophy." *Dialogue*.

————. 1975b. "Natural Languages and Formal Languages: A

Tenable Dualism." Paper presented at Stanford Philosophy of Language Workshop, February 1975.

Morgenbesser, Sidney, Patrick Suppes, and M. White, eds. 1969. *Philosophy, Science, and Method: Essays in Honor of Ernest Nagel.* New York: St. Martin's Press.

Munn, Norman L. 1971. *The Evolution of the Human Mind.* Boston: Houghton Mifflin Co.

Nottebohm, F. 1970. "Ontogeny of Bird Song: Different Strategies in Vocal Development Are Reflected in Learning Stages, Critical Periods, and Neural Lateralization." *Science* 167:950–56.

Parret, Herman, ed. 1974. *Discussing Language.* The Hague: Mouton & Co.

Peirce, Charles Sanders. 1957. "The Logic of Abduction." In Vincent Tomas, ed., *Peirce's Essays in the Philosophy of Science.* New York: Liberal Arts Press.

Peters, Stanley. 1972a. "The Projection Problem: How Is a Grammar to Be Selected?" In Peters, 1972b.

———, ed. 1972b. *Goals of Linguistic Theory.* Englewood Cliffs, N.J.: Prentice-Hall.

Polanyi, Karl. 1957. *The Great Transformation: The Political and Economic Origins of Our Time.* Boston: Beacon Press.

Postal, Paul M. 1965. "Developments in the Theory of Transformational Grammar." Mimeographed, MIT. Translated as "Nový vývoj teorie transformační gramatiky." *Slovo a Slovesnost,* Československá Academie Věd, vol. 26, 1965.

———. 1971. *Cross-Over Phenomena.* New York: Holt, Rinehart & Winston.

———. 1974a. *On Raising: One Rule of English Grammar and its Theoretical Implications.* Cambridge, Mass.: MIT Press.

———. 1974b. "On Certain Ambiguities." *Linguistic Inquiry* 5: 367–424.

Putnam, Hilary. 1962. "It Ain't Necessarily So." *Journal of Philosophy* 59:658–71.

———. 1975. "The Meaning of 'Meaning.'" In Gunderson and Maxwell, 1975.

Pylyshyn, Zenon W. 1973. "The Role of Competence Theories in Cognitive Psychology." *Journal of Psycholinguistic Research* 2: 21–50.

Quine, W. V. O. 1953. *From a Logical Point of View.* Cambridge, Mass.: Harvard University Press.

———. 1960. *Word and Object.* Cambridge, Mass.: MIT Press.

———. 1968. "The Inscrutability of Reference." *Journal of Philosophy* 65:185–212.

———. 1969a. "Reply to Chomsky." In Davidson and Hintikka, 1969.

———. 1969b. "Linguistics and Philosophy." In Hook, 1969.

————. 1969c. "Response to David Kaplan." In Davidson and Hintikka, 1969.

————. 1972. "Methodological Reflections on Current Linguistic Theory." In Harman and Davidson, 1972.

————. 1974. *The Roots of Reference.* La Salle, Ill.: Open Court Publishing Co.

Reber, Arthur S. 1973. "On Psycho-linguistic Paradigms." *Journal of Psycholinguistic Research* 2:289–320.

Reinhart, Tanya. 1974. "Syntax and Coreference." In Kaisse and Hankamer, eds., 1974.

Reiss, H., ed. 1970. *Kant's Political Writings.* London: Cambridge University Press.

Rocker, Rudolph. 1938. *Anarchosyndicalism.* London: Secker & Warburg.

Rosenbaum, Peter. 1967. "Grammar of English Predicate Complement Constructions." Ph.D. dissertation, MIT.

Ross, John R. 1967. "Constraints on Variables." Ph.D. dissertation, MIT.

————. 1971. "Primacy." Mimeographed, Language Research Foundation and MIT.

————. 1972. "Primacy and the Order of Constituents." Mimeographed, MIT.

Russell, Bertrand. 1924. *Icarus, or the Future of Science.* London: Kegan Paul.

————. 1948. *Human Knowledge: Its Scope and Limits.* New York: Simon & Schuster.

Schiffer, Stephen R. 1972. *Meaning.* London: Oxford University Press.

Schmitt, Francis O., and Frederic G. Worden, eds. 1974. *The Neurosciences: Third Study Volume.* Cambridge, Mass.: MIT Press.

Schwartz, Robert. 1969. "On Knowing a Grammar." In Hook, 1969.

Searle, John. 1969. *Speech Acts.* London: Cambridge University Press.

————. 1972. "Chomsky's Revolution in Linguistics." *New York Review of Books,* June 29.

————. 1973. "Reply to Gewirth." *New York Review of Books,* February 22.

————. 1975. "A Classification of Illocutionary Acts." In Gunderson and Maxwell, 1975.

————. Forthcoming. "Indirect Speech Acts."

Selkirk, Elizabeth. 1972. "The Phrase Phonology of English and French." Ph.D. dissertation, MIT.

————. 1974. "French Liaison and the $\overline{\mathrm{X}}$ Notation." *Linguistic Inquiry* 5:573–90.

Shuy, Roger W., and Charles-James Bailey, eds. 1974. *Towards*

Tomorrow's Linguistics. Washington, D.C.: Georgetown University Press.

Siegel, Dorothy. 1974. "Topics in English Morphology." Ph.D. dissertation, MIT.

Sperry, R. W. 1974. "Lateral Specialization in the Surgically Separated Hemispheres." In Schmitt and Worden, 1974.

Stampe, Dennis W. 1968. "Toward a Grammar of Meaning." *Philosophical Review* 77:137–74.

Steiner, George. 1974. *After Babel: Aspects of Language and Translation.* London: Oxford University Press.

Stent, Gunther S. 1975. "Limits to the Scientific Understanding of Man." *Science* 187:1052–57.

Stich, Stephen P. 1972. "Grammar, Psychology, and Indeterminacy." *Journal of Philosophy* 69:799–818.

Strawson, P. F. 1970. *Meaning and Truth.* Inaugural Lecture, University of Oxford, November 5, 1969. London: Oxford University Press.

———. 1972. "Grammar and Philosophy." In Harman and Davidson, 1972.

Suppes, Patrick. 1969. "Stimulus-Response Theory of Finite Automata." *Journal of Mathematical Psychology* 6:327–55.

———. 1973. "Semantics of Natural Languages." In Hintikka, Moravcsik, and Suppes, 1973.

Teuber, Hans-Lukas. 1974. "Why Two Brains?" In Schmitt and Worden, 1974.

Urmson, J. O., and G. J. Warnock, eds. 1967. *J. L. Austin: Philosophical Papers.* London: Oxford University Press.

Vendler, Zeno. 1967. *Linguistics in Philosophy.* Ithaca, N. Y.: Cornell University Press.

———. 1972. *Res Cogitans.* Ithaca: Cornell University Press.

Vergnaud, Jean-Roger. 1974. "French Relative Clauses." Ph.D. dissertation, MIT.

Wang, Hao. 1974. *From Mathematics to Philosophy.* London: Routledge & Kegan Paul.

Wasow, Thomas. 1972. "Anaphoric Relations in English." Ph.D. dissertation, MIT.

———. Forthcoming. *Anaphora in Generative Grammar.*

Watson, Richard A. 1968. "Cartesian Studies." Mimeographed, Washington University.

Weimer, W. B., and D. S. Palermo, eds. Forthcoming. *Cognition and Symbolic Processes.*

Weiss, Donald D. 1975. "Professor Malcolm on Animal Intelligence." *Philosophical Review* 74:88–95.

Wexler, K., P. Culicover, and H. Hamburger. 1974. *Learning-theoretic Foundations of Linguistic Universals.* Social Sciences Working Paper no. 60, University of California, Irvine, July 1974.

Whitaker, Harry A. 1971. *On the Representation of Language in the Human Mind.* Edmonton, Canada: Linguistic Research, Inc.

Williams, Edwin S. 1974. "Rule Ordering in Syntax." Ph.D. dissertation, MIT.

Wittgenstein, Ludwig. 1953. *Philosophical Investigations.* Oxford: Basil Blackwell & Mott.

Wood, C. C. 1973. "Levels of Processing in Speech Perception: Neurophysiological and Information-Processing Analyses." Ph.D. dissertation, Yale University, 1973; Haskins Laboratories, Status Report on Speech Research, SR-35/36.

————, William R. Goff, and Ruth S. Day. 1971. "Auditory Evoked Potentials During Speech Perception." *Science* 173:1248–50.

Wood, Ellen M. 1972. *Mind and Politics.* Berkeley: University of California Press.

Yolton, John W. 1956. *John Locke and the Way of Ideas.* London: Oxford University Press.

Ziff, Paul. 1967. "On H. P. Grice's Account of Meaning." *Analysis* 28:1–18.

Index of Names

Alston, William P., 194–5, 248 n.16
Aristotle, 5–6, 11, 45, 52, 234 n.23, 235 n.32
Armstrong, D. M., 235 n.27, 236 n.36
Arnauld, Antoine, 220
Atherton, Margaret, 177–9
Austin, John L., 60, 161–2

Bakunin, M. A., 132–3
Barnes, Jonathan, 218–23
Beloff, John, 246–7 n.9, 248 n.22
Berkeley, George, 8
Berlin, Isaiah, 133
Bever, Thomas G., 231–2 nn.2, 3
Bourbaki, Nicolas, 230 n.16
Bower, T. G. R., 8
Bracken, Harry M., 127, 130–1
Braine, Martin D. S., 231–2 n.3
Bresnan, Joan W., 88, 239–40 n.16
Brewer, William F., 247 n.12
Bruner, J. S., 8

Calder, Alexander, 203
Carey, Susan, 176
Cartesian ideas, 6, 40, 130–1, 138, 217, 221, 224, 252 n.41. *See also* Descartes
Chomsky, Noam, 56, 171, 187, 191–2, 206, 214, 217, 218, 220, 251 n.38; *Aspects of the Theory of Syntax* (1965), 24, 30, 95, 201, 204, 211, 218, 219, 227, 239 n.8; *Cartesian Linguistics* (1966), 126, 216, 218, 221, 227; "Conditions on Transformations" (1973a), 85, 95, 97, 150, 151, 152, 240 n.25, 241 nn.27, 33; *For Reasons of State* (1973b), 131; "Knowledge of Language" (1975a); 23, 223; "Linguistics and Philosophy" (1967c), 218–19; "Quine's Empirical Assumptions" (1969a), 190–1, 193–4, 195, 201, 249–50 n.31; *Problems of Knowledge and Freedom* (1971), 60–1, 150· "Recent Contributions to the Theory of Innate Ideas" (1968a), 218; *Studies on Semantics in Generative Grammar* (1972b), 151
Cohen, Jonathan, 204–14, 251–2 nn.38, 40, 41, 43
Cordemoy, Géraud de, 220
Cudworth, Ralph, 6–7, 146, 218, 221, 226

Darwin, Charles, 124, 252 n.43
Descartes, René, 40, 127, 146, 216–18, 224, 226, 230 n.20, 251–3 nn.41, 47. *See also* Cartesian ideas

Eimas, Peter D., 7
Emonds, Joseph E., 84–5, 242 n.41

Fiengo, Robert W., 108
Fodor, Jerry A., 231–2 nn.2, 3
Frege, Gottlob, 42, 60

Galilei, Galileo, 253 n.47